FROM SCHOOL BOARD TO LOCAL AUTHORITY

From
SCHOOL BOARD
To
LOCAL AUTHORITY

by
ERIC EAGLESHAM
*Professor of Education in the Durham
Colleges, University of Durham*

*

Routledge and Kegan Paul
LONDON

First published 1956
by Routledge & Kegan Paul Ltd.
Broadway House, Carter Lane, E.C.4
Printed in Great Britain
by The Bowering Press, Plymouth

CONTENTS

PREFACE

SOME four years ago I happened to become interested in a number of questions about educational development at the end of last century: What was the significance of that queer event, the notorious "Cockerton Case"? What really happened to the higher grade schools then and why? To what extent were evening schools involved in the educational crisis of that time? What bearing had these questions on events leading to the 1902 Act? And what part did Morant play behind the scenes? Investigation of official documents for the period showed that the answers to these questions usually given in histories of education could not be accepted. And, little though I wanted to add yet another to the list of books on education, I felt that some of the material in the government files was of such importance that it ought to be published.

The book which has resulted contains much detail. Indeed, I hope that its main value will lie not so much in putting my own point of view as in offering evidence from which those interested in the history of educational development at that time may form their own conclusions. Thus it seems to me that the memoranda by Gorst and Morant, which are here printed as appendices, afford valuable evidence which any answers to the above questions must take into account.

In this period, perhaps more than any other in educational history, it is difficult to avoid partisanship; and, if I cannot now claim neutrality, at least I started the investigation on one side of the fence, as an opponent of the school boards, pursued it in a spirit of more or less cold-blooded detection, and finished on the other side, if not as a supporter of school boards, at least with a conviction that, with all their faults, they had a much stronger case than is commonly realised, and that a systematic and extensive development of the *ad hoc* principle might in the long run have provided a sounder system of local educational administration than that established by the 1902 Act.

Obviously no finality can be hoped for for any views here expressed. The material used probably deals too much with relations between the London School Board and the Education Department.

Too little is as yet known of the development of many other school boards. And the inner history of the Education Department and the Science and Art Department has yet to be written.

The story here told rests mainly on material to be found on the files of the Education Department, the Science and Art Department, and the Local Government Board (some of which are now available at the Public Record Office). Consequently it would be somewhat misleading to include a bibliography; for while the list of books consulted would be large the views here expressed are, except where I have made acknowledgements, based on evidence found in the government files, the parliamentary debates and evidence given to the Cross and Bryce commissions.

Unfortunately considerations of space have led to the exclusion of some of the earlier (and to my mind very interesting) material dealing with the control of the London School Board by the district auditors; but I have taken account of it in my conclusions and some of that evidence may be published later in separate articles.

I am deeply indebted to Durham University for a sabbatical term devoted to pursuit of the research, and to the Ministries of Education and Health for permission to use the material in their files. I am very grateful, too, to Miss Downie and her staff in the Ministry of Education library for their kindness and helpfulness; and also to Mr. Worcester of the Ministry of Education for his invaluable assistance in unearthing material. I am further greatly indebted to Mr. Fountain, the librarian of the Ministry of Health, who so readily allowed me facilities for studying the audit files of the Local Government Board.

I must also thank Sir James Duff of Durham University and Professor Judges and Dr. Weitzman of London University who were so kind as to read the manuscript and offer comments on it; but I must add that, though I benefited greatly by their advice, I did not always follow it, and they are in no way responsible for my occasionally heretical views or for the not so occasional tediousness of my style.

Many thanks are also due to Mr. J. A. Bruce of Newcastle Royal Grammar School for reading the proofs.

REFERENCES

References to archives of the Ministry of Education are shown as M.E. . . . followed, where applicable, by the registered number of the file.

Records of the Ministry of Education which have been transferred to the Public Record Office are shown as P.R.O. . . . followed by the class and piece number of the document.

All the Ministry of Health files dealt with here have now been transferred to the Public Record Office. Consequently files marked as M.H. (referred to mainly in Chapters VI to VIII) should be consulted at the Public Record Office.

The dates quoted in footnotes may refer to letters giving final decisions in the cases in question, or to the sources of quotations, or to papers in the files giving evidence of special significance.

I

INTRODUCTION

*

ONE of the most interesting periods in educational history is that immediately before the great Education Act of 1902, during which something like an administrative revolution was effected. The story of that time is usually made to centre round the celebrated Cockerton Case, in which Cockerton, a district auditor, "disallowed" the expenditure of London School Board on certain higher grade and evening classes working under the syllabus of the Science and Art Department. He argued that the expenditure was not on *elementary* education and was therefore not proper expenditure for a school board. The school board took the case to the Queen's Bench Division and to the Court of Appeal; but both courts upheld the auditor's decision.

The case is probably the most dramatic, and one of the most important, events in educational history; since, as textbooks suggest, it led to the destruction of higher grade schools in their original form, and precipitated the abolition of school boards and the creation of a new educational system. As one writer put it, "There can ... be no doubt that the Cockerton judgment delayed reorganisation on Hadow lines by at least fifteen years and was largely responsible for the neglect of technical education which persists to this day".[1] But, as we shall see later, a brief examination of the Cockerton judgments shows that they had no such *necessary* consequences; for their main practical implication was that school boards had no power to educate *adults*, that is, in effect, no power to run evening schools. What then was the exact historical significance of the Cockerton Case? How did the crisis of 1899–1902 arise? What were the main considerations leading to the abolition of the school boards? Why was

[1] Graves, *Policy and Progress in Secondary Education, 1902–42*, Nelson, 1943, p. 32.

I

the work of the higher grade schools, with all its possibilities for technical education, so severely curtailed? If it was illegal for school boards to run evening schools, how had they contrived to do so for thirty years, and why had the Education Department not previously cautioned them as to their illegality? And what was the Education Department policy during these critical years? This book attempts to answer these among other questions.

It has long been known that a major part in the planning of the great changes at that time was played by Morant, that strange administrative giant, who entered the educational scene in 1895 as an assistant to Sadler in his office of Special Inquiries and Reports, and became private secretary to the Vice-President of the Committee of Council on Education, Sir John Gorst, in 1899, in the first instance to help him to pilot the Board of Education Bill through the House of Commons. In August, 1900, Morant was appointed to the office of "Senior Examiner" at South Kensington; but effectively he remained Gorst's right hand man until he was invited by Balfour to prepare the draft of the 1902 Bill. During these years Morant's influence on educational policy was, to a considerable extent, exercised through memoranda which he produced concerning the major problems of reorganisation; and fortunately some, at least, of these have been preserved. (See Appendices A, B, D, E.) But these memoranda, masterly though they are, give all too brief analyses of such problems and of the history behind them, and they have more than a tinge of bias. To get a balanced picture it is necessary to go back to the 1870 Education Act and consider the origins of the school board system and the essential nature of the education contemplated at that time. Thence we may trace several lines of development under that statute which will help to explain the crisis at the end of the century.

Part of the difficulty in understanding the history of education from 1870 to 1902 lies in the complexity of the system itself, and the strangeness of some of the methods by which education was controlled. Mainly as a result of the exertions of the Churches there had already grown up a system of voluntary schools, to which the government, from 1833 onwards, gave assistance by grant. The distribution of that grant, upon conditions to be prescribed, became in 1839 the business of the Committee of the Privy Council on Education, or Education Department, as it was called from 1856 onwards. But the question of State help to, or State control of, education was obviously one of intense interest, if not anxiety, to Churchmen; and it is not surprising that the plan for unsectarian education in public elementary schools proposed, before the 1870 Bill was passed, by the Radical Education League, split the government's supporters

Education could not, in fact, be considered on its own merits and, as we shall see, the weaknesses of the 1870 Act may be largely attributed to the ferment of religious discussion in which it was engendered, and which prevented clear-cut planning of its administration.

The 1870 Education Act was essentially a compromise between the principles of voluntary and those of State education. In such circumstances, a State Education Department purporting to aid impartially competing voluntary and State schools was bound to be in a delicate position. But some of the provisions of the 1870 Act itself made its task doubly difficult. Thus one section appeared to give school boards power to make a final decision on a matter closely affecting the voluntary schools.[1] Since these boards were, in the eyes of many, secular trespassers on fields which should rightly have remained under Church control, the task of a department which had to hold the balance between the system of old-established, but impoverished, voluntary schools and that of the relatively wealthy and powerful newcomers was from the outset a formidable one.

These difficulties were enhanced by the fact that the province of the Education Department and its relations with other bodies assisting education were ill-defined. For example, the help given by the Endowed Schools Commissioners and their successors, the Charity Commissioners, had enabled secondary education of a grammar school type to be given to perhaps 15,000 pupils in 1868 (increasing to over 75,000 in 1895).[2] But, on the one hand, the endowments and "charities" were not all aimed at secondary school work; and, on the other hand, there was no agreement that a comprehensive system of secondary education was either feasible or desirable. Indeed, it may be said that until 1889, when the Technical Instruction Act was passed, "secondary education" was only remotely a concern of the State, and few would have cared to say either what "secondary education" meant or who was to provide it, if not the school boards.

But these were not the only complications: for athwart the whole educational scene, and confusing the administrative picture to a degree that almost baffles the understanding, there ran the multifarious activities of the Science and Art Department of South Kensington. This offspring of the Board of Trade, constituted as a distinct department in 1853, and in part designed to educate taste and thus stimulate the production and consumption of goods of approved kinds, never entirely lost all traces of its origins. For a long time it afforded an interesting illustration of departmental

---

[1] See pp. 10–11.
[2] Graves, *Policy and Progress in Secondary Education, 1902–42*, p. 12.

irresponsibility and its incursions into education were of a varied and surprising nature. The wonder is that two such bodies as the Education Department and the Science and Art Department were able to work side by side for so long. Much of the work done by "South Kensington" was of outstanding value. Thus the achievements of the distinguished scientists who served it are well known; but the debt owed to pioneers such as Buckmaster, the organising master, should not be forgotten. (Perhaps Buckmaster's most remarkable feat was at the Exhibition of 1873 where, though a novice to the kitchen, helped by a French chef and four women assistants, he demonstrated the scientific principles underlying cookery so successfully as to be largely responsible for a fashionable craze for cookery and the teaching of it.)[1] But its constructive achievements, important though these were, must not blind us to this department's large measure of responsibility for the confusion in the administration of education in the last quarter of the century. It was prepared to examine pupils in, and give grants to, a wide and variegated range of institutions: elementary and higher grade schools, schools of science, schools of art, grammar schools, evening classes, working men's institutes, Pupil Teachers' Centres, Technical Schools, Technical Colleges, Polytechnics—all brought grist to the science and art mill.

The heart of the State "system"' (see p. 9 *infra*) of elementary education was the school board itself. This was a local body, elected to supply education under the Elementary Education Acts. Some school boards represented parishes, some boroughs; and the school board for London had a constitution peculiar to itself. To speak in a general sense of "school boards" or "school board policy" may therefore give an impression of uniformity which is misleading; for the mighty school boards of London, Manchester and Birmingham, at one extreme, bore little resemblance to a rural board, consisting perhaps of the parson and a number of villagers, at the other. All had, however, two features in common:—

(i) They were elected for educational purposes and for educational purposes alone.

(ii) They could issue a "precept" requiring the local rating authority[2] to pay to the school board treasurer the expenses of the board and, if necessary, to raise the amount by means of a rate.

The protection of ratepayers from the possibility of extravagance or illegal expenditure on the part of school boards was thus a matter

---

[1] cf. Sillitoe, *A History of the Teaching of Domestic Subjects*, Methuen, 1933, p. 24.

[2] The borough council or the parish overseers. London was again a special case, and the rating authorities included the commissioners of sewers for London and the parish vestries.

of some concern under the 1870–1902 system. The duty of ensuring that the ratepayers' interests were protected was entrusted to the district auditor for the accounts relating to the relief of the poor. Any ratepayer could attend the audit, and object to any item in the accounts, and the auditor had then to decide whether to "allow" or "disallow" the item, i.e. in effect to permit or forbid it to be charged on the rates. An appeal could be made from his decision to the Local Government Board. As the extent of the school boards' powers under the Elementary Education Acts and of the Education Department's responsibilities in controlling school boards were both ill-defined, the auditor's rôle in deciding what was or was not legitimate work for a school board was one of considerable importance.

But, complicated and confused though this "system" was, a still more serious source of difficulty lay behind. One of the ablest of modern writers on legal theory has said that "a fruitful parent of injustice is the tyranny of concepts. They are tyrants rather than servants when treated as real existences and developed with merciless disregard of consequence to the limit of their logic".[1] This is as true in administration as in law; and some of the problems of this period are only understandable if we can appreciate the varying extent to which able individuals might be slaves to outdated concepts and yet honestly believe that they were coping in an up-to-date manner with changing realities. For during the latter part of the nineteenth century the ideas and emotions aroused by the terms "elementary education" and "technical education" were everywhere changing, but they changed more rapidly in the great school boards than in the government offices; and educational facts were changing most rapidly of all.

The significance of the emotional background of ideas is a commonplace of psychological theory; but its importance in the development of our educational system is apt to be overlooked. We are too ready to think of that system as a collection of bodies, offices and buildings, and to forget that it is also a collection of mercurial ideas. We try to pin down these ideas by attaching them to certain terms; but they refuse to stay put. Rignano put a similar argument vividly thus: "As the old carapace, abandoned by the crustacean after shedding, retains the appearances of the animal which moulded it and which now inhabits it no longer, so the word which continues to represent a quite dematerialised metaphysical concept is no more than a verbal *carapace*, now completely abandoned by the intellectual content for whose symbolisation it had been originally created. Without this verbal *carapace*, the disappearance of all intellectual content would involve the disappearance of all trace of the past

[1] Cardozo, *Selected Writings*, Fallon, 1947, p. 287.

existence of such content. But the *carapace* preserves something which . . . although devoid of all intellectual content, always constitutes a valuable point of attachment and support for the corresponding emotion."[1] The simile is picturesque; but, if the comparison is to be true to life, we must recall that the "carapace" may be taken over by new tenants and that new ideas may inherit the emotions attaching to the old name. Thus today not only does the term "technical education" carry an emotional legacy from the Greeks and the Middle Ages and the school board battles of the late nineteenth century, and ideas deriving from standard works on education, but its meaning for us will even vary according to whether we have, or have not, read recent reports on Education for Agriculture, Education for Commerce or even Education for Management.

During the period 1870–1902 the terms "elementary", "secondary" and "technical" were all highly ambiguous when applied to education; but the most uncertain and shifting and the most dangerously charged with emotional assumptions was "elementary". To see the reasons for this we must next consider the Elementary Education Act of 1870 and the debates in Parliament which preceded it.

---

[1] Rignano, *The Psychology of Reasoning*, Kegan Paul, 1923, p. 255.

II

UNCERTAIN FOUNDATIONS

The Elementary Education Act, 1870

★

IF the title of the Elementary Education Act of 1870 had been "An Act for the Secular Education of the Children of Poor Labourers" it would have described more accurately the intentions of most members of Parliament of the day, and subsequent development of our national system of education would probably have taken a different course.[1] The term "elementary" could scarcely be used as an epithet an... ...ng to "education" without a social significance. Parliamentary speakers in 1870 assumed that the education provided was to be for ... ...children of the labouring poor". "How could we deal", said one member, "with the miserable children who are to be seen swarming in our s...ets, lanes and alleys, only half-clad and covered with filth and ver... ...n?" It is true that a proposal to exclude the children of parents enjoying an income of over £150 was negatived;[2] and that Forster indica'ed that in many cases it would be an advantage to have the schools open to all classes; but as a rule the social reference of "elementary" was accepted and was implicit in most of what Forster himself said. I. deed, the spokesman of the government in the House of Lords expressly stated that the Bill would deal with the children of the working classes only—although, as one speaker tartly commented, it did not say so. "Elementary Education" was in fact a euphemism for "Education of the Children of the Poor".[3]

[1] Forster was one of the sponsors for "The Education of the Poor Bill", 1867. This was described by the Cross Commission as "the parent of Mr. Forster's Bill". (*Final Report of the Commissioners appointed to Inquire into the Elementary Education Acts of England and Wales* H.M.S.O., 1888, p. 20.)

[2] *Elementary Education Bill, 1870. Debate in Parliament*. National Education Union, p. 350. See also Cross Commission *Final Report*, p. 241.

[3] The earlier codes not only enumerated the classes of parents whose children might receive State-aided education (e.g. masons, carpenters, tailors and "simple

It seems improbable, however, that Parliament would have failed to deal explicitly with the central term of the Bill had not the minds of members been so preoccupied with other issues. Indeed, the emphasis of the debate was so markedly on religious topics that the Chancellor of the Exchequer compared the House of Commons to "a fine herd of cattle in a large meadow deserting the grass which is abundant about them and delighting themselves by fighting over a bed of nettles in one corner of the field".[1]

Since problems of religious education and of State or Church control of schools loomed so large, it is perhaps not surprising that few ordinary members considered the scope and content of this "elementary" education which was to be provided. There was occasional mention of reading, writing and arithmetic; and some discussion of the probable duration of education for poor children; but such issues were not seriously tackled.

It *is*, however, remarkable, in view of this preoccupation, that the government spokesmen did not give better guidance. Even Forster's well-known description of the schools proposed was based on administrative and religious criteria. He wanted elementary education to be sufficient, efficient and suitable. "By sufficient, I mean if we find that there are enough schools; by efficient, I mean schools which give a reasonable amount of secular instruction; and by suitable, I mean schools to which, from the absence of religious or other restriction, parents cannot reasonably object.... We consider as elementary all schools that will allow our inspectors to visit them".[2] This description was sound and practical, but scarcely likely to lead to consideration of such a fundamental issue as the scope of the education which the Bill aimed at providing.

But although the scope of the education to be given was scarcely discussed, it is not difficult to discover the assumptions which governed the course of the debate. Elementary education, ran the unvoiced argument, is that given to children of paupers or of the poorest members of the working class. It is inconceivable that these should be kept at school beyond 13 or 14, or that they should learn more than the barest rudiments. Hence definition of elementary education and discussion of its secular content are superfluous. Nor is there the

policemen") but indicated that in borderline cases, such as shopkeepers, a decision could be made according to the persons a parent associated with (Revised Code, 1870, Appendix II, Rule 10 (c)). The New Code of 1871 abolished the restriction of grant to the children of labourers, but, as the Cross Commission pointed out, this made little difference, since schools with fees above 9d. a week were not recognised as public elementary schools. (Inability to pay a fee of 9d. a week was one of the three main criteria of membership of the labouring class in Codes before 1871.)

[1] *Elementary Education Bill, 1870. Debate in Parliament.* National Education Union, p. 99.

[2] Op. cit., p. 8. *Parliamentary Debates,* Third Series, cxcix, 445.

slightest need to consider when elementary education must stop, though there is some point in deciding when it should begin.

Moreover, though many fundamental issues were not adequately discussed in the debate, the very content of the Bill ensured that a wide field was covered. The essential principles of the plan were that wherever voluntary schools existed they were to be preserved and supported; and that wherever gaps existed in the provision of elementary education these were to be compulsorily filled through the creation of school boards with the duty of acting. The scheme was as simple as that—to keep the existing garment; but, wherever the Education Department decided that there was a hole, or that the cloth was inadequate, a patch was to be put on. The school boards, who were to do the patching, were to be local bodies elected for that purpose alone.

Before considering the powers and duties of school boards, it would be well to note the types of school a district might have after the Act came into operation; for some of these had to be taken into account in calculating the educational "needs" of the district:—

(i) Schools or departments of schools which did not have elementary education as "the principal part" of their work. These might give some elementary education, but were not to enter into the plan of the Act at all.

(ii) Schools or departments of schools charging fees higher than 9d. a week. No matter what education they gave, even if it was only the three R's, they were not "elementary" schools, and they were entirely outside the plan of the Act.

(iii) Schools which were "elementary" but which were not "public": Roman Catholic schools, for example, which did not accept a conscience clause. If such schools were "efficient" and "suitable", they were to be taken into account in calculating the educational needs of the district. "Suitable" had a religious meaning. Thus if there were, in District A, 600 working-class children, 200 of whom were Roman Catholics, and there was a Roman Catholic school with accommodation for 200 children, then the district would need a Board School for only 400; but if, in District B, there were 600 working-class children, 200 of whom were Roman Catholics, and there was a Roman Catholic school for 300 pupils, then this district also was taken to need a Board School for 400 pupils. That is, the accommodation in an elementary school, which was not public, was only counted as available for children for whom it was "suitable".

(iv) Public elementary schools provided by voluntary bodies (e.g. the National Society). To be "public" they had to observe

9

the "Conscience clause", they had to be open to inspection, and they had to obey the Code of the Education Department. Accommodation in such schools was taken to be "efficient" and "suitable" for everyone.

If in District C there were 500 working-class children, 200 of whom were Church of England, and the Church of England had there a *public* elementary school with accommodation for 500 pupils, then the educational needs of District C were nil.

(v) Public elementary schools provided by school boards. These differed from other public elementary schools in that they gave no denominational instruction; and in that they were supported by the rates. These were also assumed to be efficient and "suitable" for all religions.

This plan was indeed a patchwork affair and sure to run into trouble. The supporters of school boards and of voluntary schools were at one another's throats before a single school board had been created; and, as the population was expanding and the system itself was envisaged as a growing and flexible one, the possibilities of serious rivalry were obvious from the outset. What then, in this explosive situation, were to be the main powers and duties of these new bodies, the school boards? What were the powers and duties of the Education Department? What was the machinery of control and direction of competing interests?

It must be remembered that a school board only came into existence if the Department decided that there was a deficiency of "efficient, suitable, public" school accommodation in the area. But once the school board was created, it had to act; it "shall supply" the existing deficiency (s. 6). The schools which it provided had to satisfy two conditions: (i) They had to be public elementary schools complying with the Code of the Education Department. (ii) If they gave religious instruction, it had not to be denominational. The latter was the only educational characteristic distinguishing them from the general body of public elementary schools

When these new schools were supplied, the school board had to maintain them, and the performance of this continuing duty was greatly facilitated by its continuing power of recourse to the rates. Other public elementary schools had no such unfailing financial pool.

But in many ways the most interesting duty was that of providing additional accommodation; for this was the key to development and the most probable cause of future trouble. The words of the Act imposing this duty were remarkable. "The school board shall . . . from time to time provide such additional school accommodation as is, *in their opinion*, necessary in order to supply a sufficient amount of public school accommodation for their district".[1] The school board were thus not only given the duty of supplying extra school places but were themselves made judges of the extent of that duty. How would this work? In Applecombe, let us imagine, there were in 1870 700 children needing public education, and a Church of England *public* elementary school for 300 only. Accordingly, in 1872 Applecombe School Board provided a school for 400 children. But Applecombe was rapidly expanding, and in 1880 there were altogether 1,100 children needing public education in the area, though the total school accommodation was only 700. Let us assume that 200 of the 400 pupils still to be provided for were Church of England. Then, under this section and having future expansion in view, Applecombe School Board could reasonably argue that its duty was to provide a new school not for 200 pupils (those who were not Church of England), nor 400 (the total deficiency), but even 500 or 600, taking account of young children not yet at school. And it need not take into account at all Church of England plans to provide additional Church of England *public* elementary school places mainly for the Church of England children. Further, the proposed large new school would almost inevitably draw pupils away from even the existing voluntary school. One need not be a voluntary school supporter to see that to give the school boards what was, *prima facie*, complete discretion in this matter was hardly prudent. So it proved in fact, and much of the vehement hostility which finally brought about the destruction of school boards and some of their best work may be traced to the operation of this provision. There is no section in the statute specifically saying what the schools of the school board were to do. Like other elementary schools, the principal part of their education was to be elementary. But what "elementary" meant as applied to a school curriculum, the Act did not say. Almost certainly the intention of those who framed the Act was that "elementary" in such a context meant Reading, Writing and Arithmetic. This can to some extent be inferred from the language of the Codes, the practice of the schools at the time, and the debate in Parliament; and supporting evidence came at a later date from the Department.[2]

We look through the 1870 Act in vain for any suggestion that the Education Department was to perform a function even remotely similar to that of a modern Minister of Education in promoting the education of the people and securing "the effective execution by local authorities, under his control and direction, of the national

---

[1] Elementary Education Act, 1870, s. 18. (Italics mine.—E.E.)
[2] See p. 54.

policy for providing a varied and comprehensive educational service in every area"[1] or even for a notion of benevolent general superintendence of education, similar to that of the old Board of Education.[2]

The rôle of the 1870 Education Department was to be more that of a central paymaster than that of a ministry. The major instrument of control put into its hands was that every public elementary school (including, of course, every school board school) must be conducted "in accordance with the conditions required to be fulfilled by an elementary school in order to obtain an annual parliamentary grant".[3] These conditions were to be in the Education Department Code of Regulations, which was to be laid on the table of both Houses of Parliament for one month before becoming operative.[4] The dominant idea of these regulations had been and continued to be that of safeguarding public expenditure. Any public elementary school would be aided, provided that it was efficient; that is, provided that it could earn payment on results. The Code of 1871 laid down the following tariff for children over seven, subject to the school having met at least 400 times:

(1) 6s. od. per scholar in average attendance.

(2) 4s. od. for passing in reading; 4s. od. for passing in writing; 4s. od. for passing in arithmetic.

(3) 3s. od. each for not more than two specific subjects (some ten subjects including geography, history, natural sciences, natural philosophy and political economy were listed, but other subjects might be chosen). But the three R's were obligatory, and the specific subjects could only be taken by pupils in Standards IV to VI.[5]

A further important financial weapon lay in the Department's power of blocking a school board's request for a loan. Thus, though a school board could in theory build or buy a school without consulting the Department,[6] in actual fact they had to raise loans on the security of the rates, and for this they had to obtain the consent of the Education Department.

The Education Department had, however, further powers and duties under the Act. Thus it had to decide if an alleged deficiency of public school accommodation warranted the formation of a school board.[7] In making this decision, the Department had to consider, not only the efficiency, but the "suitability" of existing accommodation for children of the district.

[1] Education Act, 1944, s. 1.   [2] Education Act, 1921, s. 1.
[3] Elementary Education Act, 1870, s. 7. (4)   [4] ibid. s. 97.
[5] New Code of Regulations, 1871, Arts. 19-21, and Schedule IV.
[6] Elementary Education Act, 1870, s. 19.
[7] Elementary Education Act, 1870, s. 8, 9, 10.

The Department might also declare a school board in default and control their future action by appointing new additional members.[1] This provision seems to have been aimed at the failure of a school board to act; but it might also apply in case of failure to comply with the Code. "If the school board do or permit any act in contravention of or fail to comply with the regulations according to which a school provided by them is required by this Act to be conducted, the Education Department may declare the school board to be and such board shall accordingly be deemed to be a board in default. ... If any dispute arises as to whether the school board have done or permitted any act in contravention of or have failed to comply with the said regulations, the matter shall be referred to the Education Department, whose decision thereon shall be final".[2]

Moreover, in the event of failure of a school board to provide such *additional* accommodation as the Department thought necessary, the Department might declare the board to be in default and, in effect, supersede it with its own nominees.[3]

These powers of the Education Department did not mean as effective control as a first reading would suggest. Declaring a school board in default was too serious a step to be taken frequently. It was in fact fitted for use against gross failure on the part of some of the many very small and very backward school boards.[4] Again, while the Department could deal with a school board which failed to supply additional accommodation, it had no similar direct power of curbing school boards which decided by needlessly competitive methods to squeeze out their voluntary school rivals. It is true that there was a provision for refusal of grant to unnecessary schools, but this applied only when these had not previously been in receipt of grant. Could the Department use it against a school board providing additional accommodation, when the statute had expressly given the school board discretion in such provision? We shall see shortly how thorny a question this proved.

Clearly the Department's most effective instrument for controlling school boards was the use of the grant in conjunction with the grant regulations. To twentieth-century eyes, the nineteenth-century Code appears an all-powerful and extremely flexible instrument; for the Department could, and did, insert conditions governing sites, buildings, qualifications of teachers and content of curriculum; and indeed the whole running of the school. Unless

[1] Elementary Education Act, 1870, s. 63.   [2] ibid. s. 16.   [3] ibid. s. 18.
[4] cf. Chester, *Central & Local Government*, Macmillan, 1951, p. 69. At the time of the Cross Commission thirty-two school boards had been declared in default and members appointed by the Education Department. In addition ten had been declared in default and a fresh election ordered. Most of these forty-two boards were in remote areas. Cross Commission *Second Report*, 1887, pp. 1004-5.

the board conformed, the Department could refuse to pay any grant, or part of the grant; or—a most effective weapon—warn that the grant would be witheld another year. Unless the school board came to heel, it lost not only the grant but its very power to raise a rate; for, by not conforming to the Code, the school ceased to be a "public elementary school". But there were throughout this period certain limiting factors. The Department (as we shall see later) felt powerless to vary the "standards", no matter how outdated these might prove, and consequently was unable to adjust its regulations adequately to meet varying conditions. Moreover, the power of effectively using the regulations depended in turn on the Department thoroughly understanding and accepting the provisions of the Education Act themselves, a condition which, unfortunately, was not always satisfied. Again, the interpretation, in the field, of the Acts and of the Code itself was, as the result of a last-minute change in the 1870 Bill, entrusted to the auditors responsible primarily to another government department.

The picture so far suggested might be rather crudely described as one of local factories of elementary education operated by small boards to supplement local voluntary production. These boards had been set up by a central department to meet local deficiencies and could be goaded into action by it. Once the local bodies were created, the Department would lay down rules as to premises and staff and other conditions, but its *essential* rôle was that of paying for work done according to a published tariff. Thus effectively the school boards were on the same contractual footing as the voluntary schools for their grants.

One of the most important sections of the Bill dealt with the local financial arrangements. The expenses of the school board were to be paid out of the "School Fund". This was to contain all moneys got by school boards; or, in the words of the Act, "all moneys received as fees from scholars, or out of moneys provided by Parliament, or raised by way of loan, or in any manner whatever received by the school board".[1] Doubtless, the main purpose of this device was, as the Cross Commission stated, by throwing rates, grants and fees together, to enable school boards to remit fees or even to establish free schools;[2] but in practice it had a great additional advantage for checking school board accounts. For it meant that a school board could not legally use rate money or scholars' fees directly to pay for anything. Everything must first be paid into the fund where it would lose its identity and then, as part of the fund, become available for use.

[1] Elementary Education Act, 1870, s. 53.
[2] Cross Commission *Final Report*, pp. 27-8.

Prima facie, this was an admirable plan. Since all money received by the board went into the pool, the chances of individuals tampering with it were lessened; and since deficiencies were to be met by the rates, the school boards would combine flexibility in their planning with a sense of responsibility in their expenditure. But there were at least two possible sources of misunderstanding, which together had serious consequences. Firstly, the phrase "moneys provided by Parliament" was too general, since what was really meant was "moneys provided by Parliament for the purpose of elementary education of children". The objection seems pedantic; but, as we have seen, the Act contained only an imperfect description of the educational duties of the school board, and certainly no clear upper limit to its work had been laid down. Hence, since money might be given by parliament to other government departments without specifying the agent to be employed in spending it, there was danger of money intended for purposes not contemplated in the 1870 Act becoming mixed with the School Fund. In the second place, the school board had an all-embracing power of falling back on the rates. "Any sum required to meet any deficiency in the school fund, whether for satisfying past or future liabilities, shall be paid by the rating authority out of the local rate".[1] To get this money, the school board had simply to serve a demand or "precept" on the local rating authority. Coupled with the previous obscurities, this sweeping power was dangerous; for if we imagine that a school board had obtained £50 from parents or some government department for a purpose only vaguely covered by the 1870 Act, but the project had in fact cost £60, there was a possibility that £10 of the rates might be drawn upon to meet the difference.

From the reports of the debates on this important section, it is clear that the obvious solution of fixing the local rate and letting the imperial treasury bear the residue, whatever it might be (that is, to let the deficiency fall on taxes rather than rates), was defeated because the plan was reckless of efficiency, and under it payments by results would "vanish altogether".[2] Moreover, the same rule had to be applied to voluntary schools and it was feared that the weight of central government would almost inevitably bring them increasingly under State control.

Thus, just as discussion of religious issues had led to neglect of the need for clear definition of the scope of the Act, so difficulties of fitting in voluntary schools contributed to the failure to face the need for defining clearly the measure of central responsibility for local

[1] Elementary Education Act, 1870, s. 54.
[2] *Elementary Education Bill, 1870. Debate in Parliament* p. 396. *Parliamentary Debates*, Third Series ccii, 1637.

expenditure. But that failure was also caused by the prevailing preoccupation with payments by results; for, since efficiency was considered in terms of grant-winning powers, it was natural to look at the school board as, in a sense, a local business enterprise, whose duty it was to extract fees from parents and win grants from a variety of sources, and to keep the contribution of the rates down to the lowest possible level. The school board was not to be in any sense the partner, or the agent, of the central body in a joint enterprise; the central body was mainly a watchdog over its expenditure. Forster put it thus: "It had never been his principle, or that of the government, to decide by any regulations of the Ministry or even of that House exactly what kind of education that (secular education) should be. If they attained an efficient secular education they would have effected the object they had in view".[1] The Code and Inspectors were instruments to ensure that efficiency.

We must now see how the expenditure of the school boards was in fact subjected to constant supervision and check. This was done by the district auditor, appointed by the Local Government Board.[2] As a result an on-the-spot check on waste and illegality was established as a complement to the legislative and financial powers of the department. In doing this, the auditor had to interpret and apply not only the Education Acts but also the Education Department's own regulations. How this control by audit actually worked we shall see later. It is enough to notice here that it was a more important method of control than is usually realised.

Such was the main statute from which school boards drew their powers. In the next chapter we shall, using the evidence given to the Cross Commission, examine some of the major problems connected with the administration of the 1870 Act.

[1] *Elementary Education Bill, 1870. Debate in Parliament*, p. 447. *Parliamentary Debates*, Third Series, cciii, 69.

[2] Elementary Education Act, 1870, s. 59–62. Elementary Education Act, 1873, s. 17 and 18 and the District Auditors Act, 1879.

III

RELUCTANT TYRANTS

The Education Department before 1890

*

MANY changes, mainly of a liberal character, were made in the legislative and administrative pattern of English education between 1870 and 1890, but these were changes of degree rather than of kind, and the essential features of the 1870 system remained. But 1890 brought a period of disintegration of the old order and of an attempt to build a new: and the administrative failure of that attempt made the crisis of 1899–1902 inevitable. The failure was threefold—failure in understanding, failure in planning and failure in action; but the fundamental failure was the first. For the Education Department tried to build its new order without itself discarding the concepts of the old. To realise this we must examine fundamental problems with which the administrators of the old order were occupied, and for that purpose we could hope for no better guidance than is given by the monumental volumes of the Cross Commission.[1]

The Cross Commission is of special interest, not merely because it examined so thoroughly the working of the Elementary Education Acts before 1886, and because it had a strong representation of London School Board among its members, but also because it had access to the experience of no fewer than three persons who had held the office of Secretary to the Education Department: Lord Lingen (1849–69), Sir Francis Sandford (1870–84) and Patrick Cumin (1884–90).

Lingen had entered the Education Office in 1847, and in 1849, at the age of thirty, became Secretary in succession to Kay-Shuttleworth. During the twenty years he held that office Lingen was the

---

[1] *Reports of the Royal Commission appointed to Inquire into the working of the Elementary Education Acts*, Vols. I–VI, Eyre & Spottiswoode, 1886–8.

dominating executive force. He was largely the creator of the various regulations, and acted in complete harmony with Lowe in the latter's production of the Revised Code. Lingen would certainly have been the last to shrink from accepting a large measure of responsibility for the changes of 1862. "Mr. Lingen is quite as powerful (as Mr. Lowe)", said an outspoken contemporary article,[1] "and a good deal more offensive. It is from Mr. Lingen that all the sharp, snubbing replies proceed". But, whether that bitter comment was true or not it did not prevent Lingen's being promoted, in 1869, to be permanent secretary to the Treasury, the highest post in the Civil Service, where, till his retirement in 1885 he enjoyed scope for his capacity for "negativing claims upon the public purse".[2] What had this redoubtable apostle of educational parsimony to say to the Cross Commission, when he was called as a witness in 1887? Lingen was alarmed at the incursions of the school boards into higher education. Accordingly with his nostalgic memories of the "beautiful simplicity" of Lowe's original system, it is not surprising that, though he agreed that the three R's should be merely the necessary minimum, not the maximum, he was in favour of rigorously restricting grants to these subjects. For Lingen saw clearly the difficulty of defining secondary education on a subject basis. Once the State ceased to base its grant upon the three R's, he argued, "you cannot logically say of any subject that it is not desirable to know it". Hence he proposed to sweep all the accretions out of the Code and to have an elementary system with a grant from the government strictly limited to the elementary subjects and a similarly restricted local rate. This was, of course, consistent with his fundamental assumption that not more than 5 per cent of the pupils who entered elementary schools could profit from secondary education. It was, too, closely linked with his plan for delegating as much responsibility as possible to new local authorities—for by getting back to the simple essentials the central office would be cleared of much cluttering detail and education would present no more difficult an administrative problem for the county bodies than roads or sanitation. We shall see that both Cumin and Sandford had visions of the same kind.

The spotlight of the Cross Commission investigations was naturally centred on Patrick Cumin, the Secretary in possession, and throughout no fewer than nine days he was subjected to a searching and sometimes hostile examination. Cumin had been a permanent member of the staff of the Education Department from 1868, and had, for Forster's Bill, drafted some of the most important clauses by which religious difficulties were overcome, or evaded. As

---

[1] *Saturday Review*, 16th April, 1864, p. 465
[2] *Dictionary of National Biography* 1901–11.

Assistant Secretary he had been in large measure responsible for the legal side of the administration of the 1870 Act and was throughout closely concerned with disputes over the rights of voluntary schools. The Mundella Code of 1882 was largely his work and embodied some of his main ideas. The policy of the Department in this crucial period was founded, if not very convincingly, on Cumin's belief in strict legal correctness in the administration of the Acts; but the fierceness of his examination before the Cross Commission is not to be entirely explained by that fact. A Sudeten Scot, Cumin had a distaste for the forms of religion prevailing in his country, and, indeed, no love for fervour in any form. He was therefore unlikely to be *persona grata* to the Churches, or to clerical inspectors who sympathised with the opponents of the school boards. Yet to his colleagues in the office he was a delightful and varied personality; relying perhaps too much on personal contacts (he might be in and out of another's room half a dozen times in a day); a friend of Arnold and "Chinese Gordon"; a lover of the Classics, of poetry and of drama; suspicious of inspectors and their aptness to pose awkward local problems ("if you get an inspector on his hind legs," he is reputed to have said, "it's the devil"); with an extreme interest in the House of Commons and an instinctive sense of what would be accepted there—anything more unlike a dictatorial bureaucrat it would be difficult to imagine.[1]

Cumin's examination in 1886 was, of course, largely aimed at elucidating departmental policy as embodied in the Code. At first sight, the Code of 1886 was a liberal and flexible instrument compared with Codes of earlier days. Thus there was some easing of the rigidity of the standards in the statement that no attendance was *as a rule* to be recognised of pupils who passed out of the seventh standard;[2] and the lockstep within the standards had been relaxed by a provision that, in exceptional cases, and subject to safeguards, pupils might be excused from being examined in a standard higher than in the previous year.[3] Further, grant was made for the elementary subjects not on individual passes but on the percentage of passes;[4] pupils could be examined in not more than three class subjects (which, if taken at all, were to be taken by classes throughout the school); and scholars could also be examined in not more than two specific subjects—provided that they were also examined in the "elementary subjects" in Standard V, VI, or VII.

---

[1] *Patrick Cumin—Secretary of the Education Department*, London, Hugh Rees, 1901.
[2] 1886 Code, Art. 13.   [3] 1886 Code, Art. 109(e).
[4] Thus, while the 1871 Code promised 4s. 0d. for each pass in each of the three R's (Art. 19B.2), the 1884 Code promised "*a grant on examination in the elementary subjects* determined by the percentage of passes in the examination at the rate of 1d. for every unit of percentage". Art. 109(e).

But closer scrutiny of the Code, and of the instructions to inspectors shows that these concessions were hedged about with restrictions. And Cumin's evidence indicated both how illusory some of the advances were and how serious the danger that the Code, and the Department, would prove unable to keep in touch with educational realities as well as with legal requirements.

Cumin had a profound belief in Reading, Writing and Arithmetic as the only *essential* components of elementary education. Indeed at one point he appeared to identify elementary education with the three R's.[1] Further, his preoccupation with the elementary subjects and their incarnation in the standards led to a strange conclusion about the irrelevance of the age of children in assessing the need for accommodation for elementary schooling. Though defensible on a strictly logical basis, it reflected a lack of ability, in the Education Department, to rethink the Code in terms of changing educational facts: "As to the persons who want to go to elementary schools", argued Cumin, "it does not matter whether they are 16, 17 or 18. The question is whether they can take up the curriculum in the Code which consists of seven Standards. . . . Since the Code of 1882 there is no age specified; age is abolished. Consequently in an infant school you can have a boy of 9 or a boy of 10; and in another school you can have a boy of 14. The only question that is asked is: 'You are in this school; are you in any standard?' 'Yes, I am in the seventh Standard'. 'Very well, then it does not matter what age you are. If you are capable of taking advantage of the public provision for education and are in the first, second, third, fourth, fifth or sixth Standard, and have not passed the seventh Standard, you are entitled to go to that school.' . . . *It is a question of whether the child has passed a curriculum which the Legislature (sic) has defined to be elementary education.* . . . Supposing, for instance, that a boy had passed the seventh Standard and said: 'I do not want to go to this school to learn the elements, but I want to go for the purpose of learning Latin, or chemistry, or agriculture, and I know my seventh Standard.' I say that that boy cannot go to that school because he has passed the Seventh Standard."[2]

Here then was one safeguard of the rates; a bulwark relied on to prevent "elementary" education encroaching on "secondary" preserves: no child could go to an elementary school who was not in the standards; and the standards were the schemes of reading, writing and arithmetic prescribed in the Code. But, it may be objected, what of all the galaxy of class and specific subjects? To which Cumin replied that these were permissible auxiliaries only; valuable

---

[1] Cross Commission, *First Report*, 1886. Q. 293.
[2] Cross Commission, *First Report*, 1886. Q. 379-83. (Italics mine.—E.E.)

enough, but in no way necessary. " 'Every child in a school must be thoroughly instructed in reading, writing and arithmetic, i.e. the standard subjects; most of the children ought to be instructed in the class subjects, and some individual children may be instructed in the specific subjects'. Therefore, in the Code you cannot get beyond what is really and truly elementary education, because up to the seventh standard you must pass, and you must be taught in a standard, and these are all obligatory elements (i.e. the three R's); the class subjects and the others are incidental to the elements; but so long as you are in a standard you cannot be said to have received a sufficient elementary education. If you have any time to spare you may devote it to the other subjects."[1]

Such was the first great belief of the Education Department at this time, a belief which continued to dominate their thought even during the next decade. There had been qualifications to it, but such awkward facts were rationalised in one way or another. We have already seen how Cumin expunged the question of age from his consideration, which was perfectly logical if the pure doctrine of the standards was accepted. But the rising age of elementary pupils was presenting school boards with a choice which could not be evaded in practice. If a pupil went through all the standards by 12 or 13 and stayed on at school the Education Department virtuously paid no grant for him; but was the school board really to prevent him from entering for a Science and Art examination and thereby benefiting himself and earning a substantial grant for the board? And, if he did so, was it to be expected that the headmaster, who happened to be paid from the school fund of the elementary school, should refrain from giving such assistance as he had time to spare?

Another change in the situation was that the social implications of "elementary" education had weakened in Whitehall. As Cumin put it, there was no reason why the children of the Prince of Wales should not go to an elementary school along with the children of the poorest persons.[2] But, if this were so, on the one hand the schools were likely to have an increasingly large proportion of able pupils demanding higher education, and on the other to excite an increasing degree of jealousy among any existing "secondary" schools with whom they might compete.

But the most serious weakness in Cumin's case remains to be considered. It will be recalled that, although the system of standards was, in the Department's view, the principal and only *essential* constituent of elementary education, this left room for a residue. How was that residue determined? "A school might be an elementary

[1] Cross Commission, *First Report*, 1886. Q. 665.
[2] Cross Commission, *Third Report*, Q. 58,998–59,000.

school", said Cumin, "although it included more than elementary instruction. This is an illustration. At Birmingham they have a school for the 7th Standard alone. This school is attached to, or has attached to it, a sort of manual labour or technical school, which is supplied at the voluntary expense of Mr. Dixon. They have to settle a timetable and they have to bring it within this definition (i.e., that the principal part was elementary) because if they did not the rate would be bad (*sic*), and we could not pay a grant. So we determined that it must be shown that a larger proportion of time according to that timetable was to be devoted to reading, writing, and arithmetic, and I think we admitted drawing."[1]

We shall have occasion later to consider this interesting Birmingham school, but here we must note the remarkable nature of this statement of Education Department policy. There is a veiled suggestion that the school was the seventh standard itself, because that was the elementary part, which gave semblance of legality to the proceedings. To obtain the grant and use the rate they *had* to import the standards into the definition so that the "principal part" of the school became elementary. Accordingly the timetable for this seventh standard was reconstructed by having reading, writing and arithmetic substituted for (say) mathematics and theoretical chemistry, and the class, instead of being first year in the Electricity Division of a Technical School, became a Seventh Standard Elementary School eligible to receive grant and to use rates. It is scarcely necessary to know that the total staff of this school consisted of a headmaster, a master for projection and machine drawing, one for mathematics, one for mechanics, one for physics and chemistry, a practical carpenter, and a junior laboratory assistant to realise how shallow this artifice was.[2]

The belief in the immortality of the standards was closely related to the doctrine of the educational omnipotence of the Code. The standards were in fact the Code's creation (though they had been recognised by statute for certificates of exemption);[3] they were in theory varied by it from year to year; and the class and specific subjects were varied as the Department thought fit. The importance of the Code had greatly increased since 1870 and it had become in effect an addition to the education law.[4] Thus the Code of 1882 added a seventh Standard, and considerably altered the formula by introducing a "merit" grant, payable on general features of the school work.

[1] Cross Commission, *Third Report*, Q. 58,997.
[2] Cross Commission, *Second Report*, Q. 30,894.
[3] e.g. Elementary Education Act, 1876, Schedule I.
[4] Cross Commission, *Final Report*, pp. 36-7.

What then were the sources, and what were the limits, of this Code's power? The 1870 Act had enacted that the conditions of grant should be those "contained in the minutes of the Education Department in force for the time being", and had required that those minutes must, as a condition of coming into force, lie for a month on the table of both Houses of Parliament.[1] This might suggest that failure to comply with these conditions would simply lead to withdrawal of grant; but, as we have already seen, it was also laid down that every public elementary school must "be conducted in accordance with the conditions required to be fulfilled by an elementary school in order to obtain an annual parliamentary grant".[2] Thus obedience to the Code ("the conditions of grant") became a *sine qua non* for the legal existence of a public elementary school. Only Board schools could enjoy rate support and, as Board schools had to be public elementary schools, the Code in fact laid down conditions on fulfilment of which the rates could be used.

What then could the Code do, according to the Department? It could add standards; it could expand the definition of elementary education; it could, and did, include *prima facie* secondary school subjects like mechanics, physics and magnetism, and *ipso facto* these became a legitimate part of the work of an elementary school; indeed it stated "that any other subject" could, with the Department's permission, be taken as a specific subject. The Commissioners did not miss the significance of these claims, as the following exchange shows:—

Question: "But is not that in the Code and not in the Act of Parliament?"

Cumin: "But the Code is in the Act of Parliament."

Question: "As a matter of fact has not the Code introduced a tyranny at the Education Office to define what elementary education is?"

Cumin: "If it is a tyranny, it is the Act of Parliament."

Further questioning elicited that the Department held that all the class and specific subjects could be transformed into elementary subjects by the Code and imposed on the elementary schools.[3] Unfortunately the Commission did not take the enquiry one stage further: could the Department by its Code abolish reading, writing and arithmetic as elementary subjects (in the top three standards, say) and substitute for them Mathematics, Electricity and Machine Construction? Could it, in effect, abolish the standards, in whole or in part, and substitute for them a curriculum which had previously been considered secondary or technical? The trend of Cumin's answers suggests that, logically, he would have been compelled to

---

[1] Elementary Education Act, 1870, s. 97.   [2] ibid. s. 7 (4)
[3] Cross Commission, *First Report*, Q. 1,016–18, 1,072–77.

answer in the affirmative; for he had already claimed that the Department could, by the Code, create elementary subjects and put them on an equal footing with the three R's.

If, therefore, the Department could, in 1886, make into elementary subjects, subjects which were not considered elementary in 1870, and if further it could reduce the elementary subjects of 1870 to a small fraction of the curriculum or even abolish them altogether, it might be argued that it was claiming that it could change the whole purpose of the Act of Parliament. It was claiming in essence that a curriculum which would, in Parliament's view, have been non-elementary in 1870 could, in 1886, be imposed as elementary on public elementary schools, even although its sanction for doing so came from the Elementary Education Act of 1870, and even although an elementary school was defined in that Act as a school at which the principal part of the education was elementary. There was, of course, no suggestion that the Department could override the *express* provisions of a statute:[1] what was implied was that the 1870 Act had by one section given the Department such powers in applying its own provisions as enabled it to enlarge "elementary education" beyond anything which the 1870 Act itself could be taken to contemplate.

It must be noted that the Department claimed the power not only to fix the content of the curriculum but also the limits of accommodation, as determined by the age of children to be accommodated —if it decided that children aged two must be accommodated, that was enough to legalise provision of accommodation for two-year-olds. It claimed, indeed, the power of putting on the ratepayers burdens which it was not certain that the Act of Parliament had ever intended them to bear.[2] Cumin, of course, recognised that these powers were subject to confirmation in the law courts; what he and the Department appear not to have realised adequately was that their powers of interpreting the application of the Act of Parliament operated only within limits which, flexible though they were, were to be inferred from the Act itself, e.g. that the education to be given by school boards was only that of children. The Department was, in fact, too ready to refer to and quote its own Code and not ready enough to refer to the parent Act.

It would, however, be wrong to infer from the discussion so far that the Department was eager for despotic power. The reverse was true. As Cumin said, if it was a tyranny it was the doing of the Act of Parliament—as hastily interpreted by the Department. Force of circumstances, in the form of unexpectedly precocious children or rapidly growing schools or inconsiderately progressive school boards,

---

[1] Cross Commission, *First Report*, Q. 1,074.
[2] Cross Commission, *First Report*, Q. 1,810–12.

had compelled the Department to expand the curriculum, and alter the basis of calculation of accommodation, and it assumed that legally it had the power to do all these things through the Code, even if, as had to be confessed, the Code had been merely laid before Parliament in dummy.[1] Indeed, so far was Cumin from wanting bureaucratic power that in his scheme for future development he argued in favour of extensive devolution of power to county authorities; for to his mind the central authority was being relied on to make too many decisions: why, for example, should they be responsible for the morals of the children in every school?[2]

This was not mere theory. The evidence had already shown the reluctance of the Department to accept final responsibility for the very awkward questions connected with the supply of school accommodation, e.g. the extent to which, where voluntary schools already existed, a school board might supply overlapping, competitive accommodation.

When a school board had been created and the question arose of "additional" supply, owing to growth of population in the area, the Department held that the school board had the first right to supply the deficiency, and if they decided to do so any additional voluntary school accommodation might be deemed unnecessary, and therefore ineligible for grant. The relevant section said that the school board was to supply such accommodation as was in their opinion necessary.[3] The Department held, and in this the Law Officers supported them, that this gave the school boards *absolute* discretion as to what accommodation they should supply.[4] Of course, in the last resort the Department might refuse the school board a loan for their building, or even refuse a grant to the school when built.[5] But the Department had no power to prevent *ab initio* the supply of extra school places by school boards, and they did not want any such power.

But even before a school board was set up when the deficiency of accommodation in a district was being estimated, the thorny question arose of the extent to which an existing voluntary school, which was *not* a public elementary school, supplied "*suitable*" accommodation to the children of the district:[6] did the Church of England denominational schools supply suitable accommodation to the children of non-conformist parents already attending that school, or only to those whose parents were willing to allow them to remain there; or what was to be the criterion? This problem was obviously

---

[1] Cross Commission, *First Report*, Q. 1,021.
[2] Cross Commission, *Third Report*, Q. 59,583.
[3] Elementary Education Act, 1870, s. 18.
[4] Cross Commission, *First Report*, Q. 1,878–82.
[5] Elementary Education Act, 1870, s. 98.
[6] Elementary Education Act, 1870, s. 5.

an exciting one for Church members of the Commission; and it was likely to be an embarrassing one for any administrator; but why had the Secretary to be asked substantially the same question six times in succession?

Rev. T. D. C. Morse: "I should be glad if you would be good enough to tell me who, in the last resource, is the judge of suitability?"

Cumin: "Suitability is the simplest thing in the world to determine."

Rev. T. D. C. Morse: "Is it the Department or the school board that is to determine the suitability?"

Cumin: "The question of suitability is a question which every manager may determine for himself. If the school is a school attended by a certain number of persons, whatever the nature of the teaching may be, that school is suitable to this extent: that it gets an annual grant after a certain time."

The Chairman: "The question is, who is the ultimate judge, the Department or the managers?"

Cumin: "Supposing that you have a school which is opened by any religious body or irreligious body, and the school is more than is necessary in that district for the purpose of giving accommodation, we say to that school, 'Go on for a year and if at the end of the year you produce 30 scholars, you can have a grant.'"

The Chairman: "The question is, who is to be the ultimate judge of the suitability—the Department or the local managers?"

Cumin: "Ultimately the Department say, 'Produce 30 children and you shall have a grant.'"

The Chairman: "But the Department is the judge in the long run as to what the facts of the case demand?"

Cumin: "No doubt. If the Department have certain facts produced to them, they say, 'You may have a grant.'"

The Chairman: "The Department are the ultimate judges of the facts?"

Cumin: "Yes, they are the construers of the Code."[1]

Such sustained evasiveness was not, of course, accidental. The rest of the evidence would suggest that a direct answer would have been that the Department had had such extreme difficulty in adjusting school board accommodation to existing voluntary accommodation that the less it had to do with it the better it would be pleased; that it had tried to throw the responsibility on the localities; but that both with regard to accommodation to meet initial deficiencies (s. 5) and additional accommodation (s. 18) some school boards had proved so unreasonable that the Department had had to make final decisions, falling back, in the last resort, upon their powers of giving or withholding grant.

But the substance of the answers given by Cumin is in itself

[1] Cross Commission, *First Report*, Q. 409–14.

revealing. As far as it could contrive, the Department's test was essentially a pragmatic one. If, in the struggle for survival between board schools and voluntary schools, a voluntary school could in fact exist for a year, and show thirty children at the end of it, that fact was deemed to prove that it it provided "suitable" education for a sufficient number of children to warrant the State's authorising its continuance by means of a grant.

Looking through Cumin's eyes at the administrative position in 1886–7, we see an Education Department holding tenaciously on to the system of standards as the heart of elementary education; worried by the conflict between the interests of school boards and voluntary schools; conscious that school boards were in some cases unjust in using their powers against voluntary schools; assured of the final overwhelming powers of the grant regulations but reluctant to accept any additional responsibility for the Department. As we shall see, this position was buttressed by strong support of the auditor's decisions in restricting any activities of the school board which seemed of doubtful legality.

We have already mentioned that one of the members of the Cross Commission was Sir Francis Sandford, who had held the office of Secretary to the Education Department from 1870 to 1884, and who, from 1874 to 1884, was also Secretary of the Science and Art Department. A devoted Churchman, Sandford was credited, within the Education Department, with having been in large measure responsible for the line of tolerant compromise which Forster took with the 1870 Bill. He was a signatory of the Majority Report of the Cross Commission, which thus received the endorsement of the experience in office of one of the ablest practical men of his time.[1] Sandford's reservations to the Cross Report were partly aimed at strengthening the position of the voluntary schools and partly at defining the legal position more clearly. He proposed that there should be a statutory statement of the conditions for the recognition of public elementary schools; in effect that the then Code should be made into an Act of Parliament. He also argued that a distinct line between primary and secondary education should be laid down by law and that the term "elementary" should be defined. And he proposed that *limited* assistance from the rates should be given to voluntary schools, with *limited* representation of the ratepayers on the management of the schools.[2] These proposals must be viewed in relation to the Sandford Memorandum, proposing to abolish school

---

[1] cf. *Patrick Cumin—Secretary of the Education Department*, London, Hugh Rees, 1901, p. 12.
[2] Cross Commission, *Final Report,* pp. 232–3.

boards and transfer their functions to County Councils and District Councils, which is the prototype of the 1902 Act.[1]

From all the evidence it was abundantly clear in 1888 that the legal powers of school boards in their higher grade school work were urgently in need of authoritative definition. The Cross Commission Report itself stressed that need in no uncertain language: "As the meaning and limits of the term 'elementary' have not been defined in the Education Acts, nor by any judicial or authoritative interpretation, but depend only upon the annual codes of the Department on whose power of framing such codes no limit has hitherto been imposed, *it would appear to be of absolute necessity that some definition of the instruction to be paid for out of the rates and taxes should be put forth by the Legislature. Until this is done the limits of primary and secondary education cannot be defined.*"[2] Unfortunately, this "absolute necessity" was not fully recognised, and the story of the next decade will reveal how some of the more detailed recommendations, which presupposed the fulfilment of this major duty, were hastily or imperfectly put into operation, with disastrous results.

This chapter contains many apparent inconsistencies: a delightfully human Secretary, framing and administering inhuman regulations; a doctrine that the Code could do all, coupled with a determination that the Department should do as little as possible; and a belief that elementary education was essentially the three R's, linked to an assumption that potentially it embraced the whole field of education. Only by seeing these and other inconsistencies shall we fully realise both the fact that this was an era of transition and the extent to which terms like "elementary", "technical", "continuation" and "secondary" were apt to prove treacherous servants of those who relied upon them to convey, without definition, any precise meaning.

---

[1] Cross Commission, *Final Report*, pp. 204-7.
[2] Cross Commission, *Final Report*, p. 217. (Italics mine.—E.E.)

IV

HIGHER DAY SCHOOLS

First Phase (1870–1900)

*

THIS discussion of higher education under the school boards falls into six divisions: the background of ideas; the origins and early development of higher board schools; their position at the time of the Cross Commission; their development from 1890–1900; the special circumstances in London; and the significance of the Higher Elementary Schools Minute of 1900.

(1) THE BACKGROUND OF IDEAS

It seems obvious today that higher grade schools were an inevitable outcome of nineteenth-century conditions; for an increasingly progressive industrial community, with popularly elected school boards sensitive to local needs, could hardly accept a system which in essence clamped education down to narrow standards of reading, writing and arithmetic. By 1880 most of the large school boards had to face the problem of coping with intelligent lads who had gone through the standards before they were at an age at which their parents wanted them to leave school. Some provision was eventually bound to be made for them, either by local action or central legislation. And, in view of the vagueness of the 1870 Act, school boards, with the local electors behind them, might argue that they had a moral, if not a legal, duty to provide for their pupils the best education that the Education Department and the auditors would allow.

The Education Department, on the other hand, were baffled by the problem of administering the 1870 Act. It has been well said that judges' difficulties in interpreting a statute arise "when the Legislature has had no meaning at all; when the question which is

29

raised on the statute never occurred to it".[1] This was essentially the root of the Education Department's difficulty in dealing with higher education by school boards purporting to work under the 1870 Act.

It may, however, be argued that if the Education Department had, through their regulations, intelligently used their powers of interpreting the Act, higher education to the age of fifteen could have been firmly established on a lasting basis under the school boards. But it must be remembered that, apart from the vagueness of the Education Acts, few Englishmen had, in the early years of the school boards, any clear notion of the possibilities of State-aided higher education. The very term "secondary education" was new. It seems to have been first used by Condorcet in 1792 to describe the second of his proposed *four* stages of education. It was therefore, in Condorcet's view, as the Hadow Report implied, more akin to English central schools of pre-1944 days than to our municipal grammar schools. Secondary education, in Condorcet's sense, might therefore be considered as a second phase of *elementary* education. Matthew Arnold, who was familiar with Condorcet's writings, was largely responsible for popularising the term in England. As early as 1859 he pled with the Newcastle Commission to urge the government to organise their secondary education, and in 1864 congratulated an M.P., who had used the term in a parliamentary resolution, for having given "official stamp to that useful word *secondary*".[2] Its meaning, however, remained indeterminate. The word became increasingly common in various reports, but it did not receive full official sanction till the Royal (Bryce) Commission on Secondary Education was appointed in 1894.

Moreover, whatever the views of progressive writers like Arnold, there was for long no agreement that *any* form of higher education was to be provided by the State; for many believed that higher education was inherently education for people who could pay for it. As Lowe put it, it was a matter for private enterprise, offering scope for the ordinary principles of political economy in the form of payment by results.[3] And till the end of the century the Education Department continued to receive memorials protesting that the school boards were providing cheap higher education *to the middle classes.*

The context of ideas was further complicated by the development, during the latter half of the century, of a vigorous demand for "technical education". The need for some form of technical training

---

[1] Gray, *The Nature and Sources of the Law*, 2nd ed., Macmillan, 1948, p. 173.
[2] Connell, *The Educational Thought and Influence of Matthew Arnold*, Routledge and Kegan Paul, 1950, p. 244.
[3] R. Lowe, *Middle Class Education: Endowment or Free Trade*, Education Miscellanies. Cole Collection. Vol. 20, 1868.

had been made painfully evident by England's poor showing at the exhibitions of 1851 and 1862 and the French Exposition Universelle of 1878 which "annonçait brillamment la rentrée en scène de la France, acheva d'inquiéter les Anglais"[1] Technical education was obviously necessary; but England's discomfiture arose partly from the fact that no one knew how to fit it in to the English pattern. Anything technical was foreign to a gentlemanly education. But were the labouring classes to have the only form of higher education at State expense, and if so where was it to stop? And did this technical education differ only from secondary education in that the former was obviously useful and the latter was not? And what local bodies were to provide it (until 1888 there were no suitable local authorities)? And should the body supervising technical education be the Education Department with its experience in running a system of education, or the Science and Art Department with its experience in examining in a field so closely allied to technical education? It is against this background of unsolved problems that we must consider the rise of school board higher schools if we are to evaluate fairly the Education Department's ineffectiveness in dealing with them.

(2) THE ORIGINS AND EARLY DEVELOPMENT OF SCHOOL BOARD HIGHER DAY SCHOOLS

The school boards inherited a system built on grades of achievement, or "standards", starting at age six and roughly extending over the following six years. Once the children passed all these standards, either by learning more rapidly or by staying longer than the average child, the problem of "higher" education in some form arose. The Department might have regulated the giving of such higher education (a) by stating an upper age limit; (b) by prescribing upper educational limits; or (c) by ensuring that the board schools were restricted to the humblest strata of society. Before discussing the rise of the higher schools we may briefly consider why such restrictions were not successful.

(a) An upper age limit was never *effectively* prescribed. The Department contented itself with the statement in its regulations that no attendance would be "recognised", for grant purposes, of pupils above a certain age (e.g. 18 in 1874). As Morant later pointed out, an attempt in 1880 to enforce a clear-cut prohibition of education above a certain age (14) provoked such an outcry that it was almost immediately withdrawn.

(b) The rules of the Department were similarly equivocal about

---

[1] M. Leclerc, *L'éducation des classes moyennes et dirigeantes en Angleterre*, Colin et Cie, Paris, 1894. Quoted in Balfour, *Educational Systems*, p. 165.

31

subject-matter, for though in *theory* the top standard formed an upper educational limit, in *fact* the introduction of class and specific subjects continually obscured this boundary. Even in 1871 instruction could be given and grant earned by pupils above Standard IV in one or more specific subjects, including natural philosophy and political economy. And as from 1875 pupils could learn "class subjects"; or, if they had passed the sixth and final standard, not more than three "specific" subjects. This clearly left the door to higher education open. In 1882, accordingly, an attempt was made to restate the Department's requirements and to bring them into line with changed facts: (i) A Seventh Standard was added; (ii) the upper age limit was abolished; (iii) no pupil who had passed the seventh standard was to earn grant; and (iv) "class" subjects could be taught throughout the school and specific subjects in the three top standards. Higher education was, therefore, still possible, and the possibility was enhanced by the statement in subsequent codes that there was no reason why scholars should not remain at school after passing the seventh standard, even if they brought no addition to the funds except their fees.

(*c*) The third restriction was that board schools should not charge more than ninepence a week as fee. This might have been expected to keep away from board schools the children of ambitious middle class parents, since the fee barrier would not keep out working class pupils. But in the event many middle class parents seemed to prefer efficient, cheap schools, to inefficient, dear ones. In any case pupils from working class homes proved to be much more capable than had been anticipated. Further the restriction of the fees to 9d. a week was not so serious a handicap to school boards as had been expected, since the combination of rate-aid and science and art grants enabled them to rely less and less upon fees of any kind.

The development of board school higher education, in spite of such restrictions, was most rapid in the north of England, in districts where there was an intelligent and relatively prosperous artisan population, whose children were able to attend school full time and thus to get through the standards more quickly than half-timers in other schools; who were prepared to pay the 9d. fee; who appreciated the potential value of a longer education; and who looked to the school boards as the natural bodies to provide it.

A penetrating general analysis of the conditions leading to the rise of the higher grade schools, written by Morant, will be found in Appendix A. Here we may first usefully consider in some detail the early development of higher education at Bradford and Nottingham; for in these two cases momentous decisions were made at the outset by the Education Department.

32

In 1873 H.M. Inspector for Bradford area, after reporting favourably on the education given in a Bradford school where there were no half-timers, continued: "It would be best to have such higher elementary schools as I have described established by the school board, as the difficulties which might be too much for ordinary managers would not affect schools *maintained out of the rates,* and thus their permanence would be secured."[1] Bradford School Board were then too preoccupied with educating the poorest types of pupil to act on the suggestion; but in 1875 and later they, with the Education Department's consent, established higher schools at the maximum permissible fee of 9d. a week. To begin with such higher schools were simply public elementary schools teaching the subjects of the Code; but, since the parents were prepared to pay the higher fee, the board was able to provide better qualified staff, with "assistant" teachers in lieu of pupil teachers and monitors. At this stage it was indeed argued not only that such schools were no more costly to the ratepayer than ordinary public elementary schools, but that their eventual cost would be nil.

These first ventures aroused no departmental qualms until 1879 when Bradford proposed to establish a fourth higher elementary school. An inspector warned the Department that, although there was a need for such schools in Bradford, there was a danger that they would be used by parents who could afford to pay the fees of self-supporting schools. The problem was fully considered at the highest levels of the Education Department, and the policy for such advanced elementary schools laid down in August 1879, in a long and important letter to Bradford. The main points made were:—

(1) Conditions had changed since the institution of national elementary education. The original object of the grant was to educate the labouring classes, but the Acts of 1870 and 1876 made no attempt to define the social position of children taking advantage of public elementary education.

(2) Especially since 1875 there had been an enlargement of the scope of elementary education. The specific subjects recited in Schedule IV to the Code gave the opportunity of obtaining education "which might almost be called secondary".

(3) Managers had, to teach such subjects, obtained the services of teachers of high attainments. But, though this enabled parents to obtain advanced education for a low cost (at the expense of the taxpayer and ratepayer), few children were able to take advantage of these opportunities. But if children had the industry and the

---

[1] *Report of Committee of Council on Education,* 1873–4, p. 52. (Italics mine.—E.E.)

33

ability every opportunity should be afforded them. It was, however, necessary to avoid wasting teaching power.

(4) "To meet these difficulties my Lords are of opinion that an attempt should be made by school boards of large towns to grade the different Schools under their control by adjusting, as far as is possible, the quality of the education given to the fee paid, while at the same time, by means of exhibitions or otherwise, facilities are afforded for those who show capacity to pass from the lower to the higher grade schools.

"In the higher grade Schools the object should be not merely to give a more advanced education but to defray its cost by means of higher fees, so that the contribution of the ratepayers for the education of the well-to-do children may be less than for the children of the poor".[1]

Thus in 1879 the Department officially described higher grade schools as schools giving higher quality education in return for a larger fee to better class pupils; it recognised the use of rates on such schools; and it described some of the work in them, permissible under its own Code, as being *almost secondary*.

At Bradford the question of the content of rate-aided education was dealt with vaguely by the Education Department; but it recurred in 1880 when Nottingham School Board put forward a scheme for a "higher graded school". The board stated its objectives frankly: (a) The reorganised school under discussion would remain an elementary school. (b) The major aim would be to study the specific subjects of the Fourth Schedule of the Code, "or such other subjects as the Board may determine with reference to the requirements of local industries". (c) The pupils would fall into two divisions—a junior division comprising pupils in Standards I–IV, paying a fee of 9d. a week; and a senior division consisting of Standards V and VI and two *new* Standards, VII and VIII. (d) The curriculum for Standards VII and VIII would, in addition to the elementary subjects, include Latin, French, German, Mechanics, Mathematics, Natural Philosophy and Chemistry. (e) Pupils in Standard VIII would be prepared for the Local Examinations for Juniors of Oxford and Cambridge or London, and the curriculum of Standard VIII would be modified to meet the requirements of the examination. (f) The fee for the upper division would be 9d. a week, but pupils who had passed Standard VI in some other elementary school in the borough would pay only 6d. per week.

H.M. Inspector for the area pointed out the important issues of policy involved. Could a school board provide intermediate educa-

[1] M.E. E61/26383, "Bradford. Horton Road Board School. 23/8/79.

tion? Could it prepare its pupils for an external examination? Could it run a school for middle class pupils which would compete with the local high school?

An Education Department letter of September, 1880, agreed to the school board's proposal, but only on the understanding that the proposed upper departments should be elementary schools as defined by the Code, and it was suggested that the subjects taught should be limited to those in the Code. *"But there would be no objection to their organising a class in connection with the School, which might obtain the science grants offered by the Science and Art Department"*. The letter added a statement that the Department might in the future restrict the development of higher grade schools "in order that no departure may be made from the terms on which the Parliamentary Grant is made for primary education".[1]

It must be noted that this direct encouragement to take the courses and sit the examinations of the Science and Art Department was given in 1880 when Sir F. Sandford was head of both the Education Department and the Science and Art Department, and it may have been thought that co-operation between the two departments was assured for the future; but it is still true that the Department here incited school boards to a course which was later found to be illegal.

Then, towards the end of 1882, when Cumin had become Secretary of the Department, Nottingham School Board put forward a revised scheme which expressly proposed entering pupils for the Science and Art examinations. It was now told that the curriculum must be kept within the Code. But the mischief had been done. School boards had inferred that the development of their higher schools must be on lines laid down by the Science and Art Department's regulations, and not on those suggested by the specific subjects of the Code; and the laxity and ambiguity of the Code, especially after 1890, encouraged them in that belief.

As we shall see later, school boards had, from an early date, been urged by the Science and Art Department to promote instruction in science and art, but most schools preferred to enter their pupils for examinations in particular subjects in science or art rather than adopt the organised science curriculum suggested by South Kensington. Indeed, until 1883 there were only two Organised Science Schools in the country, neither of which was under a school board. But the report of the Royal Commission on Technical Education urged school boards to establish such schools. Thereafter Organised Science Schools developed rapidly. The movement flourished in the

[1] M.E. E97/68 3/9/80. (Italics mine.—E.E.)

North, where there was an urgent demand for training in science, however narrow the courses might be.

(3) HIGHER GRADE SCHOOLS AT THE TIME OF THE CROSS COMMISSION

We have seen something of the beginnings of higher education at Bradford and Nottingham. Manchester claimed to have had a higher grade school as early as 1877; Sheffield had one by 1880; and Birmingham had a Seventh Standard School (the first of its kind) in 1884. Certainly by the time of the Cross Commission the problems arising from the existence of these schools had crystallised out; and there was no lack of suggested solutions.

The question of the legality of the expenditure of the rates on higher grade schools stood out starkly in the evidence. This was so even where it was claimed that the higher grade schools could be run independently of the rates. Sheffield, for example, had in 1886 a school board pledged to efficiency, economy and Biblical instruction, and frankly hostile to higher grade schools being run on the rates.[1] It claimed, however, that with Science and Art grants and pupils' fees it could make the higher grade section of its central school self-supporting, even if a charge were made for the use of buildings and for a proportion of teachers' salaries. The school board itself firmly held that the rates could only justly be spent:

(a) on work which was within the Code, and,

(b) on pupils who were in the standards.

Accordingly, Sheffield School Board had decided that the Organised Science School must stand on its own financial legs; "for we determined that if it could not be self-supporting, we could not lawfully go to the ratepayers under the present system of elementary education and ask them for assistance from the rates". But the very description of the school given by the Cross Commission showed how unlikely it was that such an ideal was being maintained, even in Sheffield: separate rooms had indeed been set apart for Science and Art teaching, but the school board so worked the two systems together that some of the *standard* children were taught science under the Science and Art Department. Separate accounts had not in fact been established. Indeed the self-supporting claim for the school was based only on estimate.[2]

The essentially hybrid nature of the schools was obvious from the very curricula submitted to the Cross Commission. At Sheffield, for example, pupils in Standard VII took clearly elementary subjects along with secondary or technical subjects like machine construc-

[1] Cross Commission, *Second Report*, Q. 34,755-6. and 34, 861-2
[2] Cross Commission, *Second Report*. Q. 34,658-988.

36

tion and inorganic chemistry, and, on passing into "ex-Standard VII" they could enter either a commercial or a scientific section. In such schools and with such subjects it was unrealistic to expect headmasters to run "standards" and "ex-standards" as distinct entities for long. In very large schools, of course, it might have proved feasible. Thus the numbers for Manchester Central Higher Grade School (Boys and Girls) were: Standard V (boys only) 144, Standard VI 337, Standard VII 318, ex-Standard VII 350.[1] The ex-Standard VII group constituted in theory a distinct school, and could be largely self-supporting; but even this was, in fact, partly supported by the rates. Moreover, it appeared that the pupils still in the standard were also taking Science and Art examinations.

But the most challenging schools were those such as the Birmingham Seventh Standard School to which we have previously referred. The Birmingham witness shrewdly defined an elementary school on a basis not of subject-matter taught but of age of pupils. Hence a higher grade school like Birmingham's was clearly elementary, being designed for the children of working class parents who would be compelled to work in the factories on leaving school at the age of fourteen or fifteen. Assuming, therefore, that the pupil entered Standard VII at twelve plus, he could spend two or three years in this higher grade school and still leave at an age at which he was indisputably a child. In fact, about 120 pupils were in Standard VII and 130 in ex-Standard VII. Accordingly, argued Birmingham, since the only limit to elementary education was that the pupils must be children, the curriculum for these children could be planned with only their needs in mind. And, acting on that principle, the following courses were outlined to the Cross Commission:

BIRMINGHAM SEVENTH STANDARD SCHOOL
Three Possible Courses

	Machine Construction	Chemistry	Electricity
Mathematics	12 hours	12 hours	12 hours
Projection	5 ,,	4 ,,	4 ,,
Machine Construction	4 ,,	—	—
Electricity	5 ,,	—	5 ,,
Freehand Drawing	2 ,,	2 ,,	2 ,,
Workshop	2 ,,	2 ,,	2 ,,
Theoretical Chemistry	—	6 ,,	5 ,,
Practical Chemistry	—	4 ,,	—
Total ..	30 hours	30 hours	30 hours

[1] ibid. Q. 22,803.

D

The annual expenditure on this school (which paid no rent, as it had been lent for the purpose) was £1,479. The income for 1886 would appear to have been made up as follows:—

	£
Receipts from Science and Art Department	963
Receipts from Education Department	105
Fees (3d. per week, 250 roll, for, say, 40 weeks)	125 (approx.)
Rates (19/- per head)	238 (approx.)
	1,431 (approx.)

This school in fact epitomises the unmistakable challenge to action given by the evidence about these higher schools. The figures show that financially it was a science and art school. Its second major source of income was the rates; but, as the Education Department knew, rates could not in strict law be applied in support of a science and art school.

On the other hand, the school was *theoretically* a school for primary education. It is true that the above curriculum as first presented to the Commission was undeniably technical. But, when questioned about the Standard VII pupils, the Birmingham witness said that some slight modification might have had to be made for them; and later had to confess that the Department had insisted that for these pupils, that is, about half the school, at least twenty hours per week —*two consecutive hours each half day*—should be devoted to subjects in the Code. But, since Standard VII and ex-VII students were taught together for a number of classes, it was found necessary to inter-weave the two sets of requirements (i.e. Code and Directory) by putting a "liberal interpretation" upon Reading and Writing. Presumably visitors making awkward enquiries would find that although one half of the class (ex-VIIth) were occupied with "Theoretical Chemistry" and the other (VIIth) with "Writing" both were in fact copying down the same notes from the blackboard.[1]

The challenge to further action in this evidence was unmistakable. Obviously the main source of income of this Birmingham Higher Grade School was the Science and Art Department. Its second most important source of income was the rates. But, if the Education Department held that the rates must not be applied for the support of classes in "science and art", it had the choice of at least three methods of regularising the position of such schools.

[1] Cross Commission *Second Report*, Q. 30,854–922, 32,911–33. *Final Report* pp. 155, 314.

(a) To accept *content* as the essential criterion of what was elementary and therefore could be taught on the rates. This involved something like Lingen's plan, of enforcing a strictly elementary curriculum. The obvious way to do so at that time was to have a clean cut after the Seventh Standard, to pay grant only on Standard children, and only for the three R's, and to allow only Standard children to be taught on premises which were supported by Education Department grant.

(b) To accept a purely *administrative* criterion; in other words, to insist on school board schools working solely under the Education Department, to ensure that grant paid on subjects in the Code was adequate to meet the South Kensington competition, and to adjust the Code to meet local requirements as far as was deemed proper. (Thus some liberalisation of this highly technical curriculum might have been deemed necessary.)

(c) To accept a criterion based on the *age* of pupils taught, and to allow the school to work under the Science and Art Department if it wished to do so. This would have required legislation, as the school board realised, and a draft Bill was submitted by it to the Commission with that object.

The main proposals of the Bill affecting higher grade schools were:—

(1) That school boards should have power to teach the elements of science and art to those likely to become artisans or to engage in industrial occupations.

(2) That those schools and classes should work under the regulations of the Science and Art Department and be inspected by its officers.

(3) That the scholars of such schools must have passed the Sixth Standard.

(4) That such schools should not instruct in specific trades.

(5) That the course should not exceed three years.[1]

It is thus obvious that everyone interested in higher grade schools in 1888 must have known of their doubtful legality; but the most significant exchange came during the Cross Commission evidence from Bradford. The witness had pointed out that the development of the teaching of handicrafts was held up by the threat of an auditor's surcharge, and Lyulph Stanley, a member of the Commission (and of London School Board) asked, "Do you not think that this habit of bowing down before the auditor beforehand tends very

[1] Cross Commission *Second Report*, Appendix C (IV).

much to cripple the hands of the managers, and to restrict the education more narrowly than it ought to be restricted?"[1] Such a habit was certainly not a fault of London School Board, as we shall see later.

The Final Cross (Majority) Report saw these higher grade schools as something new, something not contemplated by the 1870 Act and therefore as of doubtful legality. "However desirable these higher elementary schools may be", it concluded, "the principle involved in their addition to our educational system should, if approved, be avowedly adopted. Their indirect inclusion is injurious to both primary and secondary instruction".[2]

(4) THE DEVELOPMENT OF HIGHER BOARD SCHOOLS 1890–1900

During the next decade the school boards neither forgot the equivocal position of their higher schools nor allowed the Department to forget it. Thus at a conference of school board representatives in 1893 a resolution was passed requesting the Education Department to support these Higher Grade Schools, subject to proper conditions (as recommended by the Cross Commission) by a modification of the system under which grants were paid by the Science and Art Department. From the published proceedings it was made clear both that these schools were being partly supported by the rates, and also that the conference was fully aware of the possible illegality of this. Thus the Brighton representative stated that, according to the Brighton auditor, they could not spend one penny from the rates on Higher Grade Schools and that therefore they had to depend upon the grant from the Science and Art Department and upon fees;[3] while other speakers reassured the conference by reminding them of the sympathy for these schools shown by representatives of the Education Department.[4]

The Bryce Report (1895) also stated that these schools could not "be supported out of the rates (although this seems in a few instances to have been attempted)".[5] The last remark was a kindly understatement; for in one case a witness had admitted that the school board had solved the problem of giving free secondary education out of the rates as far as continuation schools and higher grade schools were concerned![6] The Minutes of Evidence to the Bryce

[1] Cross Commission Second Report, Q. 35,481–4.
[2] Cross Commission, Final Report, p. 169.
[3] Proceedings of the Conference of Representatives of School Boards, Manchester 21/3/93, Manchester Market Street Press Works, 1893, p. 26 (cf. p. 28).
[4] ibid., p. 29.
[5] Report of the Royal Commission on Secondary Education Vol. I, p. 10.
[6] ibid., Vol. III, p. 377 (Plymouth).

Commission prove, if further proof were needed, that the school board representatives were themselves fully aware of the possible illegality of these schools. "At present the board secondary school (i.e. the higher grade school)" said a witness from Birmingham, "can only rightly exist if, so far as its most useful work is concerned (namely, its real secondary work), it costs the local rates nothing."[1] And he pointed out that successive Presidents and Vice-Presidents of the Committee of Council had consented to the "necessary straining" of the Education Act, 1870, in order to allow the higher grade work of the school boards to continue.

It was indeed clear that since 1888 the higher grade schools had become more markedly secondary in nature, some of them taking their pupils to a high level of work. It was clear, too, that a high proportion of secondary work was being done by elementary school teachers. It was claimed that some 11,000 pupils in Organised Science Schools throughout the country were being given secondary instruction mainly by elementary teachers.[2] Thus elementary teachers with elementary school methods had made a mass invasion of secondary education. But they were by no means satisfied with what they found there. There were bitter comments on the South Kensington system of payment by results and on the narrowly scientific curriculum which it enforced (both shortly to be considerably modified).[3] But what else could the schools do but work under South Kensington, as the Education Department refused to recognise their work?

What, then, had the witnesses for the two Departments to say to this deplorable state of affairs?

Sir John Donnelly, Secretary of the Science and Art Department at South Kensington, accepted no responsibility. The work of this department was really a sort of cross classification. It was true that it recognised Organised Science Schools and Science and Art classes; but it had nothing to do with secondary schools as such, any more than it had to do with higher grade schools as such. Its pupils might be in any kind of institution, and they might be of any age. Consequently, the Department would have no knowledge if a school (other than an Organised Science School) cut down its other subjects to an absurdly small limit in order to earn Science and Art grants.[4] In other words, the Department was an examining body; it washed its hands of responsibility for schools as such; and remained,

---

[1] ibid., III, 47. See also III, 64, 86, 272.
[2] ibid., III, 248.
[3] Already in 1894 the Directory required (p. 33) that the organised science school's curriculum should make some provision for literary subjects.
[4] *Report of the Royal Commission on Secondary Education* II, p. 134.

as one witness put it, the last stronghold of payment by results in its most extreme form.

But what was the attitude of the Education Department towards this urgent and important problem?[1] Secondary education, argued Kekewich, the Secretary, was where Science and Art classes began. But he allowed for, indeed he postulated, overlap between secondary and elementary education. The only distinctively and exclusively secondary work being done by the school boards was in the Organised Science Schools, which should therefore be taken away from the school boards. As for the other Higher Grade schools, his evidence suggested that there was not really a problem. This was so because many of the Higher Grade pupils continued nominally in the standards; and so long as they were receiving *some* instruction in the standards they were still elementary pupils and therefore eligible to receive grants and to have the rates used in their education. Hence he almost denied the existence of ex-standard pupils!

"A child is examined in reading, writing, or in arithmetic", he argued, "and not in all three, and until he has passed in the three elementary subjects [in Standard VII] he can always be examined in a standard of the Code, and I should think that although some children are still called "ex-sevenths", there are very few of them who are really qualified to be called by that name."[2] It is illuminating to consider exactly how this doctrine worked out. The regulation of the Code was (Art. 13): "No attendance is as a rule recognised . . . for any scholar who has passed in the three elementary subjects, and is upwards of fourteen years of age." Therefore, to remain in the elementary school a pupil need not take his VIIth standard examination until he was over fourteen, and, thereafter, Kekewich implied, he might be examined in Reading at fifteen, Writing at sixteen, and Arithmetic at seventeen!

Linked to this belief, that merely remaining in the standards, on however tenuous a basis, made a pupil elementary, was the argument, founded on the statutory definition of an elementary school, that if a completely non-elementary department could be attached to the "elementary" department (which would be nominally in the standards), then the whole school would be "elementary". How this worked out was made clear by Kekewich's illustration from the Birmingham Bridge St. School: "The public elementary school was merely kept up in order to enable the science classes to be added to it and in order to enable the school board, therefore, to spend the rates upon the maintenance of science classes. I daresay there were some children in that school who were practically not in the

---

[1] ibid., II, p. 110.
[2] ibid., II, p. 111.

public elementary school, *but nevertheless there was the public elementary school attached to it.* We could not tell whether there were children in the science classes who were not in the public elementary school."[1] Yet, in spite of the strange nature of these arrangements and in spite of the fact that the witness had little idea of some of the main facts (e.g. how far the children in higher grade schools were not re-presented in the standards at all), he was well satisfied with the system; for if they had an organised system of secondary education they could not get such devices as the Birmingham School in which a public elementary school was kept up merely in order that the science classes might be a tag to it![2]

The reader may ask how any government department had become attached to such hocus pocus. It was not merely that the Education Department was jealous of South Kensington and determined to support its own system of higher grade schools run by the school boards; for, as we have already implied, the demands of the majority of school boards were by no means excessive and would at this stage probably have been conceded by endowed schools, by technical education committees, and by South Kensington.

Whitehall was in fact at a loss itself to know how to distinguish elementary and secondary education; we have already stated three possible criteria which the Department endeavoured to apply (content, administration and age); but we must recall that traversing these criteria and muddling all decisions were two mental assumptions from the past. It was accepted, even by Kekewich, that social factors would continue to play a large part in determining the respective spheres of elementary and secondary education, and the conception of "standards" as an unfailing and essential hallmark of the elementary school seemed to render the rethinking of the Code impossible. Thus one member of the Bryce Commission suggested that, since it had been possible to add a Seventh Standard since 1870, the term "elementary" might be further extended by adding eighth, ninth and even tenth standards. These, he argued, could give real continuative, higher education, which would still be elementary, and ensure the *bona fide* adoption of higher grade schools by Whitehall. But to Kekewich this solution was unthinkable. "The eighth standard, if there could be an eighth standard, would be a standard like all those below it, of reading, writing, and arithmetic. . . . The standards do not go beyond the three R's, and the standards are the standards of reading, writing, and arithmetic. That is the meaning of standards *under the Act* and the Code."[3] Now it was true

---

[1] ibid., Vol. II, p. 111. (Italics mine.—E.E.)
[2] ibid., Vol. II, p. 112.
[3] ibid., Vol. III, p. 495. (Italics mine.—E.E.)

that certificates of proficiency based on examination in the standards in reading, writing and arithmetic were required for exemption purposes by various Acts (e.g. Elementary Education Act, 1870, s. 74, Elementary Education Act 1876, s. 5 and Schedule I). But these were limited to Standard IV. There was nothing to prevent the Department from modifying the requirements for later standards by means of the Code. The difficulties were really with the Code, not the Act, and with what the Department regarded as essential for the top standards. Whitehall was in a prison of its own making.

When we turn from the Bryce Report to concrete problems facing the Education Department at this time we find that some of the most revealing decisions concerned schools in Wales. There the provision of intermediate and technical education by joint education committees of the county councils had been authorised by the Welsh Intermediate Education Act of 1889 which defined intermediate education as "a course of education which does not consist chiefly of elementary instruction in reading, writing and arithmetic, but which includes instruction in Latin, Greek, the Welsh and English language and literature, modern languages, mathematics, natural and applied science, or in some such studies, and generally in the higher branches of knowledge, but nothing in this Act shall prevent the establishment of scholarships in higher or other elementary schools". (s. 17.)

In 1892 Newport School Board proposed that it should establish a higher grade school. The provision of intermediate education was a matter for the "Intermediate School Committee"; but the school board stated that it proposed to provide, neither a school for elementary education, nor one for instruction in intermediate subjects, but "one in which technical subjects, useful to children in the Artisan class, may be taught and in which they may be instructed in the principles applicable to the various trades in which they will be engaged".

It is important to realise that there was in Newport at this time no deficiency in elementary school accommodation and there was no precedent for sanctioning a loan in such a case under s. 10 of the 1873 Education Act. The Education Department, however, decided that, even in these circumstances, and in spite of the Welsh Intermediate Education Act, there was need for such a higher grade school. It was argued that there was a "prospective deficiency" (a hollow fiction in view of the alleged facts) and on these grounds it was decided to sanction the loan. But the proposal finally broke down over the question of fees. The school board had proposed a fee of 6d. a week and the Department, anxious to prevent competition with the Intermediate School where the fee was £8 per annum, insisted that the proposed higher grade school should be free.[1]

The position in England was, of course, very different from that in Wales, but throughout the country it became increasingly clear that the friction aroused by two independently organised systems of higher education could not be overlooked much longer in the field, and in 1897, on the initiative of the Incorporated Association of Headmasters, a conference was arranged at Whitehall under the chairmanship of Sir George Kekewich himself. In addition to representatives of the Headmasters' Association, and of the Higher Grade Schools, Sadler and Morant were also present. The outcome of the conference, as accepted by both associations, was issued as a parliamentary return in 1898,[2] and might have constituted an important step in the integration of the higher grade schools into the educational system. It was agreed that these schools were *sui generis* and had an important part to play in the educational system. Hence they should be recognised by the Central Authority and given adequate grants. Age of leaving was recognised as the most important single element determining the curriculum, though social conditions were also important. It was proposed that the higher grade schools should have a junior portion, consisting of Standards IV and V, and a senior portion "of three or of four years". The senior courses might be in science, or in some other course approved by Whitehall. Secondary schools, on the other hand, for pupils leaving at 17 or 19 were to give a liberal education in which immediate utility was subordinated to the "better securing of a well-trained and open mind".

We must note that the higher grade school representatives freely agreed to the restrictions of age and curriculum proposed.

From the facts established and from the agreed policy of the conference it is obvious that these schools could easily have been fitted into the pattern of schools proposed by Birmingham School Board Draft Bill at the time of the Cross Commission. But, just as nothing had been done then, so nothing was done following the 1897 conference until April, 1900, when the Department, stung into activity by the findings of the Cockerton Audit Case, but *before* the matter had come to Court, issued the Higher Elementary Schools Minute. Before considering the minute, however, we must look at developments in London.

---

[1] M.E. "Newport. Proposed Higher Grade School." 5/12/92. The failure of the proposal may have been partly a result of the violence of the local opposition where the Scheme was described as "legalised swindling, and the spending of thousands of pounds on educating the children of snobs".

[2] No. 381, 9th August, 1898.

(5) THE SPECIAL CASE OF LONDON

London had been a slow starter in planning higher grade schools, partly because the scientific type of curriculum encouraged by South Kensington was felt to be inappropriate to London and partly because of a belief that the higher grade schools of the provinces catered too much for the middle classes, and London wanted higher grade schools to be without fees. Already in 1886 the school board had planned to group children for manual instruction, in co-operation with the City and Guilds of London Technical Institute and had been in trouble with the auditor for converting class-rooms into workshops for that purpose. Then (in 1887) the board proposed to Whitehall that it should try a scheme for instructing in one school fifth, sixth and seventh standard pupils from a group of three schools. The Department replied that it *highly approved* the general principle of such grouping; and two years later approved lists of the higher standard schools with their proposed fees. Nor did the Department remain long in ignorance of the way these schools were developing; for as early as 1891 the school board was exerting pressure to have the school year changed to fit in with the Science and Art examinations in May. "The Board feel", they wrote, "that if the course of instruction under the Science and Art Department, which is applicable to the Seventh Standard, and especially to the ex-VIIth Standard, and which must end in May, is made to coincide with the general school year, there is much less likelihood of cram, or of a comparative neglect of the timetable during part of the year."[1] After this correspondence, which was conducted at the highest levels, one would have thought that there could be no serious claim in Whitehall to be ignorant of what was going on in London Schools.

Oddly enough, however, Whitehall was mainly concerned about this time with the weaknesses of these London higher schools in practice, and their failure to achieve the standard of work reached elsewhere. A memorandum by an H.M.I. brought the matter to the Education Department's attention, in the end of 1891. This was a forthright document with all the signs of having been written at the end of a tiring week, with the words of indignant headmasters ringing in the inspector's ears: "I am very anxious and somewhat indignant", he began, "at the way in which the (London) School Board is carrying out, on miserably defective lines, its splendid theory (or rather *the* splendid theory) of Higher Standard Schools.

"The idea involved is of the very highest value. If really, in every square mile of area or so, a school were organised entirely from

---

[1] P.R.O. Ed. 14/40, 30/4/91.

children in the Vth to VIIth (and ex-VIIth) Standards, with due provision for technical and chemical and other teaching, etc., etc., and with a staff of Assistant Teachers selected for special ability in Upper Standard Teaching, and with a Head Teacher famed for similar special aptitude, and if further, these schools were left un-distracted for the discharge of their Higher Standard work by having no children in attendance in either of the lowest four standards, *then* a magnificent work would be done for the higher stratum of our elementary school population.

"But I have to point out that, so far as my District is concerned, and further, as far as my knowledge of other Districts goes, the whole thing exists but on paper, and as a theory; and that, too, upon lines that hardly could be expected to reach any real practical success." There was ferment among his teachers, with some because they were losing their best pupils, with others because they did not know how to cope with the newly-grouped classes; there were inferior schools being made into higher standard schools, and good schools being broken up and degraded to "feeder-schools"; there were family school traditions being interfered with; there was lack of co-ordina-tion between "feeder" and "higher standard" schools; and there were often serious accommodation weaknesses in the latter. The memorandum ended, as it had started, on a high note of indignation about this pretentious but hollow plan.[1]

The London reorganisation of 1891 obviously had all the diffi-culties of Hadow reorganisation forty years later. The heads of the Department gave full consideration to this refreshingly outspoken document, but, in consultation with the senior Inspectors, decided that these were mere teething troubles. They were strongly in favour of the development of such schools and hoped that vigorous action by London School Board (as by excluding VIth and VIIth Standard pupils from the feeder schools) would make the scheme successful. Their reaction to the memorandum was a purely negative one ("We can do nothing"), but at least by 1891 they had been fully informed of the radical nature of the planned reorganisation *and of the plan to retain ex-VIIth Standard pupils* in the higher standard schools.

The difficulties apparently continued for some years, for in 1894 another London H.M.I. endorsed all the above criticisms.[2] One of the major practical difficulties was to make the school years of contributory schools conterminous with those of the central school but this, which involved an adjustment of inspection dates, was finally agreed to, and the reorganisation went on apace. But changes in London did not follow the pattern elsewhere. In the provinces, as

[1] P.R.O. Ed. 14/40, 26/10/91.
[2] P.R.O. Ed. 14/40, 2/3/94.

we have seen, the higher grade schools in general accepted the Science and Art Department's plans and many of them became organised science schools. In London pupils took science and art examinations, but there were only four organised science schools. The pattern aimed at in London was a commercial one. Matters finally came to a head with another memorandum in 1899.[1] Helps, a London H.M.I., severely criticised the higher standard schools in his area. He pointed to the neglect of the humanities and of music, to the lack of commercial training and to the excessive influence of the Science and Art examinations. "It seems to be doubtful", he argued, "whether chemistry and modelling in clay are suited to the needs of the majority of the scholars, and whether the Science and Art syllabus affords the training required for girls."

Helps thought that the weaknesses of the schools were largely a result of the attempt to serve two masters—the Education Department and the school board on the one hand, and the Science and Art Department on the other; but there were other factors involved, such as the desire to gain scholarships. Accordingly he called for co-ordination and guidance, and a systematically planned three-year course, instead of the practice of passing scholars into the "ex-VIIth Standard".

The Helps memorandum was warmly welcomed by London School Board; for it was in line with the policy which they had long had at heart. A conference was summoned in the end of April 1899 and attended by inspectors representing Whitehall; and by September of that year London had a scheme for higher grade schools. A definite break was made from the "Organised Science" type of school; and for boys' schools the following pattern was decided on:—

London School Board
Higher Grade School Scheme 1899 (Boys)

Registration, Scripture, Physical Exercises, etc.	$6\frac{1}{2}$ hours
Arithmetic and Mathematics	$3\frac{1}{2}$,,
Experimental Science	2 ,,
English Subjects	$3\frac{1}{2}$,,
History and Geography	2 ,,
One foreign language	2 ,,
Drawing	2 ,,
Unallotted	$8\frac{1}{2}$,,
Total per week	30 hours[2]

[1] P.R.O. Ed. 14/41, 30/1/99.
[2] P.R.O. Ed. 14/41, 9/9/99.

By the time this scheme had been adopted by London School Board, however, there had been a radical change in the educational atmosphere. The proceedings before Cockerton commenced in April, 1899; his decision was known by August; and by 8th December, as we shall see later, the Education Department was busily engaged in manoeuvring the Local Government Board into the position of adopting Cockerton's case against the London School Board. It is, therefore, not surprising that by 11th December the Education Department was making a change of front. These conferences with H.M.I.'s, wrote one high official, might seem to give the Education Department's sanction to the board's scheme. There was need to examine the board's scheme in detail, and decide if the schools satisfied the criteria of the Act of 1870. "I should very much doubt whether the principal part of the instruction is in the elementary subjects and I should ask the Board how they propose to show it. If the scholars have not passed Standard VII, they ought to be taught in that standard, but I imagine there will be many who have not passed that standard (simply because no examination is held), but are yet taught wholly beyond the standard."[1]

Accordingly, timetables were sent for and scrutinised in detail. They showed a pattern in which the skeleton of the standards was being broken. Thus in one school of nine classes four were in the upper division. These were styled Standard VII, ex VIIa, ex VIIb, ex VIIc, while another school made no pretence whatever of standards but substituted schemes of work for (1) an intermediate class; (2) a junior commercial class; (3) a senior commercial class; (4) a candidates' class; and (5) a scholarship class.

Examination of the detailed timetables, which were of a markedly commercial nature, accentuated the anxiety of Education Department officials.

They were now very much on their guard and the most obvious criterion of legality was virtuously applied. As one official put it: "All the ex VII classes . . . are *outside the Code*, and . . . it is our duty to have nothing to do with them. It seems a pity to interfere with this work which is, I think, very valuable. . . ."[2]

We have seen something of the Department's responsibility for similar developments elsewhere. But even disregarding that evidence, one may ask, how could such a situation conceivably arise in London without Education Department connivance? The official answer was that, as the classes were outside the Code, the Department did not pay grant for them and the pupils were consequently not subject to their inspectors. "When I have visited Fleet Road School",

[1] P.R.O. Ed. 14/41, 14/12/99.
[2] P.R.O. Ed. 14/41. 5/2/00.

said one H.M.I., "I have been taken into the rooms where the commercial classes were held, but my visit was unofficial, and I never reported on the work."[1]

But although Whitehall could plead official blindness in the past, it obviously could not overlook these developments any longer. An acrimonious correspondence ensued. The Department demanded an assurance that the elementary school registers had been kept entirely distinct from those of South Kensington. The school board had to confess that pupils had in fact been entered on both sets of registers, but added that no Whitehall grant had been claimed for them. Whitehall replied by sending a copy of a letter of 1888, which had insisted on complete separation of Science and Art classes from those of Whitehall; to which the school board tartly retorted that the 1888 letter had in fact ended with the Science and Art Department recognising the school in question!

It is unnecessary, however, to follow further these skirmishings as to responsibility. For already the future development of the higher day schools of school boards had been prescribed by a Minute of the Board of Education.[2] The main provisions of this important regulation were:—

(1) The school had to give an approved four year course.
(2) Pupils had to be certified by an H.M.I. as likely to profit by instruction before being admitted to a higher elementary school; and their fitness to continue in it, or to be promoted to a higher class had to be similarly certified each year.
(3) Attendances of pupils over 15 would not be recognised.
(4) Pupils were not to remain in a higher elementary school beyond the close of the school year in which they reached 15 years of age.
(5) Grants were to be on a higher or lower scale according to the inspector's report being favourable or unfavourable. They were also graded steeply so that pupils in the fourth year would attract a much higher grant.
(6) Rules were also included to prevent these higher elementary schools receiving grants from other sources, or teachers engaging in other duties (such as teaching "Science and Art" classes) during school hours.

The date of this Minute (6/4/00) is important. When it was issued the Cockerton case had come before the auditor, but not the courts. The question of restricting the age of the pupils had not been raised; indeed, as we shall see, questions of age were by agreement entirely

[1] ibid., 7/4/00.
[2] Higher Elementary Schools Minute, Cd. 127 of April 6th, 1900.

left out of the argument. It is, therefore, beyond dispute that the restriction of the age of pupils in higher elementary school to fifteen in this minute was entirely one of government policy, in no way arising from any decision in the Cockerton case, either by the auditor himself or by the courts.[1]

The steep grading of grants was part of a definite policy to recognise only those schools in which a seriously planned four-year course was provided. That policy was also behind the odd provisions by which the H.M.I.'s were in effect to check entries, control promotions and eject unsuitable scholars—a plan which proved in large measure unworkable.

Apart from its somewhat severe restriction of age, the Minute seemed beneficent on the face of it. It appeared to offer legal status to all higher grade schools and indeed to assure the creation of a system of intermediate and technical schools under the school boards; and thus to grant at long last what the promoters of the Birmingham Bill had proposed to the Cross Commission in 1887. By its substitution of a block grant it removed the objectionable features of payments on specific subjects or on science and art examinations. And it cleared the way for a rational and uniform policy for these higher schools, which had for so long suffered from duality of central administration.

But other objectives of this measure only become clear from consideration of the underlying policy.[2] The minute was prepared, at the direction of the Vice-President, Sir John Gorst, by a joint committee of South Kensington and Whitehall officials, with a South Kensington chairman and Morant as secretary. Morant took a large share in the drafting and in all the moves behind the scenes. An understanding was arrived at with the Treasury (and with Balfour personally—See Appendix B) that the Minute would be so operated that it would both prevent any expansion of the higher schools under school boards and take from them some of their most attractive features. The main features of this policy, which was essentially that of the political heads and of Morant, were:—

(i) The age limit would be strictly enforced.

(ii) The higher schools would, under the Minute, cost *less* than previously. Thus, far from new higher grade schools being created under the Minute, only a selection of existing higher grade schools would be approved by the Board of Education as entitled to the status of higher elementary school.

(iii) Their hybrid nature would be used to confine the schools to a narrow range of pupils, subjects and equipment:—

[1] See Morant's memorandum to Balfour (Appendix B).
[2] See Appendices A, B and C.

51

(a) The schools were to be "higher" and therefore restricted to the select pupils able to profit by them; but the schools were also to be "elementary" and therefore must not contain pupils who ought to have gone to (endowed) secondary schools in the area.

(b) The schools were to be "higher" and therefore must have a very different curriculum and equipment from the ordinary elementary schools. But since the schools were also to be "elementary" anything dangerously "secondary" would be barred.

The curriculum and equipment would in fact be those of an organised science school. This was partly because such schools were already in possession and provided a convenient yardstick whereby other applicants could be measured and excluded. But it was also doubtless a hangover from old ideas of what education befitted working class and middle class children respectively. The technical and scientific curricula of the higher grade schools of the industrial north were fitting preparation for the skilled artisan and therefore for the elementary school system. Commercial schools, on the other hand, had a black-coated aroma which made them possible competitors with endowed secondary schools.

But although organised science schools were to be retained as "higher" schools, they were also to be clearly marked as "elementary" by having their advanced courses taken from them and being placed under the Code for elementary schools.

(iv) The treasury, through its insistence on a strict and economical interpretation of the Minute, was to tie down the administration in Whitehall and ensure that no inconvenient concessions were made to the school boards.

To sum up: The Minute of April, 1900, was to be used in a pincer movement against the higher education given in school board day schools. The "elementary" claw of the pincers would ensure that higher elementary schools were restricted in scope, in length of school life, and in subject matter; the "higher" claw would keep them few in number, and limited to a narrowly selected range of pupils and specially equipped buildings. And the powerful arms of the pincers would rest in the unseen grip of the Treasury.

V

EVENING SCHOOLS

(First Phase)

★

From an early date there were two types of evening class, those assisted by the Education Department and those, mainly for teachers, assisted, as from 1855, by the Science and Art Department. In this chapter we shall deal mainly with the former.

In 1851 the government began to subsidise evening schools, but the assistance given was very limited, and, though grants were increased in 1855, it was stipulated that the fees paid by night scholars should equal or exceed the government grant.[1] But, though certain differences from day schools were recognised, from their commencement until about 1890 evening schools were commonly regarded as merely alternative public elementary schools, which happened to meet in the evenings.[2]

Obviously, however, such differences from day schools as age of pupils and possible numbers of attendances could not be overlooked. Even in 1862 evening attendances for scholars *under* twelve were not to be counted for grant purposes, and the 1871 regulations also excluded scholars over eighteen. But for long after that the evening school was conceived of mainly as a convenient alternative to the ordinary school for those who had not been able to get there by day and its curriculum might be limited purely to reading, writing and arithmetic. For example, the 1879 regulations applied to day and evening pupils alike, except where express reference was made to one or other type, as in the calculation of grant. But while the grant for *day* pupils included payments for average attendance

---

[1] Sadler (ed.), *Continuation Schools in England and Elsewhere*, Manchester University Press, 1907, pp. 56–7.
[2] cf. 1869 Code, Art. 38: "Schools may meet three times daily; viz. in the morning, afternoon and evening."

(4s.), for the three R's (3s. × 3), and for passes in class or specific subjects (4s.), that for *evening* pupils was 4s. for each unit of average attendance plus 2s. 6d. for each pass in each of the three R's.

In 1882 evening school pupils were permitted to take additional subjects; but the regulations required that they be examined in the three R's, before they could earn grant in such subjects. And the Education Department still regarded evening schools as strictly elementary. When, in 1886, Birmingham School Board asked for concessions in the evening school curriculum, the reply of the Education Department was significant:—

"As to modifying the conditions now imposed on Evening Schools . . . My Lords do not consider that the Department could, consistently with the Act of Parliament, establish schools, either Day or Evening, where the principal part of the instruction did not consist of the Elementary Subjects. For instance, as matters now stand, the Department would not be justified in making grants to schools in which the only subjects taught were class and specific subjects. *According to the Act of 1870, the only schools which can be provided out of the Rates are Elementary Schools, and . . . the practical meaning of the term "Elementary" has long been settled.*

"Thus the Duke of Newcastle's Commission was appointed in 1858 to consider and report what measures, if any, were required for the extension of sound and cheap elementary instruction. And their report and recommendations are confined to schools in which the curriculum almost entirely consisted of Reading, Writing and Arithmetic. . . . Finally, it is to be observed that from 1870 until the present time the code has confined the recipients of the grant to those instructed in the three obligatory subjects—other subjects being regarded as additional or incidental.

"In these circumstances *it is impossible to ignore the fact that Reading, Writing and Arithmetic are essential elements in every elementary school, and, therefore, My Lords cannot admit any evening school to receive grant of which these three subjects do not form the principal part of the curriculum.*" The Department went on to point out the impossibility of their paying grant for children who had passed the VIIth standard.[1]

This was a logical, if reactionary, statement of the legal position of the curriculum under the 1870 Act: the *sine qua non* of an elementary school was that the three R's should be the principal part of its work. All else was incidental. The rates could be spent only on an elementary school so defined. If once these truths were doubted no other interpretation of the 1870 Act could be sustained. No one could have asked for a more definite statement of what an elementary

[1] P.R.O. Ed. 10/11, 31/12/86. (Italics mine.—E.E.)

54

school then was. Two years later, however, the position was made yet more clear by an emphatic official letter as to what an elementary school was *not*: it was not and could not be a school of science and must be kept utterly distinct from that.[1] With such a precisely defined policy the Education Department seemed to have effectively stemmed back the rising tide of school board education from any encroachment on the secondary fields. How then did the dam burst? The answer can be found partly in considering evening school administration. We may note, however, that already there were signs of one gap in the dam which, from the nature of things, it was practically impossible to stop—education of the school boards' "pupil teachers", "ex-pupil teachers" and "assistant teachers". The Education Department itself insisted on their being given further education. It was clearly more efficient to do this in centres of some kind than in each school, and if it was done out of school hours the centre almost inevitably became an evening school. It was obviously going to be difficult, if not impossible, to keep the education of this élite of ex-elementary pupils even nominally within the bounds of an education consisting principally of the three R's.

Meanwhile, the narrow policy of the Education Department, with its insistence on the three R's, nearly resulted in the complete disappearance of evening schools. Thus, while in 1871 the average attendance was 83,000, by 1884 it had sunk to 24,000; and even in the North an H.M.I. could report, as late as 1887, that the evening school was almost extinct. The remarkable increases in numbers of evening school pupils during 1890–1900 was in many ways the most striking educational phenomenon of the time. Four main types were distinguishable:—

(i) The *traditional* evening school, teaching mainly the three R's.
(ii) That which met for *recreation*.
(iii) That providing a *"technological"* education under the Code. The rise of this type was most marked in the Manchester area, where under the able guidance of Wyatt, the school board clerk, classes were arranged in a wide list of subjects including cookery, laundrywork, sick-nursing and woodcarving.
(iv) More *advanced* evening classes under the Science and Art Department.

Such developments were made possible by an extraordinary series of changes in the regulations and in the departmental attitude to evening school work. First of all, the Education Department's narrow, if legally correct, definition of elementary (including evening

[1] See pp. 95–6.

school) education was shattered by the recommendations of the Cross Commission Report (1888). For the report refused to accept any such interpretation of "elementary", and called for statutory definition of its meaning.[1]

Closely linked with this challenge came two recommendations which, if accepted, would make the Education Department's definition of an elementary school unworkable. *Firstly*, it was recommended that the Code's requirement that all evening school pupils should pass in the three elementary subjects should cease to be enforced. *Secondly*, no superior limit of age was to be imposed.[2] But these proposals implied the *third*, and paramount, necessity for defining the legal limits of evening school work; for, since a school board evening school had, according to the Code, to be a public elementary school, the abolition of the three R's in any board evening school would mean the abolition of the condition of its existence (in the Department's own view). Unfortunately, however, the Department succeeded in meeting the first two requirements, but utterly failed to meet the last.

How this happened must be one of the oddest stories of departmental legislation. The 1888 Code had contained the following requirements:—

Art. 113b (iv) No (evening) scholar may be presented for examination in the additional subjects alone.

b (v) No (evening) scholar may be presented for examination in more than two of the additional subjects.

The 1889 Code was stillborn; but the 1890 Code changed these regulations to read:—

Art. 106b (v) No (evening) scholar may be presented for examination in the special subjects alone or in less than three elementary subjects, *unless such scholar* at the time of presentation produces a certificate that, having been a scholar in a Public Elementary School, he *has passed Standard V in the elementary subjects*. (In other words, an evening scholar who had passed in Standard V might elect to take additional subjects only.)[3]

But shortly afterwards the Department realised that in effect they had now come perilously near trying to repeal an Act of Parliament by means of the Code; for, if their 1886 interpretation was correct, they were now, in 1890, saying that they would pay grant under the

[1] Cross Commission, *Final Report*, pp. 145–6.
[2] Cross Commission, *Final Report*, p. 164.
[3] cf. Revised Instructions to Inspectors. *Report of Committee of Council on Education (England and Wales), 1889–90.* H.M.S.O., 1890, p. 184.

Elementary Education Acts for evening school education which was not elementary. Accordingly a Bill was prepared and rushed through parliament to authorise what had been done. It was clear from what was said in the House that this was simply intended to give statutory backing to what was said in the 1890 Code. But it would have been difficult to phrase section I of this Education Code (1890) Act more obscurely: "It shall not be required as a condition of a parliamentary grant to an evening school that elementary education shall be the principal part of the education there given, and so much of the definition of the term 'elementary school' in section 3 of the Elementary Education Act, 1870, as requires that elementary education shall be the principal part of the education given in an elementary school shall not apply to evening schools."

The first interpretation of this section is that it meant only the abolition of compulsory instruction in the three R's in evening schools; and it seems certain that the Education Department intended by this Act merely to ensure that school boards should have the power in running their evening schools of using both grant and rates to teach any combination of subjects *mentioned in the Code*.[1] The evening schools certainly would remain elementary in the sense of keeping within the regulations of the Education Department. Provided that they did so, they could teach any subjects from German to Navigation or Dairy Work, as these were in the Code. And as from 1893 they could teach them to pupils of any age.

But the section was widely interpreted in a different way. It was understood as exempting evening schools from the duty of giving elementary education in any sense whatever, and as meaning that a school board evening school might legally give secondary or technical or University education, even outside the Code. But this interpretation led to strange results. For those adopting it had to explain how school boards, drawing their funds under the *Elementary* Education Act of 1870 could, under the Act of 1890, apply these funds for purposes of *secondary* education to evening schools which the Education Department Code continued to describe as public *elementary* schools, and the income of which, the Code continued to insist, must be applied for the purposes of an *elementary* school.

But there was a further difficulty in this obscure section. It stated that it should not be required *"as a condition of a parliamentary grant"* that the evening school's education should be principally elementary. The question of legalising the use of *rates* in this newly enlarged field of evening school education was not mentioned. There can be little doubt that the Education Department had assumed that express mention of the rates was unnecessary; for the fact that the Code

[1] See *Parliamentary Debates*, Third Series, cccxliv. 1902.

prescribed a subject had come to be accepted as sufficient authority to spend rates on it.[1]

But during the crucial period, 1890–1900, the Education Department not only failed to control expenditure of rates on evening school work, it incited the school boards towards a more ambitious policy; for, as we shall see shortly, the intention of the Evening School Regulations, when, in 1893, these became separate from the Day School Code, was to encourage expansion, variety and adventuring. It was, therefore, obvious that there was increased danger of overlap with the Science and Art Department, and of school boards spending rates on classes working under that department. There were two tenuous safeguards against this. Firstly, there were provisions in the Code against students being simultaneously registered with the two departments for the same subject. But this, in fact, only prevented the gaining of double grant. Secondly, a rule was laid down in 1895, within the Education Department, that all schemes of science subjects in evening schools which were not within the schedule of the evening school code (i.e. schemes made, with the inspector's approval, by the managers themselves) should be forwarded to the Science and Art Department to see if in difficulty they ranked below the schemes of the Science and Art Directory.[2] But this rule did not prevent the mutual overlapping of schemes already in the Code and Directory, and therefore the overlapping of the apparently legitimate sphere of classes working under Whitehall with that of those working under South Kensington.

In some ways the most dangerous possibility of overlap was in the field of technical instruction where the school boards had been anxious in the first place to obtain the powers given to the county councils by the Technical Instruction Act, 1889. Here, if anywhere, there was need for clear definition of the respective spheres of the two departments; for in some areas—notably Manchester—technical work in school board evening classes was rapidly developing. The problem was discussed at the highest levels in 1893–4, but no one was prepared to say where technical education under the Education Department must end, nor how it should be co-ordinated with work under the Science and Art Department.[3]

This failure to co-ordinate provoked a sharp criticism from the Vice-President in 1897. "The Education Department", wrote Sir John Gorst, "seems only to have had before it the possibility of overlapping and consequent waste of resources between Board School and Voluntary School Managers. But Science and Art Classes and Technical Instruction Classes of County and Municipal and Urban District Councils are also liable to be overlapped by the operation

[1] See also p. 129. below.   [2] P.R.O. Ed. 9/5, p. 129.   [3] ibid., pp. 81–2.

of Evening Continuation Schools to the waste of public money. Under these conditions I doubt whether the Education Department should cast away the power which it undoubtedly possesses of refusing to recognise an Evening Continuation School which it considers to be unnecessary."[1] But merely to refuse recognition was not an adequate way of dealing with the problem. This was especially so from the very nature of the Evening Continuation School Codes themselves. These were substantially the same throughout the period 1893-7. From the outset they went out of their way to stimulate development.

They commenced with a cheerful explanatory memorandum. The avowed aims of the regulations were to give freedom to managers in the organisation of their schools; to offer a wide choice of subjects; to suggest courses of instruction in other subjects for which no such grants are paid, but which it might be desirable, for special reasons, to include in the curriculum.

Precautions were taken to avoid duplication of grants by the Education Department and the Science and Art Department[2] but, apart from these, the main changes, introduced in 1893, were in the direction of greater freedom for the schools. Attendances of students over 21 were to be recognised; no scholar was compelled to take "the elementary subjects", grants were to be paid to the school and were no longer to be based on the attainments of individual students.

It was only in the smaller schools that evening work was to follow the old stopgap plan of trying to remedy the defects of early education. Elsewhere it might be general continuative education providing a crown to elementary schooling. But it was not to be a blind alley: it might, the Department pointed out, be preparatory to Science and Art classes, or University Extension lectures or other forms of higher education.

This unusual memorandum went on to stimulate school boards to launch out into new fields, inviting experiments to render the Evening Continuation Schools more attractive—lantern illustrations, music, manual work, sketching clubs, and general recreation. Many of these activities would earn no grants, but managers were encouraged to introduce them, provided that one hour was spent on one of the thirty-eight subjects mentioned in the Code.

The whole emphasis was indeed delightfully positive, to remove difficulties and restrictions and encourage experimentation and attractive courses—to what extent at the expense of the rates the memorandum did not specify.

[1] P.R.O. Ed. 9/5, p. 186.
[2] See, for example, Evening Continuation School Code, 1893, Art. 13.

Range of Subjects (1893 Evening School Code)

The subjects named in the Education Department's schedule included: the Elementary Subjects; the English subjects; French, German, Latin; Euclid, Algebra, Mensuration; twelve science subjects ranging from Science of Common Things to Mechanics, Botany and Agriculture; four Commercial subjects; three Miscellaneous subjects; and, for women, Domestic Economy or Needlework. Grants were also payable for Cookery, Laundry work and Dairy Work—altogether a comprehensive list.

Some of the schemes given in the Code were of a very simple nature; some suggested a standard of difficulty approximating to the work of secondary modern schools today; and some were extremely ambitious. A striking example was Bookkeeping, which, at the Intermediate stage, included the study of—"Assignment, credit slips, royalties, free on board, bonded goods, debenture, underwriter, insurance, average, brokerage, commission, ad volorem, warrants, bill of lading, charter party, clearing a vessel, del credere, agent, supercargo, tale quale, vendue, scrip, Inland or Foreign Bill . . . exchange and par of exchange, agio, bill of sale, classification of vessels at Lloyd's."[1]

Such a scheme makes strange reading when, as the regulations remind us, we find that the school had to be a public elementary school, and was subject to many of the same regulations as the day elementary schools and was authorised by the Elementary Education Acts. The income of the school, as Article 90 laid down, must be applied only for the purpose of public elementary schools.

One essential difference of evening school education from day school elementary education during this period was that scholars might satisfy the regulations and earn full grant by taking two subjects only: e.g. Advanced Bookkeeping and Advanced Commercial Geography. Indeed, so far as the regulations went, it seemed that the entire work of the Evening School might be of University standard.

Yet all this superstructure of regulations and syllabuses for advanced evening school work rested on a badly-drawn section of the Education Code (1890) Act, 1890. As we have seen the section must, when drafted, have meant, "Education in public elementary evening schools need not be principally Reading, Writing and Arithmetic." These regulations (1893 to 1897), interpreted it as empowering the Department to say: "Education in public elementary evening schools may be exclusively and for every scholar at as high in level as the school boards care to provide—assuming only that the Education Department agrees."

When we turn to London School Board, it is noteworthy how

[1] Evening Continuation School Code, 1897, p. 40.

slowly and cautiously the first steps were taken. As was the general case, the evening schools were basically schools for teaching the three R's to pupils who could not come by day. But even at that early stage the problem of the upper age limit was recognised as important, and the Board consulted its solicitor, who hesitantly suggested sixteen as an upper limit—a reasonable interpretation if we assume that the 1870 Act was aimed at the elementary education of children.

The Code, however, as from 1871, prescribed twelve and eighteen as the lower and upper age limits within which evening school attendances might be reckoned for grant purposes. But was this an absolute bar to the admission of pupils over eighteen? The solicitor cautiously advised that the only safe way to keep within the law, and thus avoid surcharge, was to charge these older pupils fees adequate to cover the whole cost of instruction.[1]

The board therefore decided that while it would lend its schoolrooms for the education of the pupils over eighteen its own evening school activities would be confined to strictly elementary classes for pupils under that age. And even these classes were discontinued in 1875. Such a restricted course of purely elementary education had little to attract pupils or to excite the interest of any imaginative school board.

In 1882 the evening schools were, after a long battle, revived. Three distinct trends must be noted in their development.

(1) The classes conducted for subjects recognised under the Code had, even before 1890, almost entirely lost the old type of illiterate student who came for instruction in the three R's. And from 1890 onwards, students were increasingly free to adventure in the other subjects of the Code. Already, by the 1882 Code, the Education Department had shown how uncertain was their judgment as to the proper age limits, "No attendance is, as a rule, recognised . . . in an evening school for any scholar under fourteen or over twenty-one."[2] It is hardly surprising that London School Board showed their contempt for such uncertain guidance by admitting pupils over twenty-one, a policy checked by the auditor's surcharge of 1888,[3] but accepted by the Education Department in its positive instructions in the Code of 1893: "The attendance of persons over twenty-one years of age will henceforth be recognised."

[1] Lord Reay, *Final Report of the School Board for London*, P.S. King, 1904, p. 272.
[2] In addition to suggesting possible exceptions, this rule seems to imply attendance without recognition.
[3] *Infra* pp. 68–9.

(2) Parallel to the Education Department's evasion of a real decision as to the scope of evening classes, London School Board made similarly evasive arrangements for advanced classes. Even during the earlier years classes were instituted in subjects recognised by the Science and Art Department. The ordinary school buildings were used for these at a charge and arrangements were made by teachers. Then in 1882 the Board decided to run advanced classes, comprising both Science and Art classes and technical classes recognised by the City and Guilds Institute; but an important rider was added to the decision: "In the working of classes not recognised in the Code no charge whatever can be made on the school fund."[1] Thus in 1882 London School Board itself emphatically laid down one of the two major rules which it was found to have broken in the Cockerton Case eighteen years later.

The advanced classes were therefore farmed out to teachers. They were "entirely of the private adventure order", and the Board only exercised a slight supervision, undertaking no financial responsibility. The practice did not, however, continue into the next decade. And in 1890 London School Board went some way to regularising its position by being appointed local committee of management for Science and Art schools and classes.[2]

In no field had London School Board been more eager to play a part than in technical and commercial education; but its attempts, however well-meant, to force the hand of a laggard department, had sometimes unfortunate repercussions. Thus, in November 1889, it forwarded to the Department a copy of a newspaper cutting which stated that school boards could *not* obtain aid from the local authority, under the Technical Instruction Act, for technical instruction carried on in their schools. They could, however, with the Education Department's consent, frame *byelaws* by which a child could be exempted from school on condition of: (1) passing, say, Standard V, and, (2) thereafter attending a school giving technical instruction under the Technical Instruction Act, 1889. Moreover, the school boards could themselves run technical schools, such as that in Manchester for ex-VII Standard children. If they did this they could obtain grants from the Science and Art Department, but none from the rates under the Technical Instruction Act.

The London School Board, in forwarding the above suggestions, consulted the Education Department as to its opinion of the state-

---

[1] Reay, *op. cit.*, p. 275.
[2] Until the time of the Cockerton Case it continued to be recognised that a school board could be such a local committee. cf. Science and Art Directory 1898, s. VIIb.

ment that ex-VIIth Standard pupils were ineligible for aid under the Technical Instruction Act, and that the same applied to evening classes. And, if they were not eligible what of the suggestion of a school such as that at Manchester? The Education Department acidly replied that it was no part of its job to interpret the Technical Instruction Act.

Having thus done its best to bamboozle the Department by suggesting possible methods of using the byelaws to establish technical schools, and of running classes under the Science and Art Department; having taunted it with inconsistency in permitting at Manchester a technical school and in effect refusing the same in London; and having irritated it by a reference in the cutting to the harmful effect of Education Department restrictions—having done all these things, the Board went on to frighten it thoroughly. It pointed out that it (London School Board) had already, in October, authorised its Evening Classes Committee to open classes, in at least nine schools, in subjects specified in the Technical Instruction Act, 1889. Arrangements had in fact been made for opening four of these. The classes were to be held in the evenings for ex-VIIth Standard pupils in Art and Practical Chemistry, Manual Training, and Magnetism and Electricity. Would the Department agree to a fee of a penny per week for each such subject?

This request the Department flatly rejected. No such instruction could, they wrote, be sanctioned under the Elementary Education Acts, 1870. Nor would H.M.I. approve of such classes if they appeared in an evening school time-table.

It is indeed difficult to understand how an experienced school board came to make such a request, in such a fashion, at such a time. "I can scarcely think," wrote one very high official, "that the school board are serious. It may be some plant."

The Board in reply retracted hastily their suggestion of a special fee, and disavowed any intention of establishing separate schools for instruction under the Technical Instruction Act. They intended, they said, to conduct their evening schools in accordance with the Code and to select their subjects from those recognised by the Code (though knowing full well that these subjects were not then within the Code). From all of which the Education Department inferred that the original proposal was "to entrap My Lords into including technical instruction in a timetable of a public elementary school and approving a fee for it."[1]

But with the new Code which followed in March 1890, and the general abandonment of restrictions on evening school work in 1893,

---

[1] P.R.O. Ed. 14/39, 31/1/90.

great developments took place in the Evening Schools of London—notably in Bookkeeping, Shorthand and Cookery.

(3) But the most interesting, and in some ways most dangerous, aspect of London School Board development came from a third source. From 1885 onwards the Recreative Evening Schools Association set about liberalising the work of the evening schools with the express purpose of rendering them attractive and useful for life. Every subject taught was to satisfy two requirements—that it should have a special interest to the child, and that it should be recreative, "bringing to him refreshment and stimulus, alike to mind and body". Hence Paton, their inspiring but realistic leader, proposed to the Cross Commission that evening schools should retain the three R's, taught in a practical and interesting way; but that they should abandon the too ambitious and hard specific subjects. The extra subjects—including cookery, woodcarving, singing and rhythmical drill—were to give "a most refreshing evening of education and entertainment". Only at a second stage, when pupils were over sixteen, were there to be grants from the Science and Art Department, and more advanced instruction.[1] But the Association did not limit itself to advice; it helped to stimulate classes of a recreative nature, to provide instruments for music, for lantern illustrations and similar daring departures, and when, with its funds spent, and its mission accomplished, it dissolved in 1897, it handed on its materials and some of its tradition to London School Board itself.[2] This proved to be a *damnosa hereditas*; for when the rapidly increasing numbers excited the jealousy of rival secondary schools, and the growing expense aroused the fears of ratepayers, and the school board had, by its apparent irresponsibility, alienated too many of the Education Department officials, political opponents of the school boards made unscrupulous use of music, dancing and swimming classes as illustrations both of the Board's extravagance and of the triviality of its evening school education. There can certainly be no doubt that this association had a deep influence on the liberal development of London evening schools, though the most spectacular increases in enrolments, which expanded from 10,000 in 1889 to 79,000 in 1900, were the result of other causes, such as the changes in the regulations in 1890 and the abolition of evening school fees in London in 1898.

---

[1] Cross Commission, *Third Report*, Q. 53,021–131.
[2] Spalding, *Work of the London School Board*, P. S. King, 1900, pp. 258–9.

VI

AUDITOR'S CONTROL
OF "ELEMENTARY" EDUCATION

(London, 1870-91)

*

Modern control of local bodies by "audit" began in 1834; but the fundamental principle is an old one in English constitutional history. "Show me your Parliamentary warrant to raise this money for building your ships", said Hampden, on behalf of the taxpayers, to Charles I in 1637. And "Show me your Parliamentary warrant to use this money for running these higher classes", said Cockerton, on behalf of the ratepayers to London School Board in 1899. The points of resemblance are not merely superficial; but the modern machinery for controlling local spending is more complicated.

The audit of the accounts of the new school boards was, in 1870, aligned with the existing system of audit of accounts relating to relief of the poor. Any ratepayer *might* be present at the audit and *might* object to items in the account. But the procedure of the auditor was much more strictly laid down. Under the Education Acts and the Poor Law Acts which prescribed his duties he had little latitude.[1] Thus if any item in an account was not sanctioned directly, or by necessary implication, by some Act of Parliament, it was to be "disallowed". Where the money for the disallowed item had already been paid away (e.g. to a contractor) whoever authorised the payment was to be "surcharged", that is, made personally liable for the amount.

One result of the strict interpretation by the auditors of their strict statutory instructions was the surprising number of cases arising. Thus in 1885 the disallowances by district auditors which

[1] See, for examples, Elementary Education Act, 1870, s. 59-62. Poor Law Amendment Act, 1844, s. 32. District Auditors Act, 1879.

were referred to the Local Government Board numbered 2,832 (of which 298 involved school boards), and in 1898, in spite of the Local Authorities (Expenses) Act of 1887 which was aimed at reducing this vast total, the number was still 2,371 (220 involving school boards).[1]

There were three safeguards against possible harmful effects of the inflexible administration of the law by the auditors:

(a) The person surcharged could appeal to the Local Government Board, which would reconsider the auditor's decision on points of law and confirm or reverse it.

(b) Even if the Local Government Board confirmed the auditor's decision in law it had power, which the auditor had not, to "remit the surcharge", that is, to decide that, although the money had been wrongly spent, the person responsible (e.g. the school board member who signed the cheque) need not repay it.

(c) Instead of appealing to the Local Government Board the surcharged person could follow the more costly course of having the case taken to the courts.

Almost from its formation London School Board was involved in a series of appeals to the Local Government Board against a stream of disallowances and consequential surcharges for payments unlawfully made: gratuities given to policemen to expedite proceedings under the attendance byelaws; payments made to pupils who were employed to visit absentees; money rewards given to pupils in industrial schools; school fees paid over to a teacher as salary without first being paid into the school fund; and travelling expenses paid to teachers going abroad to learn about Swedish drill. Such disallowances, the great majority of which were confirmed by the Local Government Board, served in the mass to lay down the limits and methods of permissible expenditure. And some of the disallowances raised most important issues. Thus in one series of cases Lloyd Roberts, the London auditor, challenged attempts by London School Board to raise temporary loans to meet their current expenses under the Elementary Education Acts, because they had no express statutory authority for doing so. The issue finally went to the Court of Appeal which decided in 1880 that a school board had no authority to borrow for any purposes except those *specifically* authorised by statute.[2] It is not without importance that at the outset of this series of loan cases the Education Department had warmly supported the school board against the auditor and against the Local Government Board; and that by 1880 its sympathy had become

---

[1] Roberts, *A Treatise on Local Administration*, New Era Publishing Co., 1930, pp. 192-3. See also Local Government Board Reports for figures.
[2] R. *v.* Reed, 1880, L.R. 5 Q.B., 483.

suspicion; for the school board had used it as a stalking horse to approach the Local Government Board and the Treasury with proposals for legislation for powers to raise loans; and then, when pressed, failed to produce facts to support their case. In fact the Education Department had become convinced that London School Board were much too prone to ask for sweeping powers to meet hypothetical difficulties.

It is abundantly clear, on the other hand, that by 1880 the school board could have had no doubt that every item of expenditure not authorised by statute, directly or by necessary implication, would be challenged by the auditor. Our investigation is, however, more specially concerned with cases in which the auditor challenged expenditure on education because it was not "elementary" and we must now look at such cases in more detail.

The Cockerton Case of 1901 turned largely on questions of the school board's power to give advanced education and to educate pupils of sixteen or over; but long before that its power to provide for children under three had been questioned.

The Education Act of 1870 spoke frequently of school boards educating "children", but it nowhere defined a "child". It is true that it provided for byelaws for compulsory education between the ages of *five* and thirteen; but there was no indication that children outside these limits must not be accommodated, if they cared to come to school. Indeed the Education Department planned school accommodation according to the numbers of children between *three* and thirteen in a district and paid grant only for children over three. The question was no academic one; for in some *voluntary* schools provision was made for babies of eighteen months or so brought by elder children. Why then should school boards be forbidden to make similar arrangements, since unless this was done the older children, whose parents were at work, could not come to school themselves?

In 1873 the Education Department, though expressly not deciding the question of legality, had approved a proposal to establish a crèche as "a suitable and probably the only means" of enabling older pupils to attend school. Shortly thereafter London School Board provided twelve such rooms, fitting them out, to the dismay of conservative officials, with "babies' chairs, blankets, millpuff pillows, mattresses, waterproof sheeting, diapers, etc." Infants of eighteen months and over were to be admitted. The expenditure on rooms and equipment was disallowed by the auditor in 1879 and the surcharged members appealed to the Local Government Board.

On being consulted the Education Department supported the scheme, since, they argued, the 1870 Act defined an elementary school as one at which elementary education is the "principal part" of the education there given; which would still be the case in the school as a whole even if one room were reserved for babies.[1] But the Local Government Board would not accept this argument. They considered that "principal part" meant that a fraction of *higher* not lower education might legitimately be included in an elementary school. They then upheld the auditor's disallowance on the ground that the babies' rooms were not for the purpose of elementary education, but merely "to relieve parents of the custody of their children during school hours".

This case is especially interesting for us; for it turned on the interpretation of the same definition as the Cockerton Case and the conclusions of the Local Government Board about the functions of an "elementary" school contrast markedly with those of the judges in the later case. Moreover, the sympathetic note in the Education Department's letter should be mentioned: "My Lords see no reason why a school board should not have power to provide for younger children in its schools, though not required to do so by the Education Department." The issues at the lower end of the age range were thus settled for the time being, although the school board made further representations on the subject.

At the upper end of the range there was a notable lack of challenges by the auditor on the ground of the age of the pupils. Indeed in only one case in this area was the issue *merely* one of age. In 1887 two members of London School Board were surcharged for authorising payment of the salary of a teacher at an evening school: "Because the said salary was paid for the instruction at an evening school of pupils above twenty-one years of age, and school boards are not authorised in law to incur any expenditure out of the school funds in respect of pupils of that age . . ." To counter this argument, however, the school board were able to quote the ambiguous terms of the Code (Art. 13): "No attendance is as a rule *recognised* . . . in an evening school for any scholar under fourteen or over twenty-one", which the board, not unreasonably, had interpreted as implying that no *grant* could be earned for the instruction of adults, but that it was open to the board to instruct them provided that they met the whole of the deficiency out of the rates. Moreover, on certain forms the Education Department required to know the numbers of pupils over twenty-one on the books of the schools!

The Education Department, however, supported the auditor. In arriving at their decision they concluded that scholars over twenty-one were placed in exactly the same position by Article 13b of the Code as ex-Standard VII pupils were by Article 13a, i.e. school boards were not entitled to instruct them out of the rates. Unfor-

---

[1] M.H. 27/132, 8/3/80.

tunately this argument was not sent in full to the Local Government Board, who, in affirming the decision, simply mentioned that they had consulted the Education Department who thought the auditor right "having regard to Article 13b of the Code".[1]

But if the question of the permissible upper limit of age was left strangely alone by the auditors before 1900, the question of the limit of the school board's lawful interest in education was not. In 1881 the London Board received an emphatic warning that the field of higher education was not within their province and that they must not spend the rates upon it.

It happened thus. In 1880 the auditor disallowed London School Board's expenditure of £280 on an investigation of the Educational Endowments of London. He did so because there was not "any authority in law to defray such expenditure out of the School Fund". Thereupon the surcharged member appealed to the Local Government Board and gave the following reasons for the investigation, which had been conducted by an Educational Endowments Committee.[2]

(a) Since in building schools London School Board had to take into account all the available accommodation, they ought to have a full picture of the educational situation in the area. Otherwise unnecessary expense might fall upon the ratepayers.

(b) The school board, subject to its not spending out of the School Fund for purposes other than elementary education, had statutory power to become trustees for educational endowments and charities by s. 13 of the Education Act, 1873. They therefore felt that they should ascertain not only what endowments had already been devoted to educational purposes but what might be made available and "would thus ultimately reduce the expense of the education borne by the School Fund".

(c) The Endowed Schools Commissioners and the Charity Commissioners were in the habit of consulting London School Board about London Trusts.

For all these reasons it was urged that the school board needed full information about the trusts and endowments in their area, and therefore that an enquiry about them was an important and necessary part of their work.

The school board's objectives were made clear by the resolutions appointing the Educational Endowments Committee and authorising its work:—

(i) A resolution of 1871 appointed the Committee to ascertain what was known about endowments and bequests in the area and

---

[1] M.H. 27/135, 8/3/88. [2] M.H. 27/132, 4/8/80.

available for purposes "of the general and *technical* education of the people".

(ii) A resolution of 1875 required an investigation of endowments providing for the *higher education of scholars in elementary schools* and especially for the development of *technical instruction.*

(iii) A resolution of 1877 required the committee to ascertain the facts "with regard to any endowments which may be available for public elementary education or *the higher education* of the class of children receiving elementary education within the jurisdiction of the Board."[1]

A report on educational endowments had at length been issued by this committee in 1879. It called attention to the powers of the school board to accept endowments, and to the possible need for legislation if the board were to apply the funds for purposes other than elementary; it stressed the need for secondary educational advancement; and it proposed the establishment of "Higher Elementary Schools" for purposes of commercial and technical education. Its proposed exhibitions for technical or commercial education were to be for less than four years.

From these three resolutions and the report it is clear:—

(*a*) that the board did not regard themselves as tied to elementary education as it was then understood; (*b*) that the "higher education" in which the board were interested was not to be carried to an advanced level; and (*c*) that they were conscious that legislation might be necessary if they were even to dabble in such fields.

As London School Board themselves realised, the answer to the question whether they had power to interest themselves in such matters depended upon the interpretation of s.13 of the Elementary Education Act, 1873, the relevant part of which stated: "A school board shall be able . . . to be constituted trustees for any educational endowment or charity for purposes connected with education . . . *except that nothing in this section shall authorise the school board to expend any money out of the local rate for any purpose other than elementary education.*"[1]

There was some division of opinion in the Local Government Board on the merits of the case. On the one hand, it was argued that since the section empowered the board to act as trustees it, by implication, gave them power to make any enquiries necessary before they could be made trustees. On the other hand, it was shown that, while the board's resolutions contemplated higher and technical education, the proviso to the section clearly showed that expense arising out of this section was to be limited to elementary education. The case went to the highest levels in the Local Government Board

[1] Italics mine.—E.E.

and it is significant that one of the final minutes concluded with a personal flavour most unusual in these austere records: "Upon the whole I am disposed to support the view of the Auditor, and I am glad to be able to so do, as it is not good policy to encourage this great School Board in their disposition towards lavish expenditure."

The decision of the Local Government Board was sent to London School Board in a long letter which, after reciting the facts of the case, and pointing out that s. 13 of the 1873 Act, on which the school board relied, contained an important proviso, went on: "Looking to this proviso the (Local Government) Board think that it may be taken to have been *clearly the intention of the Legislature that no expense should be charged on the local rates in respect to any matter relating to higher education.*" After showing further why the enquiry itself was unnecessary for the school board in the discharge of its duties or the exercise of its powers, the letter confirmed the auditor's decision that the expenditure was unlawful.[1]

This case alone, with the controversy which followed in its wake, is adequate proof that the London School Board must have been fully aware of the Local Government Board's opinion that legally their province was elementary education only, and that if they wished to go into the field of higher education they must either take the matter to court or run the risks attendant on illegal action.

The remaining cases showing the control exercised over London School Board's development of education may, for our convenience, be grouped into four classes according to the main reason for the disallowance: (i) Because the instruction was not given in a public elementary school; (ii) because it was not in material recognised as "elementary"; (iii) because the instruction was not given to pupils at an elementary stage; and (iv) because the instruction was really under the Science and Art Department and not the Education Department.

(i) *Not in a Public Elementary School*

Until a school became a recognised public elementary school a school board could not legally spend rates on it; and recognition involved approval of the timetables and rate of fees by the Education Department. At one time London School Board were, in the Education Department's opinion, somewhat lax in consulting them about the proposed fees, and, on taking transfer of a voluntary school, were apt to fix the scale themselves and, after notifying the Department but without waiting for their approval, to open the school at a provisional rate of fees and confront the Department with a *fait accompli.*

[1] M.H. 27/133, 4/7/81. (Italics mine.—E.E.)

71

In 1883, however, the Education Department decided to take a stand and advised the auditor that Denmark Terrace School had not been approved by them till some time after it opened. The auditor accordingly disallowed London School Board's expenditure of £132 upon the salaries of teachers, gas, and rates during the period of transference:—

"Because sections 7 (4), 14 and 17 of the Elementary Education Act 1870 and Article 90 of the Code not having been complied with, the said school was not approved by the Education Department until the 2nd day of November, 1883, and did not become a Public Elementary School within the meaning of the Act until that date: ...

"Because the said school was not a "Public Elementary School" ... and there is no authority in law to incur any expenditure out of the School Fund in the maintenance of or in connection with any school which is not a Public Elementary School."

The school board claim, that the scale of fees finally approved by the Education Department on 2nd November was in fact that originally proposed by the board on February 8th, could have been countered by the Department argument that their hands were forced by the opening of the school at that scale; but at any rate the law was clear. Since neither timetables nor fees had in fact been approved, the school was not, during the period in question, an approved Public Elementary School and the payments were unlawful. The auditor's decision was therefore confirmed.[1]

Clearly approval by the Education Department was a *sine qua non* for the status of "Public Elementary School". But how far in practice could the Department, through the Code and through any influence they had with the Local Government Board, safely stretch the terms of the various Acts of Parliament? A complete answer cannot be given until after we have considered the Cockerton Case; but certainly during the period 1890–1900 the Department attempted some degree of gentle stretching.

(ii) Not Recognised "Elementary" Material

The school board had, in 1885, arranged, as an experiment to be held out of school hours, a class in work with tools for boys in the VIIth standard. The instruction, they said, was "not strictly speaking technical training nor handicraft, but simply instruction in the use of tools". They defended themselves against the disallowance which followed by claiming that the expenditure was justified under Art. 17 of the Code (which provided that instruction might be given in "other subjects than those specifically mentioned in the Code" but that no grant would be paid for such instruction). The Education

[1] M.H. 27/135, 22/10/85.

Department, however, agreed with the auditor's decision that "neither the Elementary Education Acts nor the Regulations of the Education Department (the Code) contemplated that a school board should provide instruction in a handicraft out of school hours". In 1887, accordingly, the Local Government Board, who felt that on such a point they must be guided by the opinion of the Education Department, confirmed the auditor's decision.[1]

Moreover, even expenditure on printing papers for a Joint Committee of the School Board and the City and Guilds of London for considering the promotion and advancement of technical education was disallowed in 1889 on the ground that the law did not permit a school board to "provide instruction in technical education at the cost of the School Fund".

But if a subject was in the Code the opinion of the Education Department as to its "elementary" nature was bound to be almost conclusive, and from 1890 onwards there were practically no challenges on the ground of subject matter.

(iii) Not to Pupils at "Elementary" Stage

Towards the end of 1885 a meeting of London School Board electors asked the Local Government Board to meet a deputation to protest against the Pupil Teacher Centre system being charged on the rates:—

"*1st*, Because the advantage of the system, if advantage there be, cannot possibly, in any great degree, be confined or secured to the Ratepayers of London; and

"*2ndly*, Because the Education Acts of 1870 and 1873 give no authority to school boards to provide such a system at the expense of the Ratepayers".[2]

The Local Government Board, perhaps disingenuously, asserted that these were questions for the Education Department, and apparently did nothing further about the protest; but, commencing in 1886, there was an outbreak of London disallowances of expenditure on the instruction of pupil-teachers, ex-pupil teachers, assistant teachers and teachers. Throughout that somewhat confusing series of cases the Local Government Board consistently consulted the Education Department, and, although the two Departments sometimes disagreed, the former appeared to be anxious to follow any lead given by the latter. The cases may be considered in four sub-groups.

(a) Instructing Pupil Teachers at a Centre

The auditor disallowed expenditure by the school board on a Centre at which they gathered pupil teachers from surrounding

---

[1] M.H. 27/135, 28/10/87   [2] M.H. 27/135, 28/10/85.

schools for instruction. He argued that the Centre was not a public elementary school, and that therefore the school board were not entitled under the Elementary Education Acts to maintain it. They could not lawfully maintain a school for pupil teachers out of the School Fund.

The Education Department, on the other hand, were sure that the instruction of pupil teachers need not be at the school where the pupil teacher taught. The *Code* did not specify where the instruction was to be, and the Centre did not pretend to be a school: "The building is not hired or used by the board *as a School*, but only for the purpose of fulfilling their obligations under the memorandum of agreement with the pupil teachers, and the expenditure so incurred is really part of the expenditure which the Board are entitled to incur in maintaining each of the Public Elementary Schools to which the pupil teachers taught in this building belong."

The Local Government Board noted that there was no express power of providing accommodation for teaching pupil teachers in the Elementary Education Acts but went on: "It can only be argued that there is an *implied* power to provide what is necessary for their purposes and that one of these is instruction to pupil teachers." Accordingly the board decided to reverse the auditor's decision; but, in doing so, it was clear—and the letter to the school board made it clear—that they were relying heavily on the opinion of the Education Department.[1]

(b) Payments to Instructors of Teachers or of Ex-pupil Teachers

The first dispute under this heading arose in 1886 over expenditure on Saffron Hill School of Art where day classes consisted of pupils from neighbouring board schools, but evening classes were attended chiefly by teachers under the board.

The London School Board, in meeting this challenge, contended that instruction to teachers was within the spirit of the Code, and indeed of the 1870 Act, since they had been advised by their solicitor in 1874 (and the solicitor was of the same opinion in 1886) that the board might incur expenditure "in subjects which directly or indirectly advance the work of providing elementary education to children" (not a cautious opinion).

The auditor attacked the very right of the school board to maintain a Science and Art School; but the Education Department, in their advice to the Local Government Board, gave him only partial support: "My Lords", said their letter, "are disposed to concur in the opinion of the Auditor, so far as Teachers under the School Board are concerned: but my Lords see no objection to the existing

[1] M.H. 27/135, 10/3/87. This decision was overturned by the Court of Appeal in 1902. (*Infra* p. 152.)

arrangements as to the Teaching of Drawing so far as they affect Pupil Teachers and ordinary pupils." The Local Government Board letter announcing the decision was, however, more cautious. They recited the Education Department's opinion that the school board could not legally maintain a School of Drawing for the instruction of adult teachers, and went on: "Upon this view of the case, and as the proportion of the sum of £10 7s. 10d. (the total disallowance) representing the cost of instruction to adult teachers is not distinguishable, the Board, *without on this occasion going into the question as to how far the instruction could legally be provided for pupils and pupil teachers,* confirm as lawful the decision of the auditor".[1]

Shortly afterwards the auditor disallowed payments to Instructors of ex-pupil teachers at a Cookery Centre, "because school boards are not empowered to pay Salaries for the purpose of instructing ex-Pupil Teachers in Cookery". Unfortunately the Education Department confused this issue with that of the case below (i.e. payments to ex-pupil teachers themselves). Consequently the Local Government Board disregarded their advice and, feeling that payments for instructing "ex-pupil teachers" must come under the same rule as payments for instructing the ordinary teachers at Saffron Hill School of Art, affirmed the auditor's decision.[2]

(c) Payments to Ex-pupil Teachers

The auditor in 1886 disallowed £7 10s. 0d. paid to ex-pupil teachers themselves as assistant instructors of cookery. His five reasons were:—

(1) Because it was not legally competent for school boards to pay Salaries or to incur expenditure in training persons to become instructors of Cookery.

(2) Because such ex-Pupil Teachers were not articled Pupil Teachers.

(3) Because the persons aforementioned were not Teachers within the meaning of the Elementary Education Acts.

(4) Because school boards had no lawful authority to engage and pay Instructors of Cookery.

(5) Because the said school board had no authority in law to make such payments out of the School Fund. In effect, the school board cannot pay *instructors* of trainees; these trainees are not pupil teachers; they are not teachers; and where is the authority to pay *them* as "instructors" of cookery?

The Education Department argued that the auditor's first reason was irrelevant as these payments were not to instructors of students but to the ex-pupil teachers themselves. Moreover, they pointed out

[1] M.H. 27/135, 18/11/86. (Italics mine.—E.E.)
[2] M.H. 27/135, 14/12/88.

that payment of teachers of cookery was specifically allowed in the new Code. But their main point was "that the persons who receive these payments are employed to *assist* the principal teacher—in instructing the scholars in Cookery, and that the payments are made to them on that account, and the fact that they may receive additional remuneration in the shape of instruction for themselves in Cookery with a view to their becoming principal instructors does not . . . affect the question of the power of the Board to pay them these sums as salaries for the instruction they give."

The auditor emphatically challenged this argument. He had no difficulty in showing from the very letter of appeal and from the minutes of the school board that this was a thinly disguised scheme for training ex-pupil teachers to meet the serious shortage of cookery teachers. Its object was to obtain a supply of qualified instructors, not to obtain assistance to the principal teacher.

In reply to this forceful statement the Department had to admit the object of the scheme, but claimed that it was not necessarily illegal because of that: for the sum paid to these "assistant teachers" was a reasonable return for their services. The Local Government Board, thereupon, in 1888 reversed the auditor's decision. In their final letter they referred as usual to the views of the Education Department; but themselves held firmly that "the Auditor's first reason . . . is inapplicable, because, although these persons may have received instruction, it was not for this that they were paid, but for their services in instructing or assisting in the instruction of children belonging to the schools of the School Board."[1]

There the matter rested; but if, as the Education Department finally admitted, the object of the scheme was to train teachers the Local Government Board were not being entirely consistent here, and the decision may not have been a wise one.

(*d*) *Payments for Instructing and Examining Teachers of Swedish Drill*

This was a case of disallowance of payments made for instructing and examining teachers for a certificate in Swedish Physical Exercises. When consulted the Education Department agreed with the auditor's decision, comparing the issue somewhat casually with that of payments to instructors of ex-pupil teachers (*supra* pp. 74–5). The Local Government Board, though suspecting that the Education Department had not fully appreciated the distinction (for this case involved the instruction *and examination* of teachers), stated in their letter announcing the decision (1891) that "having regard to the view expressed by the Education Department in regard to the instruction of ex-Pupil Teachers the Board consider that the School Board are not empowered to employ persons to instruct *or examine* teachers."[2]

[1] M.H. 27/135, 6/12/88.   [2] M.H. 27/136, 17/12/91. (Italics mine.—E.E.)

In 1892, however, the Department, in response to prompting from the school board, raised with the Local Government Board the question whether in future they would allow the school board to pay for *examining* teachers. "My Lords, after careful consideration, are of opinion that the Board may reasonably pay a fee to a qualified person to examine and test the competence of any teachers in special subjects whom the Board propose to employ to teach these subjects . . ."

This letter, asking in effect for a partial reversal of a decision arrived at by agreement only six months previously, put the educational cat among the local government pigeons: it was noted that the Education Department had changed their attitude; that their action might put the Local Government Board in a difficult position; and that the Education Department were always confusing remission and reversal (and there were indeed signs of confusion).

But after a lengthy investigation of similar cases in which the Education Department had been consulted the Local Government Board refused to budge. They admitted that it might be competent for the school board to examine teachers to decide if they were *qualified* to give instruction; but in the case under review they had employed an officer to instruct teachers by means of classes. The examination had been at the end of the course; it had been supplementary to the course; and its object had been to ascertain the results of the course. Moreover, this view was borne out by the resolution of the school board itself, which had been to make a payment "for services rendered as Temporary Instructor in Swedish Exercises".[1]

This long discussion of cases involving the instruction of pupil teachers and ex-pupil teachers has some importance for our central problem. It shows that the question of the upper limit of elementary education was still a live one. But it also forms a background to the problem of Science and Art Schools and Classes which we must briefly consider.

(iv) Science and Art Schools and Classes

In London the only case of this type was that of Saffron Hill School of Art which we have already mentioned (p. 74). Here we must note that in his first two reasons for the disallowance the auditor challenged the very basis of the school:

"(1) Because the said School Board have no authority in law to establish or maintain a Science and Art School at the expense of the School Fund.

"(2) Because the said Science and Art School is not an Elementary school within the meaning of the Education Acts . . ."

In these two points Roberts here anticipated by fifteen years

[1] M.H. 27/137, 14/11/92.

much of the substance of the Cockerton Case. Unfortunately, however, this case was settled on another of the auditor's points, that of the illegality of the classes for teachers; but the Local Government Board explicitly left the question of the legality of the other Art classes undecided.

We shall also see later that the school board received very emphatic warning about spending rates on Science and Art Schools and classes in a letter sent to them by the Science and Art Department in 1888 and in other correspondence with the Education Department.

Practically all the audit cases discussed so far involved decisions of Lloyd Roberts, the District Auditor for the London area. In 1891, however, Roberts left that post; and the manner of his going requires some notice, for it marks the end of an era in the audit of London School Board accounts. Roberts, a barrister, had been appointed in 1871 by the Local Government Board, under s. 60 of the 1870 Act, to audit the accounts of the London School Board. He was the first London auditor to be appointed by the Local Government Board, previous appointments having been made by chairmen of the Boards of Guardians. The post was at first a very heavy one, since, as was officially noted on his retirement (in 1904), "before his appointment the work had been most inefficiently done and the accounts were in a very unsatisfactory state. By his energy and devotion to his duties he succeeded in entirely rectifying this state of things and especially in getting the rates promptly collected and properly accounted for, thus securing for the ratepayers much money which would otherwise have been lost."[1] On the legal side of his work he had certainly shown vigour and independence, and yet his decisions had usually been upheld by the Local Government Board. But the 1888 case (concerning the payment of ex-pupil teachers as assistant instructors) involved a marked divergence between the viewpoints of the Education Department and of the auditor, and, although Roberts had the better of the exchanges on paper, the Local Government Board decided to support the Department, and reversed the auditor's decision. But an even more direct clash of opinion occurred in 1890. Roberts disallowed some £6,000 paid by London School Board to stockbrokers to buy stock for a Superannuation Fund. The Board had no express statutory authority for doing so; but the teachers had given their consent to the deductions being made from their salaries, and on this ground London School Board appealed.

Roberts argued that the school board could not put the superannuation scheme in force till they got statutory authorisation:

[1] M.H. 32/104, 3/12/04.

"Their attempt to do so is wholly unauthorised and beyond the scope of their duties and further is forestalling the ultimate decision of the Legislature which may or may not confer such powers. . . . The school board have not paid to the Officers and Teachers the full amounts of the salaries which have accrued and the Officers and Teachers have not acknowledged the receipts of such full amounts; therefore the school board in making the investments have not acted as the Agents or Trustees of the Officers and Teachers, but have directly applied the School Fund for the purpose of making such investments. . . . The procedure of the school board is devoid of any statutory authority and in the not impossible event of this fund becoming insolvent I venture to think a very serious charge may be cast upon the School Fund of the District."

This was indeed a poser for the Local Government Board. The final point at issue was whether a school board could legally undertake such a trust as the creation and administration of a Superannuation Fund. The teachers had certainly agreed to the deductions; but they had not expressly agreed to the money being invested in specified securities in the names of specified persons. If these persons made away with the securities, would the teachers be able to sue the school board successfully for the money? The Local Government Board were in such doubt that they consulted the Law Officers, who advised that, since the teachers had consented to the scheme, the school board were within their powers in making the deductions and investing the money.

Accordingly, in July 1890, the Local Government Board reversed the auditor's decisions and held that the school board creation of a Superannuation Fund was lawful.[1] On being told of this decision Roberts replied that he proposed to have nothing to do with the audit of the Superannuation Fund. "These deductions will appear in the accounts of the School Board as an expenditure of the School Board under the heading of Salaries; and from that moment such deductions do not further affect the School Fund, but such deductions form a separate Fund distinct from the School Fund.

"The District Auditor has no power to audit and examine such separate fund and therefore as I have no authority I do not propose to take upon myself any obligation of Audit with respect to the Superannuation Fund, especially as it is not yet determined whether or not the Officers and Teachers are to have some share in the management of the Fund."

The following year (1891) Roberts was, against his will, transferred to the post of Inspector of Audits. There can be little doubt that his too vigorous reaction to the decisions of the government depart-

[1] M.H. 27/136, 8/7/90.

ments (and perhaps his too sweeping challenges of school board expenditure) was the main cause of his transference. Certainly no question was ever raised of the high quality of his work as District Auditor. Indeed, on his retirement as a result of ill-health in 1904, the President of the Local Government Board wrote: "I profoundly regret this most unfortunate necessity. A better Public Servant the King never had."[1] It is no great speculation that, if Roberts had been allowed to continue as District Auditor after 1891, earlier, and probably less catastrophic, decisions would have been obtained from the Local Government Board both on the question of Science and Art expenditure in London schools (which he had already raised in 1888) and on the question of the permissible age of evening school pupils (which he had raised in 1887).

[1] M.H. 32/104, 3/12/04.

VII

AUDIT IN ECLIPSE

(London, 1891-99)

*

COCKERTON must at first have appeared to be a much more comfortable bedfellow than his predecessor, Lloyd Roberts. His disallowances were less concerned with matters of educational policy; some of his cases on appeal were less well argued; and his decisions suffered more frequent reversals.

First we may consider a series of cases involving prize distributions. The London School Board had organised a general competition in drawing and needlework, involving some 450,000 children, and the prizes were distributed at a general meeting. Cockerton disallowed the expenditure on the hire of the hall; and the Local Government Board, who were nervous lest the practice should lead to payment for entertainments at prizedays, upheld the disallowance. This was not necessary educational expenditure.[1] A similar decision was reached in 1894 in the case of a hire of a hall for an evening school's prizegiving, though the London School Board argued that such a distribution, in so wide a grouping of schools, had a stimulating effect on both attendance and interest.[2]

But in 1898 Cockerton's disallowance of 6s., paid to a teacher for keeping order at a prize distribution, was reversed. The payment, he argued, being merely for an additional service, was not a duty assigned to the teacher under Section 35 of the 1870 Act. But it seemed to the Local Government Board that, apart from any specific enactment, the school board could "reasonably and therefore legally"—not an entirely convincing phrase—pay for the keeping of order, especially with a view to the protection of their property. Moreover, since the school board could, under s. 35, have appointed some officer other than the teacher to do this work, it seemed that

[1] M.H. 27/136, 6/1/92.   [2] M.H. 27/137, 30/10/94.

the appointment of someone already in their service to do this additional duty was covered by the section.[1]

Two cases, bearing superficial resemblances to the Endowments case,[2] may be taken to illustrate how during this decade the human factor was increasingly affecting the course of decisions. In 1891 Cockerton surcharged the school board for expenses in connection with a report of the proceedings of a Manchester conference on the Education of the Deaf. When consulted about the appeal, the Education Department advised the Local Government Board that the report of the proceedings was "likely to be useful in that part of their (i.e. the school board's) work which is connected with deaf and dumb children" and asked the Local Government Board to "exercise their equitable jurisdiction in remitting the surcharge". This was a confusion of issues, assuming that the last phrase meant that the Education Department wanted the Local Government Board to confirm the auditor's finding that the initial payment was illegal, but to relieve the school board members from the obligation of paying the surcharge. The Local Government Board were in doubt about what to do; for, if the education of deaf and dumb children was one of the school board's duties, and this expenditure was likely to further it, it could be argued that the payment was not illegal. But, since there was no firm guidance from the Education Department, the auditor's finding was confirmed.[3]

The above was Cockerton's first case with the London School Board. We may contrast with it one which, though it commenced in 1898, was not decided till 1901. It arose at the instance of the Religious Education Union, who alleged that the London School Board had been canvassing parents in St. Marylebone to induce them to support a claim for more board school places, although there was a "thoroughly efficient" voluntary school in the district. A ratepayer, prompted by the Union, claimed before Cockerton that expenditure on such canvassing was *ultra vires* of the school board, since it was no part of their duty to hunt about for persons who might possibly be persuaded to ask for extra free school accommodation. There was some difficulty in finding an item connected with such expenditure. Eventually the auditor disallowed 3s. 1d. spent by a clerk of the school board in travelling to the district to visit the homes of voluntary school parents to check up on vital returns.

The dispute had, however, been protracted and the school board now argued that the clerk had been investigating charges of inaccuracy against one of their officers (i.e. in statements about the opening of the case itself). This defence was technical, if not disingenuous; but the auditor's reply to it was scarcely judicial. "It

[1] M.H. 27/138, 11/5/98.   [2] *Supra* p. 69.   [3] M.H. 27/136, 17/2/92.

seems to me evident", wrote Cockerton to the Local Government Board, "that the sum disallowed was inseparably connected with what appears to have been an absolutely illegal proceeding on the part of the school board, namely, making enquiries of parents as to whether they required free education for their children. These enquiries, it appears to me, the school board had no power whatever to undertake." But this sweeping language did not convince the Local Government Board. Even if the initial investigation had been *ultra vires*, the school board was not, surely, precluded from investigating the conduct of their officers in such proceedings? Another Local Government Board opinion frankly disapproved of the case having been brought at all: "It seems to me to be going too far to say that the school board misrepresented the object for which the information was obtained, and I think the District Auditor would have been well advised to have allowed the expense . . . It is undesirable as a principle that the Auditor should be in conflict with the School Board for London on questions relating to their powers, unless he is on very safe ground." The Local Government Board were prepared to reverse the decision, but before doing so consulted Cockerton again; putting to him their legal grounds for doing so: but even in meeting these Cockerton was betrayed into an extravagant generalisation. "The case now in question", he wrote, "is apparently part of an attempt by the school board to supplant the voluntary schools and thereby exercise a power which the legislature has never conferred upon them." The Local Government Board, however, held to their opinion and reversed the auditor's decision.[1]

Cockerton's famous case, which we shall shortly consider, commenced with his audit in April, 1899. He was successful before the court of Queen's Bench in December, 1900 and again before the Court of Appeal in April, 1901. The above "Canvassing Case" was finally disposed of in September, 1901, and clearly the Local Government Board were anxious lest this auditor, who had previously been relatively quiescent, should now lose his head and embark on a hostile policy towards the school board.

But a further case, which commenced in 1892, involving reversal of the auditor's decision, suggests that there had been some change in the Local Government Board's attitude. The school board had hired a voluntary school centre for the instruction in cookery of girls coming from a school a mile away. The auditor disallowed a payment of £8 to a teacher in the centre, because she was not a legally approved school board teacher, and because the teaching was not done in a school board centre. The Education Department supported the school board, for there was a provision in the Code permitting in-

[1] M.H. 27/139, 21/9/01.

struction in Cookery, "whether or not it is given in the school premises or by the ordinary teacher of the school, provided that special and appropriate provision approved by the inspector is made for such instruction". But this did not meet the auditor's points, that the payment was not to a school board teacher, nor for work done in the school board school. Finally, however, the Education Department persuaded the Local Government Board that, since the school board had power to provide additional accommodation (under s. 18 of the 1870 Act), and since the arrangements had been approved by the inspector (as the Code required), and since the Education Department had themselves allowed grant in respect of these arrangements, the expenditure should be allowed. Accordingly, the auditor's decision was, after years of argument, reversed.[1]

We must note that here the Education Department was prepared to argue the case on legal grounds as well as those of policy; and with some tenacity. The legal argument involved considerable straining of the section of the Act; but the Local Government Board finally agreed to this, and the terms of their decision suggest that they were being influenced by policy and by arrangements made under the Code to a greater extent than ever previously.

During this long series of surcharges of London School Board there were very few in which the Local Government Board, when it confirmed the auditor's decision, did not "remit" the surcharges. Hence, though surcharges operated as a brake upon development in any direction considered illegal by the auditor, they did not operate harshly against individuals, nor, apparently, prevent London School Board exploring the borderland between the lawful and unlawful exercise of their powers. In one case, indeed, in 1892, the school board decided to go on with a drill competition in the Albert Hall, after having been warned by their Finance Committee that expenditure on a similar object had been disallowed in 1878 and that the proposed expenditure would probably also be disallowed. It was; but, as the Education Department said that the objective was a good one, the surcharge was remitted.[2]

We must now, however, consider a case which throws fresh light on the attitude of London School Board towards these audit cases. It is the last of a triad of cases dealing with the power of a school board to pay the costs of legal actions, the first two of which serve merely as a background to the third.

In the first, the school board employed their own solicitors to conduct the prosecution of a man who had grossly libelled a school mistress. The prosecution was successful and the man sent to prison; but the auditor surcharged the school board with the solicitor's

[1] M.H. 27/138, 9/10/96.   [2] M.H. 27/137, 21/10/92.

costs, because they were not themselves the actual prosecutors and there was therefore no obligation upon them to pay the costs.[1]

The second case was very similar in principle. A teacher had, outside the school playground, intervened to protect a crippled scholar from two other boys, who thereupon attacked and severely wounded him. The school board paid the costs of prosecuting the offenders and the responsible lad was sent to prison. The school board were, however, surcharged with the expenditure, again because they had been under no obligation to pay the costs.[2] In both these cases the board, though legally at fault, had considerable moral justification and in both the Local Government Board, though affirming the auditor's decision, remitted the surcharges.

The third case was altogether different in character. X, a member of London School Board, had, in a committee of the board, made the following statement about Y, a contractor: "The question of retention money, I take it, depends upon the character of the man. Now here is a well-known fact: this is Y, and we know that Y is a man without any means at all and ten years ago he was a carpenter. . . . I take it that you would not give a job of £16,000 to a man who ten years ago was a carpenter—only a carpenter working at the trade with his hands." Y successfully brought a libel action against X and was awarded £200 damages. By various devices the school board endeavoured to accept responsibility for the costs of the defence, and two members of the board who signed cheques for payment of the costs were surcharged by the auditor. The Local Government Board confirmed the surcharges. Moreover, since the jury had expressly found that the libellous statements were not made *bona fide*, and since the school board clearly had no authority for paying these costs, the Local Government Board, after deliberation, decided not to remit the surcharges.

This unusual decision produced another appeal from the surcharged members asking for remission and strongly protesting. "We would point out that if, in similar circumstances, members who sign cheques in this way and under legal advice are to be made personally answerable for payment of the money, there will be great difficulty in getting members of the Board to sign cheques at all." The argument is not without force. We have noted how, in this list of surcharges of the London School Board, the Local Government Board had become almost automatic in its remission of surcharges; and this case was thought to be of sufficient importance to be put to the President by Sir Hugh Owen (author of *Education Acts Manual*) in the following terms. "The sum in question is part of the costs of the School Board in defending an action brought against one of their

[1] M.H. 27/136, 5/9/91.   [2] M.H. 27/137, 22/10/92.

members on account of statements, made by him at a meeting of a committee of the Board, which were alleged to be slanderous. This defence was undertaken by the school board although they were advised by Mr. Wright (now Mr. Justice Wright) that they were not empowered to do so, and against the protests of several members of the Board.

"The jury found that the statements which formed the subject of the action were not uttered by the defendant *bona fide* and believing them to be true.

"It would seem that neither legally nor equitably should the rates be charged with these costs." And so it was decided.[1]

The case obviously suggests the existence of a reckless, if not defiant, attitude towards the law on the part of the London School Board; but it also implies serious limitations in the system of control by surcharges. Here was a great school board, thoroughly familiar with the constant danger of surcharge, embarking deliberately on a flagrant violation of the law; yet the surcharge, which must have been clearly foreseen, provoked this application for its remission almost as of right. On the other hand, even in the extreme case which we have just described, the protests of the surcharged members had some cogency. The work of a school board would be seriously jeopardised if every member, asked to sign a cheque for some item of its expenditure, drew back if he did not know the legal authorisation on which it was based. Such considerations made the Local Government Board very ready to remit surcharges.

We may now endeavour to gather some of the main conclusions of this survey of the control by audit of education in the London area and relate them to the situation in 1898 (the year to which the Cockerton surcharge related).

(*a*) In every field except evening school education London School Board had received warnings about the limits of their powers; and they must have known what legal risks they were taking. They knew of the auditor's methods and that he conceived it to be his duty to look, not at educational necessity, nor at educational expediency, but at statutory authorisation or its absence. They knew that every form of expenditure from the School Fund must be strictly accounted for, and that the auditor and Local Government Board thought that a school board's province was elementary education only. They knew too how consistently the Education Department had been consulted since 1885, especially on questions of the upper limits of elementary education and how strongly they relied upon the Code as a criterion of legality.

(*b*) On the other hand, there had been a gradual slackening in the

[1] M.H. 27/137, 28/2/94.

challenges by the auditor involving questions of high educational policy, perhaps connected with the change of auditor in 1891, when Roberts was replaced by Cockerton. There had, too, been a somewhat higher proportion of reversals of the auditor's decisions with consequent loss of prestige. These changes may have contributed to a false sense of security on the part of the London School Board.

(c) As from about 1885 there had been an increasing tendency for the Local Government Board to rely upon the advice of the Education Department in audit cases involving London School Board. In some cases this had apparently led the Local Government Board to pay more attention to considerations of policy than had previously been the case. This may also be the explanation of the increase in the proportion of important cases in which the auditor's decision was reversed.

(d) From about 1890 there had developed in the Education Department, firstly, a tendency to rely increasingly on the Code for authority rather than on Acts of Parliament; secondly, a disposition to try to influence the Local Government Board in the direction of what was, in the Department's view, expedient; and, thirdly, and, not quite consistently, an increasing feeling that the responsibility for *legal* decisions was that of the Local Government Board.

(e) In the great majority of cases in which on appeal the Local Government Board confirmed the auditor's decision against London School Board it also remitted the surcharge. That is, the surcharged members were finally excused and any loss fell on the ratepayers. If carried to excess (to such an extent that the surcharge became a threat which was never fulfilled), this policy of remission of surcharges would obviously have produced a feeling of contempt for the whole process of audit. That stage was never quite reached in London; but there were signs that it had come to be accepted in the school board that, unless there was a recent and very directly relevant precedent of a surcharge, any doubtful line of expenditure might be somewhat lightheartedly embarked upon.

(f) In view of the last three conclusions it would be surprising if London School Board had not by 1898 begun to feel that to persuade the Education Department of the expediency of a course might be almost as important as keeping within the strict letter of the law.

VIII

SCIENCE AND ART EXPENDITURE AND ELEMENTARY SCHOOLS IN THE PROVINCES

(1870-1900)

★

W E have seen how ill-defined were the duties and powers of school boards; and how different were the functions of the Education Department in controlling them from these of the Ministry of Education today. But we have still to consider the impact of the activities of the Science and Art Department at South Kensington on the elementary schools.

The methods and influence of South Kensington cannot be understood without some reference to its origins and aims. The Department of Practical Art was established in 1852 at the Board of Trade. Its objects were three: (1) General Elementary Instruction in Art, as a branch of national education among all classes of the community with the view of laying the foundation for correct judgment, both in the consumer and the producer of manufactures: (2) Advanced Instruction in Art; and (3) the application of the Principles of Technical Art to the improvement of manufactures, together with the establishment of Museums.[1] It will be noted that potentially the work of this department, with its frankly utilitarian objectives, cut right across the field of education at all levels.

In 1853 the Department of Practical Art was merged in the Department of Science and Art, which was created for the purpose of "supplying scientific and artistic instruction to the industrial classes" of the community.[2] Within this Department, under the Board

---

[1] *First Report of the Department of Practical Art,* Eyre & Spottiswoode, 1853, p. 2.
[2] *First Report of the Department of Science and Art,* Eyre & Spottiswoode, 1854, App. A, p. 1.

of Trade, were clustered the Government School of Mines and Science applied to the Arts, the Museum of Practical Geology, the Geological Survey, the Museum of Irish Industry, the Royal Dublin Society, and the Department of Practical Art. In general the Science and Art Department was to continue the work of the Department of Practical Art, and it had similar proposals for helping science and art instruction at all levels. Thus examples of artistic and scientific work, including mechanical models, electrical models and geological diagrams, could be supplied even to schools for the primary education of the poorer classes. The Department came under the Committee of Council on Education in 1856; but this did not imply any merger with the Education Department.

From the outset the Science and Art Department was eager to stimulate the learning of science and art by the creation of scholarships, the payment of prizes and the giving of grants, and it is with these activities that we shall be concerned.

Since it had such wide objectives it was clear that the creation of school boards in 1870 was a matter of great interest to the Science and Art Department. This was not merely because of the possibility of teaching science and art in the elementary schools, but because, for the conduct of examinations in science and art, some form of local organisation was necessary and was not always easy to arrange. Accordingly, as early as 1871, the Science and Art Department wrote to school boards thus: "It appears to My Lords that the Boards elected under that Act (of 1870), if they are willing to charge themselves with the responsibility and will act for the Science and Art Department, may render highly important services towards the furtherance of Science and Art instruction by making more complete the local organisation provided for in these rules" (i.e. rules in the Directory for the conduct of local examinations).[1] Thus early the larger school boards were offered contact with the Science and Art Department's examination system, and before long many were involved in one way or another.

The principles on which South Kensington operated its examinations at this time were stated with admirable clarity by Captain (later Major General Sir John) Donnelly, then head of the Science Division, and, as from 1884, executive head of the Science and Art Department until the time of the Cockerton Case.

Some of the examiners for 1870 had written devastatingly severe reports on the work of the science candidates. Donnelly put these in their proper setting in relation to the system operated: "It is of the greatest advantage to teachers", he wrote, "to have their work

---

[1] *Eighteenth Report of the Department of Science and Art*, H.M.S.O., 1871, p. 32.

criticised in the sternest way, and their shortcomings pointed out without the least remorse."

Then, after extolling the achievements of payments on results, both in showing teachers their deficiencies and giving the Department a thoroughly trustworthy view of the state of instruction in the country, Donnelly had to admit that the system had weaknesses, such as cramming. Some critics had even suggested that the examinations should be restricted to pupils of certificated teachers. "It seems always to be forgotten", retorted Donnelly, "that the very best criterion of a teacher is the result of his teaching. It is by that, and by that alone, that he is now judged. . . . The teaching can be tested, and if it is secured what is the object of trying to discover in a perfunctory way beforehand whether A.B., who proposes to provide it, is likely to be able to do so or not? It is illogical and contrary to the principle of paying only on results to introduce such a restriction. If a teacher produces nothing he gets no pay, and very soon gives up the attempt to teach. *The object of the State is to have results; the machinery for producing them is immaterial,* and so long as they are obtained the less the machinery is restricted by interferences the better."[1]

Force of circumstances later compelled the Science and Art Department to lay down curricula and inspect premises for Organised Science Schools. These were not necessarily schools in the ordinary sense at all. They might consist of as few as twenty students. But they had to consist of pupils who had passed out of Standard VI; and the laboratories and timetables had to be approved. Moreover, by the end of the century, under pressure of public opinion, the timetable in these schools had to devote ten hours per week to literary subjects; and payment by results was abandoned in 1895-7. But, although the Department's procedure was considerably modified, the sombre philosophy underlying payment by results continued to dominate its relations to schools.[2]

We have already seen something of the problems created by the overlap of this department's activities with those of the Education Department in the case of London School Board. What of the provinces? No attempt can be made here to give an overall picture, but a number of illustrations may serve to suggest the development of a general policy.

As early as 1873 Liverpool School Board was awake to the need for scientific and technical instruction and wrote to Whitehall pointing out that at least the elements of scientific knowledge should

---

[1] *Eighteenth Report of the Department of Science and Art,* 1871, pp. 50-2. (Italics mine. —E.E.

[2] It must be emphasised that these criticisms are directed solely against the Science and Art Department's examination policy so far as it affected school board higher schools and evening classes.

be imparted to the country's future artisans. They accordingly proposed to establish in Liverpool a department of Technical Education under a competent head who was to be an itinerant lecturer, visiting the board schools in succession. Through his lectures teachers and pupil-teachers would become qualified to give lessons to the pupils, and where pupils showed special aptitudes for scientific knowledge they were to be formed into special classes and given technical or vocational training. But, asked Liverpool, would this be legally within their powers?

Whitehall had doubts if such education was within the scope of a school board's duties and powers, as laid down in the 1870 Act. But three arguments in favour of the school board's plan were advanced by various Education Department officials. (1) If some physical science were introduced into the Pupil Teachers' Course presumably the school board could make special arrangements for training pupil teachers and organising such classes. (2) The school board were also school managers, and as such could act in connection with the Science and Art Department. (3) Some instruction in technical subjects could be regarded as "elementary". Confronted with these arguments on the one hand and its legal doubts on the other, the Education Department was at a loss.[1] Finally, South Kensington was consulted and the head of the Science Division replied: "I am a little doubtful as to what the Liverpool School Board mean by Technical Education. But, supposing that they propose to teach the branches of Science towards instruction in which aid is given by the Science and Art Department, their classes would receive the ordinary payments under the Science and Art Directory.

"Classes for teachers have been very successfully worked at Manchester and other places. . . . These Teacher Classes, from the previous knowledge and training of the teacher-pupils, are very remunerative. So much money may be earned on payments on results on these picked pupils that the cost to the Liverpool School Board need be but small. If they organise the classes, finding the room, etc., any science teacher would be delighted to take them without further payment than what he would earn on the results."

But still the Education Department was troubled as to the legality of any charge made on the School Fund for such a purpose, and the possibility of such expense being challenged by the auditor. Finally, they wrote to Liverpool School Board suggesting that the latter should communicate with the Science and Art Department as to the nature and conditions of the grants available in aid of such a

[1] It may be noted that these three arguments (the further education of pupil teachers, the dual rôle of school boards and the obscure meaning of "elementary") were never adequately dealt with during the separate existence of the Whitehall and South Kensington Departments.

scheme. The Board would then be able to judge what contribution from the School Fund would be necessary. But, concluded the Education Department, "My Lords do not consider that the Rates could properly be charged with the cost of carrying out the proposal."[1]

The Liverpool Board, however, in spite of this caution, determined to carry on with the formation of Science and Art classes in its *evening* schools. Further, in 1877 they informed the Education Department of their plan for systematic instruction in elementary science in the higher standards of all their schools after consulting with Major Donnelly and Professor Huxley and "other gentlemen of scientific eminence". The school board, now, however, suggested specific scientific subjects *in the Code* which they were prepared to teach, and the plan for grouping higher standards in day schools was approved.

It must be noted that the possibility of South Kensington and Whitehall provinces overlapping had already been realised. Thus the 1871 Code contained a provision prohibiting the claiming of Education Department *grant* for specific subjects for scholars who had received grants from the Science and Art Department,[2] and this regulation was subsequently made more explicit. The difficulty throughout was the question of *rate*-support for classes not run under Education Department auspices.

From an early day some school board classes were self-supporting. This did not necessarily mean an unambitious curriculum. Thus in 1881–2 Salford School Board's Science and Art Classes included Drawing; Practical, Plane and Solid Geometry; Machine Construction and Drawing; Building Construction; Mathematics, Stages I and II; Applied Mechanics; Sound, Light and Heat; Magnetism and Electricity; and Animal Physiology. The fee for the session, admitting a student to any three of these classes, was three shillings. As the Clerk to Salford School Board explained, "The classes have been approved by the Science and Art Department and are held under the conditions laid down in the Science Directory. They are all held in the evening, and are attended chiefly by adults of the Industrial Class, pupil teachers and assistant teachers. None of the students are children attending elementary schools. The payments made to the teachers consist of the grants received from the Science and Art Department on the results of the May examinations. The teachers receive no other remuneration."[3]

This Salford plan only illustrated the logical outcome of the South Kensington policy. If the machinery producing the results

---

[1] P.R.O. Ed. 16/166, 3/7/73.
[2] New Code of Regulations, Art. 21.
[3] P.R.O. Ed. 16/185. Letter to Education Department, 18/4/83.

was no concern of the state, classes could be "farmed out" to teachers in this way. The plan seems to have been widespread in the north but the departments became opposed to it in policy and by 1891 an explicit regulation against such farming out appeared in the Directory (p. 3).

From 1874 to 1884, when Sir F. R. Sandford was secretary of both departments, the dangers of overlapping spheres must have seemed less serious. But thereafter ensued a period in which the need for clarifying the legal position was fully appreciated. Thus in 1886 the Education Department informed the Southampton School Board that the Department was not empowered to recommend a loan for the erection of schoolrooms for other than elementary education, nor was it aware of any provision in the 1870 Act which would enable the school board to provide for such an erection out of the rates or out of the school funds.

In 1886, too, other school boards (Leeds, Birmingham and West Ham) became restive about restrictions on their powers of giving higher education. Thus Leeds asked for legislation to enable school boards to have schools giving a three-year course, in connection with the Science and Art Department, to pupils who had passed the VIth Standard of elementary education. It also asked for relaxation of the Code to permit more advanced teaching of pupils in the higher standards; and it pointed out that instruction of ex-VIIth Standard pupils was of doubtful legality.[1] Birmingham sent a deputation which, in addition to pressing for power to hold Schools of Science, asked for concessions for school board evening schools.

The Education Department reply, in dealing with the request for schools of science, plainly foreshadowed the provisions of the Technical Instruction Act, 1889: "My Lords do not consider that School Boards have authority to establish Schools in connection with the Science and Art Department, nor are the Government prepared to introduce a Bill giving such authority to School Boards until the whole question of Technical Education has been more fully discussed in Parliament. . . . *If authority is to be granted to provide and maintain Schools of Science out of the rates, it might be better given to such Local Representative Boards as would be created under a Local Government Act.*"[2]

In 1888 the Department made a most explicit statement of policy in a case which fully illustrated the dangers in the situation. During 1886 Brighton School Board had asked the Education Department if they might give higher education to older pupils in an elementary school. The Education Department saw no objection to their retaining children over fourteen in the VIIth standard, provided that

---

[1] P.R.O. Ed. 10/11, 7/12/86.
[2] ibid. 31/12/86. (Italics mine.—E.E.)

their parents thought they would get benefit from the instruction. But attendances were not to count for grant purposes. In reply the school board pointed out that few children were involved, and that the Code permitted pupils who had passed the VIIth standard to be re-examined and recognised for grant if the Education Department inspector had previously permitted it (Art. 13). Moreover, the Directory[1] expressly stated that the managers of an Elementary School under the inspection of the Education Department might permit their premises to be used for science teaching provided that this did not interfere with the primary purposes of the elementary school. Further the Department's own instructions to inspectors said that there was no reason why a scholar who had passed the VIIth Standard should not continue to attend school, even though he brought no addition to the funds except his fee.[2]

In reply the Education Department warned the school board that the auditor might disallow expenditure on any object for which aid from the parliamentary grant was forbidden by the Code. In the following year the auditor disallowed £20 in the Brighton School Board's accounts, the excess of expenditure (£313) over income in the form of private donations and grants (£293) received by the school board in connection with the establishment or maintenance of an Organised Science School. He challenged the power of the school board to pay out of the School Fund any part of the costs of the Organised Science School.

The letter of appeal of the surcharged members to the Local Government Board dated 12/8/87 is of importance; for it traverses much of the ground covered by the defence in the much more famous Cockerton case:—

"(1) It is contended that the Organised Science School established in connection with the York Place School is a section of the Ordinary Elementary School set up under the sanction of the Education Department, and under the control and management of one headmaster.

"(2) Section 3 of the Elementary Education Act, 1870, states that 'the term elementary school means a school at which elementary education is the principal part of the education there given', clearly implying that something beyond elementary education might in certain cases be imparted.

"(3) Out of 445 scholars . . . but 65 have been, during the past six months, entered in the registers of the Organised Science School; the remainder of the scholars receive nothing beyond elementary education; and they are subject to the examination of the Inspectors

---

[1] *Science and Art Directory*, 1886, p. 6.
[2] *Revised Instructions to Inspectors*, 1886, p. 16.

of the Education Department; therefore elementary education is without doubt the 'principal part of the education' given in this school.

"(4) Although no grant is received from the Education Department on account of the scholars taught in the upper section of the school a much larger grant is obtainable from the Science and Art Department on their behalf. Moreover, the Board were encouraged to establish a Chemical Laboratory in the building in order properly to carry on the education of these scholars by the offer of the payment, by the latter department, of one half of the cost of the fitting up of this laboratory; which share, £80, has since been received by the Board. Further, the Board were advised by an Inspector of that Department to have this upper section of the school recognised as an 'Organised Science School' (see Sec. 33 of the Directory of the Science and Art Department). This has been done and a capitation grant of 10s. per head has been promised in accordance with the terms of Section 37 of the same Directory.

"(5) The Science and Art Department is a co-ordinate body with the Education Department, the Lord President of Council, with the Vice-President of the Committee of Council on Education, being responsible to Parliament for the expenditure of the funds administered by these Departments. It would follow therefore that if the expenditure in dispute is declared to be illegal the Science and Art Department have been partners in the illegality."

The letter further pointed out that for many years payments had been made by the Science and Art Department to the large majority of Brighton Schools under a Section of the Directory which, among other things, *expressly* authorised payments to scholars in public elementary schools within the meaning of the Education Acts.[1] And there were other sections of the Directory which expressly provided for science teaching in elementary schools.

The Brighton letter was indeed a complete and challenging statement of the school boards' position. The Education Department, on being consulted by the Local Government Board, stated that in their opinion the surcharge should be confirmed. They then (14/12/87) made an important statement of policy: "It may be convenient to explain the principles on which this department acts with reference to the Science and Art Department.

"(1) An Organised Science and Art School is quite distinct from a Public Elementary School. In such a school the money paid by the Science and Art Department to the managers thereof forms no part of the Receipts or Expenditure of the School as a Public Elementary School.

[1] ibid. Clause XLII.

"(2) No child can be considered as a scholar in a Public Elementary School, who is not on the Register of the School, and is not receiving instruction in one of the seven standards.

"(3) If a Public Elementary School includes a class of Standard children, who are also under instruction in subjects for which grants are made by the Science and Art Department, the grants so made form part of the legal receipts of the School.

"(4) The rates cannot legally be applied to supply instruction in any subject which is not recognised by the Code, and taught to the children in standards."

On the strength of this advice the Local Government Board confirmed the auditor's disallowance on 2/2/88, quoting the Education Department's letter in support of the decision. Moreover a copy of this letter was sent by the Science and Art Department to London School Board.[1]

The letter may appear, on first reading, decisive. And, indeed, had the school boards observed the spirit of its instructions, which were speedily made known to them, or had the departments enforced them or even consistently tried to enforce them, the Cockerton case could not have arisen, at least as far as day schools and classes were concerned. But some of the provisions left a loophole for evasion, indeed almost an attraction to it. As was pointed out during the Cockerton case, the letter had been aimed at the Brighton Organised Science School, when it was a school composed *entirely* of ex-standard scholars. The school was altered after 1888 and conducted in connection with an ordinary seven-standard school, and thereafter there had been no complaint. In other words the departments winked at the existence of the science and art classes, because the principal part of the instruction was now elementary!

 With the death of Cumin early in 1890 there came a radical change in the policy of the Education Department, which was shown in an altered attitude towards expenditure on Science and Art schools and classes. It is true that the department at the outset held to the legal view expressed in the Brighton letter, but its manner of doing so betrayed serious weaknesses. In 1892 the Education Department reduced the grant to a Leicester Higher Grade School, because, by charging a fee of 6d. a week to all its pupils, it infringed the provisions of the Elementary Education Act of 1891 (which made the great majority of public elementary schools free). The school protested vigorously and the following facts came to light.

The school was a public elementary school with an Organised Science School attached. The permissible fee in the lower part of the school was 4d. per week. In 1891 all the school above Standard

[1] M.H. 12/12787, 2/2/88. M.E. E62/6341.

VI was converted into an Organised Science School; and the permissible fee of 4d. in the lower part of the school was *increased* to 6d., while the fee of 9d., in the Organised Science School, was *reduced* to 6d. The argument of the managers in essence was that the reduction of the fee in the Organised Science School could be treated as a *quid pro quo* for the increased fee in the lower section of the school. The Education Department inferred from this that the strictly elementary part of the school (214 pupils) was being used to bolster up the finances of the small Organised Science School (81 pupils) and insisted on separation. "This Organised Science School", they stated, "is not a Public Elementary School, and does not and cannot receive annual grants from this Department, nor can any fee grant (paid under the 1891 Act to reduce or abolish fees in public elementary schools) be paid in respect of scholars attending the school.

"My Lords do not understand how the lowering of the fee in the Organised Science School from 9d. to 6d. and the consequent loss of fees to that School furnishes any ground under s. 4 of the Elementary Education Act, 1891, for granting the consent of the Department to an increase of fees in the Public Elementary School." And the Department went on to enquire if the headmaster and teachers of the public elementary school were used in the Organised Science School.

The Leicester School admitted that the two departments were conducted under one roof and the class and specific subjects taken in the elementary school were such as to dovetail into the work of the Organised Science School. The Organised Science School was in fact part of the Public Elementary School and therefore a flat rate of fee for the whole was justifiable. The science and art classes of 1890 had been treated as part of the public elementary school; and the fact that they were in 1892 called an Organised Science School was a mere change of name.

It was true, also, that the headmaster both supervised and taught lessons in all classes in both departments, but how could the Department argue that his teaching in the Organised Science School was an infringement of the Code's rule restricting his work to the public elementary school; for not only had the head of the Leicester School previously been in a school similarly organised, but the Leicester Committee had been in touch with all the Organised Science Schools in the kingdom and the same arrangement had been approved without exception and was now being practised in them all!

The Department could not contest the facts. "I cannot find", wrote one official, "that in Brighton, Birmingham, Sheffield or Manchester Higher Grade Schools (all of which, I understand, have Organised Science Schools attached to them) we have ever enquired whether the same Head Teacher is responsible for both the Public Elementary School and the Science School." But his superior thought that this had been a mere omission. Accordingly, the Department insisted on the apportionment of the Leicester headmaster's salary, and maintained their decision about fees. Renewed protests from Leicester only produced the lame reply from the Education Department that if they had sanctioned elsewhere similar arrangements for use of staff in both schools (Public Elementary School and Organised Science School) it was because the full facts were not brought to their knowledge.[1]

We need not enter further into the intricacies of this case. It is enough to note that in 1892–3 the Education Department were squarely faced with the challenge that throughout the country elementary headmasters working under the Code were being freely used to teach in Organised Science Schools under the Directory. They considered the practice illegal, and compelled the Leicester School to conform to their conception of legality. But they did nothing about the other schools.

In 1893 Macclesfield School Board figured in an odd case in which the Local Government Board adjudged lawful expenditure very similar to one of the sums disallowed later in the Cockerton case. The auditor had disallowed the school board's payment of the examination fees of evening school students who competed for prizes given by the Union of Lancashire & Cheshire Institutes. The Union's objects were, by the prizes it offered, to promote primary, secondary and technical education in Mechanics' Institutes, School Board Evening classes and similar associations. The distribution of examinees for 1890 showed clearly where the emphasis lay; for of the 20,300 competitors, 20,000 were in commerce, art, science or technology and only 300 in elementary subjects.

The Local Government Board, in consulting the Education Department, recited the facts of the case and concluded thus: "The Board understands that the Union acts as an Examining Board as regards subjects which the school board are legally empowered to teach and under these circumstances it may be urged that the payment by which the school board secured for students in their evening school the right to present themselves for the Examination conducted under the direction of the Union was not illegal." To which the Education Department sent the following remarkable reply: "My Lords do not consider that a charge for the cost of examination for prizes and certificates is admissible in the accounts of a School under Article 90 of the Code, i.e. it is not a necessary part of the expense of maintaining the School. Hence, one infers, the Education Department thought the charge illegal.

[1] M.E. E89/1, 30/7/92.

98

"Their Lordships have no reason, however, to differ from the view which is suggested at the end of your letter." (That is, the Education Department here say that the charge is legal!)

The Local Government Board could, of course, make no sense of this reply; but decided to reverse the auditor's decision on the grounds that the promotion of primary education was included among the objects of the Cheshire Union. This, in view of the later Cockerton case, was certainly a wrong decision and illustrates to a marked degree the weakness of such divided responsibility; for, if the Education Department was at fault in giving such superficial attention to the facts of the case, the Local Government Board was equally in error in not consulting them further.[1]

Presumably, the Education Department were not interested in the Macclesfield case, but they showed no such detachment from a number of surcharges for sums paid by Tottenham School Board for scientific apparatus during the period 1892–5. In the first case the question of the nature of the classes involved was not raised. The auditor simply objected to expenditure on a tellurium, a hekto-graph, a microscope and a school museum as being unnecessary or unsuitable for elementary education. The Education Department, however, were "decidedly of opinion" that the auditor's decision should not be upheld. "School boards", they said, "have a large discretion as to the completeness or incompleteness of the apparatus they provide to aid in the teaching of the subjects taught in their schools, as they have in the subjects taught . . ." Accordingly, the Local Government Board reversed the auditor's decision.[2]

In the second Tottenham case the auditor disallowed sums spent from the school fund on scientific apparatus for science and art *evening* classes. The Education Department, however, argued that the auditor's decision should be reversed on the somewhat hollow grounds that (*a*) the classes, though run by a local science and art committee were really controlled by the school board (presumably acting as such a committee), and (*b*) the apparatus was needed for instruction in specific subjects under the Code (presumably by day pupils). In once more reversing the auditor's decision the Local Government Board relied strongly upon this advice from the Education Department.[3]

But the most revealing decision of all occurred in 1898 when the Assistant District Auditor for Swansea disallowed the school board expenditure on school alterations and improvements made, at least partly, for the purpose of an Organised Science School.

The school board, in a letter of 14/6/98, claimed that the expenditure had been incurred in respect of an elementary school,

[1] M.H. 12/1001, 1/2/93. [2] M.H 27/141, 14/10/92. [3] M.H. 27/141, 28/9/95.

which consisted of two parts: (*a*) a lower or Standard Section (Standards IV to VII) and (*b*) an upper or ex-Standard Section, extending over two or three years. Both sections were under one headmaster and the staff was interchangeable. They claimed that this arrangement of an elementary school was justified by the 1870 Act (s. 3) since the principal part of the education was elementary.

From the opening of the School in 1882 till 1892 instruction in the Upper Section was practically the same as that given in the "School of Science" in 1898, grants being received from the Science and Art Department upon the results of individual examination of Scholars. On the suggestion of the inspector of the Science and Art Department an Organised Science School was formed in 1892.

The building in question was erected in 1892—from plans approved and out of loans sanctioned by the Education Department for a "Higher Grade School", mainly for the upper or ex-Standard Section. The accommodation proved insufficient, however, and improvements and alterations were recommended by inspectors of the Science and Art Department. These were designed to secure better organisation and efficiency, partly in the Lower or Standard Section, and partly in the Upper or ex-Standard Section. Alterations specified, the school board stated, included altering a lecture room and utilising it as a Physical Laboratory required by the Science and Art Department for instruction in Physics in the School of Science, or as a classroom for instruction in Physiography or other subjects, should the "School of Science" be discontinued. . . . "All the alterations are necessary improvements of the school as a whole, and the alterations to rooms used solely or mainly by the upper of ex-Standard section are such as would be required if the "School of Science" were to be discontinued."

The Local Government Board asked the auditor to stay his hand and consulted with the Education Department, who on 27/6/98 wrote to the Local Government Board stating that an Organised Science School was not an elementary school; but that they were considering the matter of a loan. The Education Department on 25/7/98 decided to sanction the loan for the work carried out. But still the auditor held to his surcharge on the grounds (*a*) that the school board had no power under the Elementary Education Acts to provide accommodation for an Organised Science School, and (*b*) that teaching in an Organised Science School was secondary education, and in Wales secondary education was provided for by the Intermediate Education Act (Wales), 1889.

The Education Department, on being consulted again, assumed that the surcharge challenged the expenditure under the loan sanctioned by themselves. They further argued that, since their letter of 27/6/98, the School Board for Swansea had satisfied the Department that the works in question were required for the further efficiency of the School as a Public Elementary School independently of the partial use of one floor of the School as an Organised Science School. To this the auditor retorted that the expenditure disallowed and surcharged was incurred solely in providing accommodation for an Organised Science School, for example, for a Physical Laboratory and Balance Room.

The Local Government Board, very conscious of the shakiness of the Education Department's arguments, again asked for their comments on the auditor's allegations, to which the Education Department replied on 18/1/99, "When Their Lordships arrived at the decision referred to in their letter of 8/12/98, They did so on the specific ground that They had been satisfied that the whole of the works in question, including the laboratory and other rooms mentioned by the District Auditor, were required for the further efficiency of the School as a Public Elementary School, irrespective of their use by the Organised Science School, and that they might therefore be properly provided by the school board under the powers conferred on it by the Elementary Education Acts."[1]

The argument is too shallow for serious consideration. It would suggest that, if a local authority is empowered to build a house for X out of the rates, it can therefore build a house for X and Y out of the rates and give Y free use of it, provided that he does not interfere with X. Moreover, the correspondence with the school board showed quite clearly that the alterations and improvements were *primarily* aimed at benefiting the school of Science. But the Education Department letter is specially interesting as representing the high-water mark of its policy towards higher grade schools during the '90's. It was written shortly before the argument before Cockerton commenced, and if it showed, on the one hand, a healthy desire to help school boards to establish and develop Schools of Science, it also showed, on the other, dangerous irresponsibility towards legal considerations. The letter is, of course, completely at variance with the Brighton letter of 1888.

[1] P.R.O. Ed. 16/397.

IX

DEPARTMENT AND
SCHOOL BOARD

A Contrast in Attitudes

*

W E have already seen what a cold reception the proposals of the Leeds and Birmingham School Boards, for legislative recognition of school boards' achievements in technical and higher education, met from the Education Department in 1887. Some at least of the Education Department's predictions were realised. The Cross Commission Majority Report recommended that the control of technical education should be placed in the hands of municipalities, and, somewhat inconsistently in view of later events, that it should be controlled at the centre by the Education Department and not the Science and Art Department.[1] The Technical Instruction Act, which followed in 1889, was a serious blow to the hopes of school boards. It gave to local authorities (county and borough councils created by the Local Government Act of 1888, and urban sanitary authorities) a limited power to "supply or aid the supply of technical or manual instruction" out of the local rate.

It is true that the Act expressly preserved the existing powers of school boards with respect to the provision of technical instruction; but this seemed almost a mockery. Too well these boards knew on what insecure legal foundations their experiments in secondary and technical education rested. Moreover, the Act did not protect what they had done, but only what they had *legally* done or already had legal power to do. And although school boards might enlist the help of local authorities in running schools or institutes to which grants were given by the Science and Art Department this was likely

[1] Cross Commission *Final Report*, p. 218.

to prove a Trojan horse; for the price of such help was representation of the local authority on the management of such schools—providing further experience for the local authority within the citadel of secondary and technical education.

Yet, black though these omens were, throughout the first half of the ensuing decade an era of new educational hope and indeed of definite promise for the work of school boards seemed to have commenced. The Elementary Education Act of 1891 made the majority of public elementary schools free and greatly reduced fees in the remainder; the age of exemption was in 1893 raised from ten to eleven; and payment by results was in large measure abandoned by the Education Department in 1890 by their abolition of grants for the three R's, though it continued in the Science and Art Department till 1897. Further, the whole spirit of the Education Codes was changed.

What of the man at the helm during this critical period, Sir George Kekewich, who was appointed Secretary to the Education Department in 1890, in succession to Cumin? The figure of speech may raise doubts, for during this decade education suffered from the too frequent changes of government—Hart Dyke, a progressive Conservative, was succeeded in 1892 by a Liberal, Acland; who in turn was replaced by Gorst, a determined reactionary, in 1895. But, though the political Vice-President was in control, the permanent head was, of course, the source to which the schools had to look for a measure of continuity of policy.

Indeed, in his lively memoirs, Kekewich has himself claimed a considerable measure of responsibility for the policy of the period, contrasting it somewhat contemptuously with that of his predecessors. Kekewich, originally destined for the Church, then business and next the Bar, had, in 1868, through the influence of his father, a member of parliament, been appointed as an "Examiner" in the Education Department, which was at that time "admirably organised for jobbery and a refuge for incompetence".[1] He commenced his work as Secretary in 1890 with the excellent assumption that he must place the schools first and the office afterwards, and therefore must relax every control which was not absolutely necessary. In thus planning he was not so entirely different from his predecessors as he himself suggests. As the Cross Commission Minutes of Evidence show, Lingen, Sandford and Cumin all desired a planned devolution. But they had planned a very conservative *laissez-faire* with powers devolved to large bodies, with relatively fixed statutory conditions. Kekewich was more inclined to throw the reins on the horses' heads—not always a policy in the best interests even of the horses.

[1] Kekewich, *The Education Department and After*, Constable, 1920, p. 4.

The Cross Report and the prevailing climate of opinion were indeed favourable to reforms. But Kekewich appears not to have realised that the cumulative political effect of his relaxations required a jealous safeguarding of each step of progress made. The changes made were vast:

Firstly, a relaxation of educational controls with the new Code of 1890 brought increased possibilities of adventuring in subject matter—elementary science, drawing and physical exercises were all encouraged. At the same time there came the cessation of the practice of examining in the VIIth Standard, at the top of the school. Moreover, the requirement that elementary school subjects should be taken by evening school pupils was relaxed.

Secondly, the financial control exercised by payment by results was greatly reduced. A school's whole outlook no longer need be concentrated on the three R's. What then of the glittering prizes dangled before it by the department at South Kensington, where payment by results was, till 1897 at least, still an attractive prospect?

Thirdly, and simultaneously with these changes, there came a change in attitude in considering appeals from the auditor. As we have seen, during this decade the Education Department began, to an ever-increasing extent, to exert pressure on the Local Government Board to accept decisions which were substantially decisions of policy not of law.

Finally, the abolition of fees (brought about by the "Free Education Act", 1891,[1] and later extended to evening schools in London) and of the age limit in evening schools meant that a variety of other agencies interested in secondary or technical education, already alarmed by the rising standards of board schools, saw some of their own best pupils attracted by the cheap or free education given by the boards' evening schools.

But it was not merely a matter of relaxation of controls. School boards had been *incited* to adventure in areas of doubtful legality. This, it was true, had been largely the doing of the political heads. Mundella, for example, said at the opening of a Manchester Higher Grade School, "I believe money has never been better laid out than in this Central School, and, as the representative of the Education Department, I thank you",[2] and had indeed pressed the Welsh authorities to establish similar schools.[3] This encouragement continued during the period 1890–5 and was cited by the school boards

---

[1] More accurately, though less commonly, described as the "Assisted Education Act".

[2] Quoted in *Leicester Post*, 26/12/00.

[3] cf. Armytage, *A. J. Mundella*, Benn, 1951, p. 216. Mundella's remarkable circular, issued in 1882, suggested advanced elementary schools which would enable pupils to pass on to college.

in conference in 1893 as a sure ground for confidence in their higher grade work.

In 1895, however, with the return of a Conservative government, there appeared a serious threat to the future of the school boards, and to their higher work; for the new Vice-President of Council was destined to play an important and sinister part in coming events. Sir John Gorst had a picturesque background. A Cambridge Wrangler, he had spent some time as a Civil Commissioner in New Zealand (1862–3), acting as intermediary between the government and Maori rebels; but a journal he produced so excited the hostility of the Maoris that they raided the printing office and carried off press and type. Gorst was ordered to withdraw. On his return to England he went to the Bar, entered Parliament, took silk, and became Solicitor General (1885–6), Under Secretary for India (1886–91) and Financial Secretary to the Treasury (1891–2).[1] He was certainly an interesting figure; fresh and stimulating in his speeches, and never ready to spoil a striking story by a too close regard for facts— one cannot avoid being fascinated by his apparently irresponsible waspishness. But as we shall see later, Gorst had a mixture of malice and tenacity of purpose which boded ill for his enemies; and among these the school boards took first place.

In 1896 Gorst introduced an Education Bill, which, though it did not survive ordeal by parliament, was to have posthumous importance. It was obviously based on the Sandford memorandum. The government was alarmed by the desperate financial position of many of the voluntary schools and the bill was designed both to bring them relief and to achieve a measure of local co-ordination.

The county council was to agree with the Education Department on a scheme for appointing a committee to act on its behalf as local education authority to meet local needs. This authority was to supplement and not supplant existing bodies like school boards. One main function was to distribute a special grant to aid the hard-pressed voluntary schools; but there were other possibilities. This local education authority *might* be given by the scheme the power of administering both the Education Department grant and the science and art grants for the area, and it might take over public elementary schools when school boards defaulted.

For our present purpose the most interesting provisions related to education other than elementary. Not only were education authorities to take over the county council powers under the Technical Instruction Acts; they were also given powers of supplying other non-elementary education and of inquiring into the education given by any school within their area. Moreover, the Education Depart-

[1] *Dictionary of National Biography*, 1912–21, pp. 218–19.

ment might, on application of the education authority, or of the school board, "make an order transferring to the education authority for any county any school, or department of a school, within the county maintained by a school board and providing education which, in the opinion of the Education Department, is other than elementary."[1]

Gorst's introduction of the Bill had a superficial cleverness which won him applause. He presented the measure as, on the one hand, bringing aid to the hard-pressed voluntary schools and, on the other, establishing a paramount local education authority in every area. The latter was indeed to be a localised Education Department round which was to be built a new decentralised system. On these new bodies were to be thrown the duties of administering the parliamentary grant (including that for science and art), and of inspection. The decentralisation of the Code would follow these arrangements. And just as the school boards were originally presented as "supplementary" to the voluntary schools, so the localised Education Departments were to supplement the work of a school board in higher and in elementary education. For the main idea of decentralisation Gorst claimed a long and honourable lineage: the reports of the Newcastle Commission of 1861, the Schools Inquiry Commission of 1868, the Technical Instruction Commission of 1884, the Sandford Memorandum of 1888, and the Bryce Commission of 1895.[2] Gorst's major aims in this were, he argued, to aid a hard-pressed Education Department and to prevent conflict and overlapping. But it soon appeared that the devolution was designed to subordinate the school boards to the more conservative county councils, to freeze their educational expenditure and to maim then in their advanced work. Gorst, in spite of his opening flourishes, made a poor showing in the later stages of the debate, and the opposition speakers were merciless in their attacks. Asquith showed the financial inconsistencies of the proposals and the unreality of the devolution;[3] Harcourt indicated how imperfectly the government understood the details of their own scheme and claimed that it was largely a plan to convert an educational minimum which the Education Department had established into an educational maximum;[4] Dixon stressed the threat to the valuable work of higher grade schools such as those in Birmingham and showed how the Bill would in fact call a definite halt to the progress of school board work;[5] Trevelyan demonstrated that the Newcastle and Cross Commissions

[1] Education Bill, 1896, s. 12 (3).
[2] *Parliamentary Debates*, 4th Series, xxxix, 526–46.
[3] ibid. xl, 567–95.
[4] ibid., xli, 1168–76.
[5] ibid., xl, 637–44.

in putting forward their plans had in fact kept the control of parliamentary grant in the hands of the central authority;[1] and Mundella summed up the Bill as "this revolutionary, reactionary and insidious measure."[2]

Government supporters challenged the extravagance of the school boards and one alleged that they had "with the same lax regard which they had shown for the limitations by statute of their duties with respect to money . . . been extending their prerogatives into the domain of secondary education", pointing out, for example, that the money to pay for the Sheffield higher grade school building "came from funds supposed to be allotted to the teaching of young children in elementary schools. It had been said that if Parliament would only leave secondary education alone for ten years, the elementary teachers and school boards would have got the whole system into their hands."[3]

Balfour frankly agreed that the plan was gradually to do away with school boards, and admitted, "I rejoice to think that a step has been taken under this Bill which may put both primary and secondary education under one municipal authority, which shall prevent overlapping and waste, and be able to superintend, from the highest to the lowest stage of primary and secondary education, the whole curriculum which the children may be expected to pass through."[4] But Balfour's avowal of his determination to end the school boards in the hope of getting one single authority was so much at variance with Gorst's disingenuous suggestions, and with the dislike of the county councils themselves for his plan, that Harcourt remarked "the conflict of authorities on the Bench opposite is as remarkable as the conflict of authorities he (Gorst) is about to create in this Bill."[5]

Finally, the Bill was withdrawn; partly because of the objection of the county councils to a scheme which had been amended to give non-county boroughs power to appoint an educational committee, an amendment accepted against Gorst's advice; partly, doubtless, because of the government's own disagreements; and partly because of the success of the determined opposition. As Balfour said, "in five nights we have passed two lines—fourteen words".[6]

[1] ibid., xli, 1376-7.
[2] ibid., xl, 1035.
[3] ibid.. xl, 1029-30. Sir E. Clarke.
[4] ibid., xl, 1247.
[5] ibid., xli, 1219.
[6] ibid., xli, 1573. We should note that when increased financial assistance *was* given to the Voluntary Schools (by an Act of 1897) the distribution of grants, which in the 1896 Bill was at the discretion of the education authority, subject to the department's sanction, was firmly placed in the hands of the Education Department.

It had been accepted that when the Gorst Bill of 1896 failed a special measure to aid voluntary schools would follow, as it did. What had not been anticipated was that the framework of county co-ordinating bodies thus rejected by parliament would come back in a new guise by the simple use of South Kensington Regulations. By Article VII of the 1897 Directory an organisation for the promotion of secondary or higher education within a county or county borough might notify its willingness to be responsible for Science and Art instruction within its area. The rights of managers of existing schools and classes (including school boards) were indeed preserved; and they might even establish additional schools and classes; but the permissive Clause (VII) re-introduced the possibility of a co-ordinating county authority. Once it was called into existence, grants would in general be made to managers of new schools or classes only if they were "acting in unison with" the co-ordinating body. Gorst's administrative camel, which had, in 1896, been expelled by parliament with some ridicule from the door of the school board tent, thus, in 1897, poked its unwelcome head under the flaps at the rear.[1]

But no dislike of Gorst's methods should blind us to the seriousness of the need for establishing local co-ordinating bodies. There was indeed general agreement on the necessity for removing friction. The disagreement arose in trying to find a compromise between vested interests on the one hand and principles of co-ordination on the other (cf. proposals of Bryce Commission).

The acceptance of a plan for national secondary education made central co-ordination as necessary as local; and the Board of Education Act (1899) was merely a first step towards the Bryce suggestions for a national system. But after 1899 much still remained to be done. Within both departments there had, of course, long been uneasiness about possible overlapping of their respective spheres. Thus, it was usually accepted in the Education Department that for "specific subjects" such as chemistry, magnetism and electricity, and mechanics, the Code schemes should be on a lower plane than those for similar subjects in the Directory. But although the thorny problem of "co-ordination" was raised from time to time (e.g. in 1893) it was not seriously tackled. Another field in which the confusion was in fact resolved was that of teachers working for both departments, for it was decided in 1894 that before either department should cancel or suspend such a teacher's certificate it should be considered, by joint conference if necessary, whether the other department should do likewise.[2]

But such attempts at co-ordination left the major problems alone.

---

[1] cf. Allen, *William Garnett*, Heffer, 1933, p. 67.
[2] P.R.O. Ed. 9/5, pp. 81-2, 119.

We have already seen how, though a conference of Higher Grade and Secondary School representatives was held in 1897, nothing was done about the decisions till 1900; and even more regrettable was the failure to take legislative steps to safeguard the position of the school board evening schools against possible trouble-making.

Clearly, trouble could not be far distant. It would be difficult to imagine a more explosive administrative situation than that under the Duke of Devonshire's remote Presidential control in 1897–9. On the one hand was Gorst, the Vice-President and political representative in the House of Commons; a self-willed, able and mercurial individual, ruling over two departments, the spheres of which overlapped at many points; a firm believer in co-ordination from first principles; Gorst, who had just suffered parliamentary defeat in his plan for bringing the school boards, the agents in effect of the senior department, under the county authorities, the agents in effect of the junior department. On the other hand was Kekewich, head of the senior department, who had rather too openly espoused the cause of the school boards, but who, though a reformer at heart, seemed incapable of seeing the major problems of organisation clearly. Moreover, Kekewich was an incorrigible pragmatist, and time and again had professed a policy because it was "in the line of least resistance". At South Kensington, the junior department, the long rule of Donnelly was drawing to a close.

It only remains to point out that relations between Whitehall and the greatest of the school boards had for some time steadily deteriorated, for a number of reasons. *Firstly*, in the Education Department's eyes the London School Board had in its relations with the auditor and its appeals against his decisions been often prepared to play a smart rather than a judicious game. Its moves were regarded with suspicion by Local Government Board and Education Department alike, even during a period when the general policy was favourable to school boards; for on a number of occasions it had somewhat overbid its hand; and the fact that the Education Department was neither very penetrating nor very consistent in its legal decisions made matters worse.

Secondly, a similar policy had made the Education Department (officials and political heads alike) suspicious of London School Board proposals for new sites and additional school accommodation for London. Thus the London School Board had, for their own reasons, been late starters in providing higher grade schools and by the end of the century were urgently needing new sites, and were not very considerate in their mode of getting them. For example, on 26th September, 1898, London School Board wrote asking for approval of Site X for a Higher Grade School. On 8th October the Education

Department replied, suggesting an alternative, to which London School Board replied on 25th October that Site X was the cheapest and best situated and that, as the option of purchase only extended to the middle of October, the Board had, as a matter of emergency, already arranged for its purchase. The Education Department could do nothing but agree to this *fait accompli*, but the repercussions on relations can be imagined.[1] Moreover, in other negotiations about sites during this period London School Board were not above using their power of compulsory purchase as a lever in a way that seemed to the Education Department to savour of sharp practice.[2]

Thirdly, the general problem of accommodation in the London area was an increasing cause of tension. The reasons for this were partly historical. The earlier correspondence between London School Board and the Education Department about accommodation gives a modern reader an acute feeling of unreality. Absenteeism was so rife that it was the practice of London School Board in calculating accommodation needs to deduct 23 per cent from the total number of children in the area. But in 1881 they proposed that they should take some account of pupils over thirteen now attending school, and that they should deduct 20 per cent only, to which the Education Department replied that the London School Board deductions had been made "not from the number of children actually enumerated but from a hypothetical total obtained by adding 10 per cent to the number enumerated". The practice had apparently originated with the difficulties of attendance officers in counting the children in the area; but it was agreed that, with improved methods of enumerating, a flat rate of $12\frac{1}{2}$ per cent should thenceforward be deducted from the number of children actually counted. This illustration serves mainly to show that during the early period London School Board enjoyed a great measure of flexibility in its calculations of accommodation.[3] But, with rising standards of accommodation, the increased leaving age, and London School Board aims for higher standard schools, the basis on which accommodation should be calculated became a matter of acute controversy. We should recall that the Cross Commission had approved of the rule of the Education Department that ten square feet should be "the minimum accommodation provided for each child in average attendance, in all school buildings in future to be erected".[4] But, although the Code laid down a similar criterion in its building rules, it accep-

[1] P.R.O. Ed. 14/3.
[2] ibid., 24/3/99, 17/4/99.
[3] P.R.O., Ed. 14/2, 9/4/81. The mention of flexibility in calculating accommodation is not of course intended to minimise the very real *practical* difficulties which faced London School Board in its early days.
[4] Cross Commission, *Final Report*, p. 209.

ted a calculation of eight square feet per child for schools already receiving annual grant.[1] In actual practice, as from 1889, the general rule for the country, tacitly accepted by London, was to calculate accommodation on a basis of a ten square feet minimum for board schools and eight square feet for voluntary schools.

Then in 1898 the Secretary incautiously told a deputation from Burton Latimer that "in estimating the needs of the parish they were entitled to base their application on ten square feet per child". Thereupon London School Board, assuming hastily that what held for an obscure country district would equally apply to London, adjusted their accommodation figures by making an allowance of ten square feet for all voluntary schools. Consequently, their total of places, counted as already available, showed a drop of 34,000 on the previous year.

This great change the Education Department would not accept; but it knew well from past experience that it was helpless in dealing with general figures for such a large unit as London. Hence, though it would have been reasonable to discuss the figures area by area, and though in fact it seemed that the London School Board had not consistently applied the ten square feet rule throughout, the Department simply refused to consider the general problem and proposed to decide each question "in accordance with the particular circumstances of the case", and persisted in this attitude in spite of further challenging approaches from the school board.[2]

It is unnecessary to enter further into the merits of the dispute, beyond noting that London School Board's claim for considerably increased accommodation—which was a strong one—was not considered on a general basis, largely because of its method of presenting sudden large-scale demands, of a nature calculated to produce a feeling of helpless dismay in the Department.

It is against this background of increasing tension that we must view the London School Board statement in their letter of February 1899, that they intended in their proposals for accommodation to base their calculations, not on the number of children above thirteen who might be expected to attend school, but on those actually attending, and among these *they proposed to include children over fourteen.* "The number over fourteen attending school . . . is always small, but the Board do not consider it to be their duty to turn such children out of school, nor do the Board suppose that their Lordships desire them to do so. It is obvious, however, that such children if in school are occupying school places and must be taken into consideration."

[1] Day School Code 1898, Art. 85a and Schedule VII (7).
[2] P.R.O., Ed. 14/2, 3/2/99–16/3/00.

But, as we have seen, the Code provided (by Art. 13) that as a rule no attendance would be recognised (by the Education Department) for any scholar who had passed in the elementary subjects and was upwards of fourteen years of age. The Department had thus an answer ready to hand, if such a request should be felt unreasonable. It was felt, however, that *"in spite of Article 13"* the school board should be allowed to provide for children of fourteen who actually attended school, even though their attendances might not be counted for grant purposes. Accordingly the Education Department stated that they would be prepared to consider applications based on the London School Board's proposals.[1]

We must note, therefore, that, in spite of increasing tension about London accommodation problems, as late as February, 1899, the Education Department had accepted the principle that London School Board might provide places for pupils who, because they had passed all the standards or were over fourteen, were no longer eligible for grant under the Code. Surely after this the Education Department could not reasonably deny its own support of the London School Board's provision of some out-of-standard education for such pupils?

---

[1] P.R.O., Ed. 14/2, 27/2/99.

X

THE CRISIS

*

In 1898 London County Council, on the advice of its Technical Education Board, decided to apply for recognition as the residual authority for secondary and technical education under Gorst's Clause VII Scheme. This obviously threatened to deprive London School Board of any possibilities of expansion, and they accordingly appealed to the Science and Art Department against the application. An enquiry was held at South Kensington on 1st February, 1899, in the presence of Gorst, and with Donnelly, Secretary of the Science and Art Department, in the chair.

William Garnett, secretary of the Technical Education Board (previously Professor of Mathematics at Nottingham, and then Principal of Durham College of Science, Newcastle), who was present representing London County Council, has told the story of the meeting.[1] The school board representatives claimed to be the superior local education authority, and suggested that London County Council were trying to jump their claim. In their argument, which went to extravagant lengths, they mainly relied on the Education Code (1890) Act, 1890; for, since that Act disposed of the requirement that evening school classes should be in any way elementary, as far as *evening* schools were concerned the school boards already had the whole field of education, up to and including University education, within their proper field of action. Moreover, even higher grade day school education could include much non-elementary work, since the school board held that Section 3 of the 1870 Act, which said that the "principal part" of education in an elementary school should be elementary, meant that so long as the majority of

[1] W. Garnett, *A Retrospect. How the County Council became the Local Education Authority for Londoon on 1st May, 1904.* Reprinted from the *Educational Record*, April 1929.

pupils in a school were having elementary education the rest could do work at any level.

The main battle centred round the effect of the 1890 Act on the evening schools. The London County Council representatives argued that the school board's interpretation of it would not hold water if the full title, "An Act for the Purpose of making Operative certain Articles in the Education Code, 1890" were taken into account. They suggested that the Act was merely to legalise items in the Code which appeared contrary to the 1870 Act.

The Science and Art Department, under Gorst's direction, finally decided to accept London County Council's application under Clause VII, but it was not till after Cabinet approval had been given that the decision was published.

But the sweeping nature of London School Board claims under the Code Act had alarmed Gorst. He told Garnett, after the meeting, that the London School Board interpretation of the Code Act was new to the Education Department. Accordingly, he asked Garnett how an authoritative interpretation of that Act could best be obtained.[1] Garnett suggested a challenge of London School Board accounts before the District Auditor. But, since the complicated nature of the accounts made it very difficult for a private individual to raise such an issue before an auditor, he suggested that Camden School of Art, as a ratepaying corporation with full-time officials, would be well suited for the job. Gorst accordingly wrote to the chairman of the Technical Education Board, who in turn wrote to the chairman of the Camden School of Art. With that the train was laid.

Black, the headmaster of Camden School of Art, proved to be indefatigable in his unravelling of London School Board accounts and registers. He was not, of course, disinterested. He acted both on behalf of Camden School and of the London Technical Education Defence committee and his reports of his investigation reveal the remarkable hostility that London School Board had aroused among its rivals. He established beyond any question that the board schools had engaged in "duplicate registration"; that is, that pupils had been entered on the Whitehall registers (thus in effect qualifying for rate-aid) though no grant had been claimed for them from Whitehall, and also on South Kensington registers (thus qualifying for Science and Art grant). This practice whereby London pupils obtained both rate-aid as elementary pupils and the higher grant as Science and Art pupils, Black flatly attacked as fraudulent.[2]

---

[1] A strange question from a one-time Solicitor General to a scientist.

[2] M.E. *Camden School of Art and Science Corporation. Head master's Report on Rex v Cockerton.* Botolph Printing Works, 1901.

Black obtained legal assistance from Hales, a member of the Camden School Board of Governors, who later acted as solicitor before the auditor. With Garnett's assistance, and Gorst in the background, they proved a formidable team. Black searched the registers and accounts. Garnett and Hales attacked the school boards by letters and articles in "Education"[1] and it is noteworthy that Wm. Hales (whom we can identify under the thinly-disguised pseudonym of "HMW") even at this stage tried to focus the controversy on the point that was to him crucial, the status of the evening schools.

But, readers may ask, what part did Morant play in this developing crisis? As is well known, he arrived back in England from Siam in 1894, and in 1895 was appointed Assistant to Sadler, the Director of the new office of Special Inquiries. We have already seen how he, with Sadler, attended the 1897 Conference on higher grade schools. His biographer[2] has told how, in working for this conference, Morant was astonished to discover that the higher grade schools "rested upon no legal basis whatever, and that they had in fact been established and carried on in open defiance of the law of the land". He, as Allen tells us, carefully investigated the legal position concerning the Brighton and Southampton Cases (1888) and inserted a reference to them in the Report upon Swiss education which he was writing. The School Boards, wrote Morant, "have frequently been told by the Central Authority that they cannot take any such steps as would involve the School Board in any expense for this purpose (of providing higher grade schools), that it would be illegal to spend their rates in such a manner, inasmuch as they were only empowered by the Act of 1870 to use the rates to provide Elementary Education." And a footnote referred to reports of the cases in the School Board Chronicle.[3] On 26th December 1898, Allen continues, Morant showed the passage to a confidential agent of Dr. Garnett and gave him the facilities of the Department Library for following up the evidence of the illegality of these higher grade schools. Thus, when the Clause VII inquiry took place, on 1st February, 1899, Garnett had in his hands all the evidence required not only to disprove the school board case but also to suggest to Gorst the approach through the auditor.

The story has certainly lost nothing in the telling; but whatever weight we attach to its recital of events it must be reconciled with the following facts.

(1) To say that the higher grade schools rested on "no legal basis whatever" is an overstatement. Their position was one of doubtful

---

[1] *Education*, April 1st–29th, 1899.
[2] Allen, *Sir Robert Morant*, Macmillan, 1934, p. 118.
[3] *Special Reports on Educational Subjects*, Vol. 3, p. 47.

legality only; and it is probable that those which had maintained themselves without recourse to the rates were on a legally sound footing.[1]

(2) The *questionable* nature of the position of these higher grade schools was no secret. Thus the school boards in their 1893 conference had openly recognised their need for legal authorisation of their higher grade school work. There had also been references to this need in the evidence before the Cross and Bryce Commissions and in the House of Commons debates.

(3) Allen's description of Morant's insertion in his Swiss Report of "a few illuminating sentences" coupled with a sly reference to the School Board Chronicle's account of the Brighton and Southampton cases is highly suggestive. It is as if Morant were laying a mine which must at all costs be concealed from his chief, Sir G. Kekewich. It is a good story, which has indeed been improved upon;[2] but it is not convincing. The narrative is unjust to both Kekewich and Morant. Allen implies that Kekewich knew that these schools were illegal, suppressed any question of their illegality, and would have pounced on Morant for even hinting at the possibility. The truth was that Kekewich was a well-meaning drifter, who was prepared, if he could, to give the school boards the benefit of the doubt and had indeed influenced the Local Government Board in that direction. He was certainly not the knave that Allen's story would imply.

(4) Allen's narrative seems even stranger when we examine Morant's actual Swiss Report. We should recall the nature of these reports. In the first volume Morant had written an account of the French System of Higher Primary Schools, and in the course of a comparison with English education bluntly argued that in many towns and villages in England money was being unwittingly wasted in giving a boy "either an education which is quite unsuited to his capacities and which will leave him stranded and out of employment at the end of it, or else a base, fraudulent, and spurious imitation of education. . . ."[3] This is scarcely the language of one who worries about whether his chief will think him indiscreet; still less of one who would slip in a footnote reference to a twelve-year-old audit case in order to wreck the educational system of which he disapproves.

But when we turn to Morant's later article on "The Organisation of Education in Switzerland" our incredulity is increased. It is a vigorous, and fearless, comparison of the Swiss and English systems; with an attack on the English grant system, on its use of local tax-

---

[1] P.R.O. Ed. 11/2, "Opinion of Law Officers", 24/7/01.
[2] cf. Lowndes, *The Silent Social Revolution*, O.U.P., 1937, pp. 76–8.
[3] *Special Reports on Educational Subjects*, Vol. 1, 1897, p. 335.

ation and on its legislative provisions, or failures to provide, for secondary and higher grade and elementary education. And among these challenges comes a direct attack on school boards for illegally spending the rates on Higher Grade Schools, "inasmuch as they were only empowered by the Act of 1870 to use the rates to provide Elementary Education".

There is here certainly an attack on school boards; but no one reading this report with an open mind could accuse Morant of conspiratorial intentions; one cannot fairly call a man Guy Fawkes if he drives up to the House of Commons in an enemy tank with a machine-gun firing. Yet, says his biographer, "these few sentences and the small footnote, hidden away as they were in the big Third Volume of 'Reports on Educational Subjects' were not likely to attract much attention and they appear to have passed the scrutiny of Sir George Kekewich without observation." One must surely qualify this description. The report was placed first in the volume. On the second page of the text Morant pointed out the interest and the value to Englishmen of the Swiss comparison. "We can find in Swiss experiences of modern educational developments the most pregnant of warnings, as well as the most convincing illustrations of general principles; and this in a field where there has been almost no surrender either of the truest of democratic methods, or the best of aristocratic guidance, of the greatest freedom of local and individual initiative and effort, or of the firmest retention of a rational form of wise central control."[1]

Or take two pages on: "None the less, nay rather the more, as has before been hinted, is it possible to find very many points in which Swiss educational systems are fruitful of suggestions to a country like our own where variety of type and freedom of individual effort have been so strenuously preserved not only in Secondary education, but also in all except the mere administrative aspects of Primary education." This is a strange way to avoid attention. Nor does the reader lack challenging comparisons throughout the Report: as for example, where in dealing with "The Principles of State Control in Education", Morant attacked our lack of system and planning;[2] and the allegedly hidden reference comes during as vigorous an onslaught on the English system of financing education as it would be possible to conceive. Consider how he writes, three pages before the "hidden" passage: "Taking the foregoing three typical examples as fair specimens of the Swiss systems of Central Participation in local expenditure on Education, is it not evident that they one and all afford an infinitely more rational and intelligible

[1] *Special Reports on Educational Subjects*, Vol. 3, 1898, p. 8.
[2] ibid., pp. 23-4.

method for apportioning the central and local shares in educational expenditure than is afforded by our complicated English system . . . ?"[1]

Anyone who carefully reads the Reports, and in particular the Swiss Report, after reading the implied imputations against Morant's good faith in writing them, should ask himself: Would any writer expect such passages, criticising the whole structure of English education, not in one paragraph only but for pages on end, to escape the eyes of his chiefs? Morant knew that the reports would, like their predecessors, be directly brought to the attention of the Secretary. Did he then write an attack on the whole English educational system in the hope of concealing from the head of the office, to whom the report was addressed, a sly reference to the "School Board Chronicle" of 1888? And are we really to believe that Morant thought that Sadler, the editor, would fail to read this most outspoken report, by his own assistant, which was placed at the forefront of the volume?

Is it not more likely, in view of all the evidence about audit cases so far reviewed, that Morant knew that the office attitude was one of perplexity and helplessness about the whole issue, that they had serious doubts as to the legality of the school board position, and that they hoped that matters would somehow sort themselves out; but that they felt that the risk was that of the school boards and that the Department would only venture to make decisions when compelled to do so? And was not Morant in this article openly, almost defiantly, calling for reforms which he deemed imperative?

What use was made of this carefully concealed bomb? We are told that Morant, on Boxing Day, 1898, showed Garnett's representative the passage in the Swiss report calling attention to the untenable position of the school boards (i.e. in running higher grade schools on the rates). The result was that "on the evening of that day decisive proof of the illegality of the School Board's position was in Dr. Garnett's hands".

But contrast this with Garnett's own account of the argument at the departmental enquiry on 1st February, 1899, when this bomb was to be used. The case for the school board rested mainly on the Education Code (1890) Act, 1890, which dealt only with evening schools and which they claimed gave them unlimited power over all types of higher education. Garnett's task was to demolish that argument by showing that the Act had a very limited purpose indeed. So much was this the case that in one account of the proceedings[2] Garnett only mentioned higher grade schools in a paren-

[1] ibid., p. 44.
[2] W. Garnett, *A Retrospect. How the County Council became the Local Education Authority for London, on 1st May, 1904* p. 8.

thesis; and in another he did not mention them at all, and the account was confined throughout to a description of the argument about evening schools.[1] But had Morant overlooked the evening schools in his report? On the contrary, immediately after attacking as illegal the expenditure on Higher Grade Day Schools of rates which, by the Act of 1870, the school boards might only spend on elementary education, he had written:

"Similarly when, twenty years later, it was decided that in England and Wales the provision of Evening Schools giving *purely Continuative or Higher Education* (*instead of mainly Elementary as before*) might *advisedly* be made a function of the Primary Education Authorities, it was necessary, in order that this might be done, that a special Act should be passed (1890) *to give this specific authorisation* by removing from school boards the disability previously entailed on them under s. 14 (1) of the Act of 1870 taken in connection with s. 3, which required that in every school maintained by a school board "the principal part of the Education given must be elementary". Moreover, even when this considerable extension of school board powers into Higher Education was given it was specifically stated to be for the provision of *Evening* Schools; no mention was made of its extension to the provision of Day Schools for a similar purpose." That is, Morant treated the Code Act (1890) as having altered fundamentally the nature of school board evening schools, making it no longer necessary that they should be public elementary schools[2] and as having given school boards a "considerable extension" of their powers into Higher Education. In other words Morant put forward a modified form of the *School Board's* interpretation of the 1890 Act.

Thus Garnett's task on 1st February 1899 was, according to his own version, mainly to rebut an argument which Morant had himself adopted!

Before considering the issues which were raised and the judgments given in the Cockerton Case itself, it is necessary to have a general picture of the development of the case, and of some of the moves connected with it.

The audit case, which was heard before Cockerton, the District Auditor, during April and May, 1899, really consisted of two parts:

(1) Various schools, including Camden School of Art, and ratepayers' representatives, objected to London School Board expenditure on Science and Art schools or classes. Hales was solicitor for all these parties. In June, Cockerton decided against

[1] W. Garnett, *Educational Work of the London County Council* (Private circulation), p. 23.
[2] Hence his reference to Section 14 (1) of the 1870 Act. Italics mine.—E.E.

London School Board and surcharged school board members with the expenditure they had sanctioned. The school board decided to have *this* decision brought before the High Court.

(2) Hales, in his private capacity as ratepayer, and unsupported by the other parties, challenged all the London School Board expenditure on evening schools, lock, stock and barrel.

On this latter issue Cockerton decided *for* London School Board and allowed the expenditure. Hales appealed to the Local Government Board. This evening school issue was never pushed to a conclusion by Hales, but the opinions of the Education Department given in January, 1900, were very revealing (*infra p.* 129).

The Local Government Board were loth to take up the main case. The auditor was himself entitled to engage counsel and the Board, since they were not directly interested themselves, were anxious not to give an impression of antagonism to the school boards. The Education Department permanent officials were equally reluctant; but Gorst had no such hesitation. At his direction a letter was written to the Local Government Board asking them to take up the case and to employ "counsel of eminence". Later he himself wrote to Local Government Board officials begging them "most earnestly" to take the case up and have the Law Officers instructed to argue it,[1] and continued this pressure by correspondence and personal interview; but, as the Local Government Board were still reluctant, he approached both the Treasury and the Attorney General, to discover what steps were necessary to have the Law Officers engaged on the case. The Treasury finally agreed and had already instructed the Law Officers to support Cockerton, when, towards the end of April 1900, the Local Government Board decided that, as some of their own decisions on audit appeal cases might come in question, they were themselves prepared to take up the case.[2]

Having thus achieved his object Gorst now sat back and watched the Local Government Board deal with the unpleasant infant he had so industriously fathered on it. He carried this detachment so far that when the Local Government Board, on 14th July, 1900, sent to the Board of Education a draft "Special Case" (giving an outline of the facts and issues involved), which the solicitors wanted returned urgently, the case was, on Gorst's instructions, returned, on 24th July, with a simple comment that "the Board of Education, not being parties to the Record, are not bound by the statements in

[1] M.H. 27/141. Letters, 4/4/00, 9/4/00. P.R.O. Ed. 14/25, March–May, 1900.
[2] cf. Gorst's statement in the House of Commons on 7th July 1901: "As to the Cockerton judgment the Board of Education had nothing to do with either the case, the judgment or the prosecution of the appeal." *Parliamentary Debates,* 4th Series, xciii, 984.

the case", but that so far as they knew they had no objections to make.

In fact, however, the Board of Education had important comments to make, especially on the matter of ex-Standard pupils. Gorst's hurried, and somewhat unkind, letter of 24th July was the result of a question in the House of Commons about the delay in bringing on the Cockerton Case. To this questioner Gorst replied on 23rd July (while the papers on the Case were still in the Board of Education), "I am not aware of any cause which prevents the London School Board audit case being now submitted to the Queen's Bench Division. The Board of Education is not a party to the record, and has no right to interfere in the case. I do not know what step it is possible for the Board of Education to take to expedite the proceedings . . ."[1] Could duplicity go further?

Gorst's policy had, during these manoeuvres, forced the permanent officials into a position which, in view of the history of higher grade schools, was a singularly unhappy one. Higher grade schools had, as we have seen, been encouraged and stimulated to further efforts by various Vice-Presidents and by Kekewich himself. It is true, on the other hand, that the rashness, one might almost say the arrogance, of London School Board had produced a suspicion of its motives and ambitions which alienated its friends within the office. This is probably the only explanation of the fact that Gorst's proposals to have the Law Officers engaged, at the Department's request, in fighting a case against a school board for carrying out what was in large measure the Department's own policy, did not produce threats of resignation from his senior officials. The Local Government Board's change of heart in fact saved the Education Department from the ignominy of appearing to conduct against a school board a case in which, as it finally transpired, the crucial point against the school board (its claim to educate *adults*, i.e. in evening schools), was one in which the Education Department were confident that the school board was in the right, and in which it was thought to be protected by the Department's own legislation and regulations.

[1] *Times*, July 24th, 1900.

XI

THE ARGUMENT AND
THE JUDGMENTS

*

W<small>E</small> may conveniently consider together all the arguments which
were raised at the various stages of this long battle. The Cockerton
Case raised two main issues:—

(1) Could school boards lawfully use the rates in conducting
schools or classes, whether by day or evening, under the rules
of the Science and Art Department?

(2) Could school boards educate adults out of the rates?

The argument and the judgments may be approached with this
division in mind.

SCHOOL BOARDS AND THE SCIENCE AND ART DEPARTMENT

From the outset there could be no doubt that the powers of the
school boards had to be derived from the Elementary Education
Acts and, in particular, from the parent Act of 1870. Even school
board counsel had to concede that point. But if this were so, counsel
for the auditor argued, clearly the case against the school board was
proved; for the Acts were Elementary Education Acts, and the principal Act (of 1870) was "an Act to provide for public *Elementary*
Education in England and Wales".

It was true that the definition in Section 3 described an elementary
school as "a school or department of a school at which elementary
education is the principal part of the education there given . . ." but
this was a definition, indicating which of the existing voluntary
schools might be considered as "elementary". It did not deal mainly
with Board Schools. Indeed it did not necessarily deal with Board

Schools at all; for Board Schools were public elementary schools *of a special kind,* and if the rest of the Act showed that Board Schools must be *exclusively* elementary, then the definition would not affect them. At any rate, the definition was not legislative in the sense of conferring a power to use rates on secondary education.

Moreover, the responsibility of the Board Schools to the Education Department was clearly established by the 1870 Act. For every school provided by a school board must be a *public* elementary school (s. 14 (1)) and a public elementary school must, among other things (such as being open to inspection) be conducted under the Code (s. 7 (4)).

Finally, from start to finish of the Act there was no mention of the Science and Art Department (South Kensington). That was an essentially separate body from the Education Department (Whitehall). Its funds were given by a separate vote, and its Directory of regulations was entirely distinct from the Whitehall Code.

What answer could the school board give to this challenge? The argument was long, commencing before the auditor in March, 1899, and concluding before the Master of the Rolls in March, 1901; and it was extensive, ranging over all the statutes and regulations from 1870 to 1898; and it gained in piquancy from the fact that Asquith, the school board counsel, arguing for the power of governmental regulations, was an ex-Home Secretary and Prime Minister in the making; but substantially the school board case could be reduced to three divisions.

Firstly, it had been the practice for school boards to conduct science and art classes as part of their ordinary work since shortly after the 1870 Act was passed. This had been recognised by the Education Department, the Science and Art Department and the Local Government Board. Indeed, Parliament itself had recognised that the practice existed by referring to school boards as being possibly "in receipt of aid from the Department of Science and Art".[1] But such "recognition" could scarcely be construed as conferring a positive power to use the rates on science and art classes.

But, *secondly,* the school board practice of having science and art classes had been the only reasonable one in the circumstances. Admittedly the first duty of the school boards under the 1870 Act was to supply public school accommodation for children requiring elementary education; but once that was done surely any excess accommodation might be made available for other purposes? The Department had never forbidden the attendance of older pupils.[2]

[1] Technical Instruction Act, 1889, s. 1 (1) (d).
[2] With the exception of a short period in 1880. See p. 31, *Supra.*

Moreover, since 1891 the Education Department had power to direct that free school accommodation should be provided in any area for pupils over three and under fifteen.[1] If, therefore, a pupil had passed out of the Standards at age thirteen, and was consequently no longer eligible for Whitehall grant, but remained at school for another two years, it was reasonable that he should be free to take the South Kensington examinations. Thereby he would earn money and *reduce* the charge on the rates.

Thirdly, the vital, and more strictly legal, part of the school board argument hinged on the interpretation of the 1870 Act, using three main lines of defence:

(i) The elasticity of the term "elementary education".
(ii) The breadth of the interpretation of "elementary education" by the Education Department itself.
(iii) The argument that if the principal part be "elementary" the School Board had a free hand as to the residue.

Let us see how counsel argued for each of these.

In arguing that the term "elementary" was an elastic one, counsel for the school board carried conviction up to a point. The legislature had not interpreted "elementary" for a very good reason—education was growing and would develop, and it was neither necessary nor desirable to pin down the public elementary school to a conception of the three R's, for example, as the basis of its work. But this argument would only go so far—the court might find it difficult to deny that Algebra was part of elementary education; but it could draw the line at Analytical Geometry.

The Department's power of interpretation gave a second and independent line of defence; for even if a subject such as Animal Physiology would not normally be understood as elementary education, the fact that the Education Department had included it in the Code made it elementary education for the purposes of the 1870 Act. And if it were elementary education in that sense it was pedantic to say that the same material became non-elementary immediately it appeared in the syllabus of another department (i.e. the South Kensington Directory).

It was easy to show that the limits set by the Department as indicated by specific subjects were always wide, and had greatly expanded. Thus, even in 1871, as Asquith pointed out to the Court of Appeal, the Code, signed by Forster himself, included among its specific subjects geography, history, grammar, algebra, geometry, natural philosophy, physical geography, the natural sciences, political economy, and languages. But by 1898, argued counsel, it had

[1] Elementary Education Act, 1891, s. 5.

become so frightfully unelementary "that probably not more than three or four judges could pass examinations in the subjects specified: 'Algebra, Euclid, Mensuration, Mechanics, Chemistry, Physics, Animal Physiology, Hygiene, Botany, Agriculture, Horticulture, Navigation, Latin, French, Welsh, German, Book-keeping, Shorthand, Domestic Economy and Domestic Science'". This list of subjects certainly showed that the Department's limit to "elementary" subjects was vague. And there was no lack of illustration that the teaching of these subjects might go to considerable lengths.

The schemes in the Code overlapped considerably with those of the Science and Art Department. Was it really argued that it was illegal for school boards to use the rates to teach under the Directory the very material which it would have been lawful to teach under the Code?

But even more significant, if the Education Department's recognition could make a subject legally "elementary", was their recognition of overlap. Thus Article 101[1] stated that no scholar might be presented for an examination in any specific subject in which he had been examined by the Department of Science and Art. Here was official recognition of South Kensington subjects overlapping with those of Whitehall. As Asquith put it, "You may take them (the specific subjects) under Whitehall, or you may take substantially the same thing under South Kensington and this Whitehall grant is not to be given for the specific subject if the scholar has been examined in it by the Department of Science and Art. It is to prevent duplication of grants, but it shows very clearly that with regard to this area they are dealing with common subject matter—the same subject may be taught either as a specific subject under the Code or as an Art and Science subject under the Directory."

Indeed it seemed to Asquith to be largely a matter of accident or departmental convenience which department was responsible for a particular subject. Thus drawing had for a number of years been taught in the elementary schools with a statement in the Whitehall Code that the examination in drawing would be made by South Kensington and the grant would be paid by South Kensington. No one had ever questioned the legality of that arrangement. *It seemed therefore, that a mere statement in the Whitehall Code authorising the holding of the Science and Art classes under South Kensington would have prevented the action arising!* "If that Article (sanctioning such an arrangement), were in the Code, according to the contention of the other side, the whole of this expenditure would become legal. Why? Because it would then be expenditure authorised by Whitehall, although not paid out of the elementary grant as defined by the Act of 1870, but

[1] Day School Code, 1898, p. 24, Rule (IV).

paid by South Kensington out of the grant in respect of Science and Art and paid in respect of subjects prescribed by and examined by the South Kensington and Science and Art Department! This arrangement as regards drawing has been a battledore and shuttlecock arrangement. It has been at one time under South Kensington and at another time under Whitehall, and it seems an absurd thing to suggest that the school board would be perfectly justified in spending the rates upon these drawing classes the moment they were taken under the Whitehall Department, and yet that the expenditure would become illegal when precisely the same instruction was given under a grant given by a different Department. My Lords, there is no substance in it. It makes illegal, upon a mere question of form, if I may say so, that which is substantially the same thing."[1]

The weaknesses of this school board contention were exposed by the Master of the Rolls during the argument in the Court of Appeal.

Master of the Rolls: Supposing the Education Department had recognised that under the Act a ratepayer was to pay for teaching the child Hebrew, what would you say?

Asquith: The Education Department had absolute power to do that, certainly. I do not shrink for a moment from that. The Education Department may do so tomorrow by a stroke of the pen.

Master of the Rolls: I should want some authority for that.

Asquith: It would have to lay its Minutes on the table of the Houses of Parliament. That is all.

Master of the Rolls: You cannot tax a man without some statute imposing a tax to be levied on him.

Asquith: No, my Lord.

Master of the Rolls: Do you say the Code has the same effect as an Act of Parliament?

Asquith: It has if the Act of Parliament give it that effect.

Master of the Rolls: Where do you get that?

Asquith: Out of the Act of 1870.

Master of the Rolls: I have not seen that yet. My proposition is, of course, they may regulate and say what is elementary education and so on, but supposing they prescribed something which it is perfectly plain was not elementary education—that my ploughboy should be taught Greek at the expense of the ratepayer. What then?[2]

But the school board had a further and vital line of legal argument, in its interpretation of part of the definition given in Section 3 of the 1870 Act. "The term 'elementary school' means a school or

---

[1] Shorthand notes of proceedings before Court of Appeal. Second Day. pp. 67–9.
[2] Shorthand notes of proceedings before Court of Appeal, pp. 91–2.

department of a school at which elementary education is the principal part of the education theregiven."

If a majority of the pupils in a rate-aided school were being taught elementary education under the Code, then, the school board argued, the residue could legally be taught anything else whatever. The practical implication of this strictly logical interpretation was that in each school of 1,000 pupils relying on the rates the school board need only teach elementary education to 501 pupils. To the rest it could teach whatever it thought fit: grammar school education perhaps in the majority of its schools, technical college work in a few, and in one or two, courses of university standard to which the rest of the schools would contribute pupils. Thus one school board might operate a complete educational system.

The school board claims were in fact pitched at a very high level. Asquith argued that, as long as he kept the principal part of the education elementary, he (i.e. the school board) had "the right to go as high as ever I can and the bigger the grant I can get from South Kensington the better." As one Lord Justice put it, on this argument the school board might employ University professors, the very first men in the country, to teach the more advanced parts of the curriculum. But, as the Court made clear, it was only when this argument was linked to the teaching of adults in evening schools that the sweeping nature of its challenge could be fully appreciated.

THE EDUCATION OF ADULTS. EVENING SCHOOLS

It is strange that the importance of the question of the age of pupils to be taught was not grasped by Cockerton, nor, at the outset, by the ratepayers' representatives. Indeed all the parties to the main case agreed to treat the issue as if the question of the education of adults had not arisen. But the courts were not prepared to decide merely by the nature of the subject matter what was the statutory limit to the school board's powers. In their view the Act of 1870 was aimed at the education of children. That was the essence of the whole matter, on which even the question of the permissible content of elementary education depended.

The school board proved to have a poor defence on this question. The 1870 Act bristles with references to the education of children. An attempt was, indeed, made to suggest that wherever the word "child" occurred in the Act there was a reference to a corresponding duty on the parent's part and that otherwise the word "scholar" was used; but the briefest reference to sections of the Act will show how little foundation there is for such a claim.

Clearly, the question of age was vital for evening schools, and the longer the case continued the more obvious did the paramount importance of the evening schools become. From the outset at least two men appear to have grasped this fact. Garnett (Secretary of the London County Council Technical Board) in his accounts of the origin of the Cockerton Case tells how he based his argument on the evening schools and on the implications of the extravagant school board claim under the Education Code (1890) Act 1890.

But a more vigorous, if more extreme, attack on the school board was made by William Hales, who was solicitor to the Camden School of Science and Art. Hales, acting as a ratepayer, and independently of all the parties to the case, in an audit action which he conducted simultaneously with the main Cockerton Case, claimed from the outset that *all* the evening schools of the school boards were illegal. The fact of the existence of officially recognised evening meetings of elementary schools before and at the time of the passing of the 1870 Act would seem to be fatal to his contention in its *extreme* form. Cockerton accordingly turned down Hales' argument and *allowed* the expenditure on an evening school teacher which Hales had challenged. Hales appealed to the Local Government Board and in a long letter[1] sought to show that the Education Code (1890) Act, 1890, on which both the school board and the Education Department strongly relied, gave the school boards no authority to run Evening Continuation Schools at the expense of the rates.

Hales argued that the 1890 Act could only be understood as applying to voluntary schools which had no power of coming on the rates. For school board evening schools which drew on the rates were left subject to all the requirements of the 1870 Act. "It is therefore demonstrably clear that it is only a Board School constituted under and conforming to all the provisions of the Act of 1870 which can supplement its funds by recourse to the Local Rates, and an Evening Continuation School is not in any sense such a school.

"A Board School under the Act of 1870 cannot at one and the same time be a school in which the principal part of the education there given *is* Elementary as defined by the Day School Code and a school at which the Education there given is *not* Elementary but is in accordance with the Evening Continuation School Code."

Then after arguing that power to spend the rates must be construed strictly in favour of the ratepayers, Hales concluded: "Unless it can be shown that the Legislature has *expressly* authorised School Boards to charge the expenses of Evening Continuation Schools, which are not open to children but only to adults, upon the School Fund any such application of the rate is entirely illegal."

Now it may be noted that this was substantially the view of the

[1] M.H. 27/141, 16/10/99.

Education Code (1890) Act, 1890 later taken by the Courts.[1] Faced with the Hales dilemma immediately after the auditor's decision the Local Government Board put it to the Education Department, whose reply, given on 27th January, 1900, was significant: "My Lords . . . have no authority to interpret the terms of the Education Acts. But for the purposes of Their own administration, They have never questioned that a School Board have power to conduct Evening Schools in accordance with the Code of the Education Department in force for the time being; *and to charge any expenses arising therefrom to the School Fund.* They take it that the intention of Section 1 of the Education Code (1890) Act, 1890, was to enable evening schools, *whether provided by a School Board or not,* in which the principal part of the instruction given was other than elementary, to receive grants from this department as Public Elementary Schools, and They are, therefore, of opinion that the Auditor's decision in this case under consideration was rightly given."[2]

Hales' arguments were substantially (though not entirely) endorsed by the decisions in the main case and he therefore did not trouble to follow up his private appeal to the Local Government Board; but the documents in this odd, forgotten case furnish interesting evidence:

(i) that the many parties to the main case, including Cockerton himself, underestimated the significance of the issue of age;

(ii) that the Education Department considered that the school boards could, under the Evening School Code, charge the rates with education of adults, for it was expressly stated in the explanatory memoranda to the Evening School Codes from 1893 onwards that the attendance of persons over 21 years of age would thereafter be recognised; and

(iii) that the Department assumed that the 1890 Act empowered school boards to give non-elementary education, provided that they kept within the liberal limits laid down by the Evening Continuation Schools Code.

When school board evening class expenditure came to be discussed in the main case, it was quickly obvious that the 1890 Code Act was a broken reed, and the school board were once more thrown back upon the interpretation of the Elementary Education Acts. It could, of course, be shown that there were evening classes in existence before 1870 and at the time of the Act passing. But they were certainly not doing advanced work. Moreover, the 1870 Act so

[1] To say this is not, of course, to accept Hales' attack upon school board evening schools as such.

[2] M.H. 27/141, 27/1/00. (Italics mine.—E.E.)

129

explicitly contemplated the education of *children* that the fact of adults attending evening classes proved nothing. As one judge put it, "The practice could not enlarge the Act."

The school board also showed how frequently and how explicitly the Codes recognised the attendance of adults. But, in the first place, the Code could not give sanction to school boards to educate a class of pupils, not contemplated by the Acts; in the second place, the Codes did not purport to deal only with *board* evening schools, and the fact that they applied to adult pupils did not mean that these adult pupils must be in board schools; and, in the third place, the Codes only recognised for purposes of grant; they did not expressly purport to lay down the conditions on which rates could be spent.

The judgments of the Court of Queen's Bench, delivered on 20th December, 1900,[1] may be summarised as follows: The Education Department and the Science and Art Department were in 1870 "separate in name, separate in local habitation, separate in constitution, and separately entrusted with public funds to be administered by each department independently of the other". And although there was some overlap in the subject matter, the schemes of the Directory were of a much more advanced character than those of the Code.

Now the very condition of the existence of a school board laid down by the 1870 Act was a deficiency of schools for elementary education. A board school must be a public elementary school and must be conducted in accordance with the regulations of the Code. In a public elementary school the principal part of the education must be elementary, but the school might go beyond mere elementary education if the school board were so minded—provided that it kept within the rules of the Whitehall Code. "So long as the board school is devoted principally to elementary education, there is not only no provision, express or implied, that the instruction shall not go beyond it, but a distinct intimation that it may, and that the only condition expressly imposed as to the *quantum* of education is that it must at least come up to the lowest standard required in order to obtain a parliamentary grant—i.e., must satisfactorily teach the obligatory subjects. . . . There is, however . . . a very important and a very reasonable practical limit imposed on the education to be given at board schools. From first to last the whole series of Acts relating to this subject, which are invariably designated as the Elementary Education Acts, deal with children." The judgment cautiously refrained from defining "children" but suggested

[1] R. *v.* Cockerton, L.R. 1901, 1 Q.B., 322. The quotations are from the very lucid and comprehensive judgment of Wills, J.

that the upper age limit probably lay some where between sixteen and seventeen.

What then of the evening schools, where so high a proportion of the students were not children? The evening school regulations, the judgment continued, merely stated the conditions upon which the Education Department were prepared to make grants. "It appears to me, again, to have been perfectly within the competence of the department to lay down the conditions under which it would make grants, and I am not in the least surprised that where it found schools *de facto* fulfilling those conditions, the grant followed as a matter of course. But to argue, as has been done, that such action on the part of the department sets the school board free to teach at the expense of the ratepayers to adults and to children indiscriminately the higher mathematics, advanced chemistry (both theoretical and practical), political economy, art of a kind wholly beyond anything that can be taught to children, French, German, history, I know not what, appears to me to be the *ne plus ultra* of extravagance. If the Acts of which the primary object was elementary education and the whole object was education for children are to be transformed into Acts for the higher education—education of a kind usual rather in a college of a university than in a school—of grown-up men and women, it must be done by Act of Parliament and not by a stroke of the pen of a Government department. The department has never affected to do anything of the kind, or to do more than lay down the conditions under which a grant of money may be earned." Thus the evening school regulations so far as they applied to adults would cover grants to such institutions as working men's colleges rather than to rate-supported school board schools.

The Education Code (1890) Act, 1890, which stated that it should not be required as a condition of parliamentary grant to an evening school that the principal part of the education there given should be elementary, was similarly explained. It laid down conditions of grant only. It applied to voluntary evening schools as well as board schools. And it did not alter in the least the powers and duties of school boards and "certainly does not confer an entirely new power to teach adults by the aid of the rates."[1]

But although the court was emphatic in its decision that school boards could not, out of the rates, either teach adults or teach science and art classes (under the Directory) it considered that such work could be carried on by school boards provided that they could raise

[1] This interpretation of the 1890 Act was more or less forced on the court because the significance of the change introduced by Article 106 (v) of the 1890 Code (that pupils having passed Standard V could thereafter be examined in the additional subjects alone) was overlooked; presumably because the change had first appeared in the 1889 Code which was not put into operation.

subscriptions or donations sufficient to cover their expenditure without recourse to the rates.

The court therefore upheld the decision of the auditor. The Court of Appeal's judgment, delivered by the Master of the Rolls on 1st April, 1901, confirmed the findings of the court below. Indeed it narrowed rather than enlarged the possible scope of school board work, emphasising not merely that the Elementary Education Acts only authorised payments out of the school rates for the elementary education of children, but also that the Whitehall Code was not necessarily conclusive as to what was elementary education.[1]

What were the *practical* implications of these decisions?

(1) It must be remembered that the judgments related to the accounts for the years 1897 and 1898, when the Whitehall and South Kensington Departments were entirely distinct. As from 1900, however, the two departments were merged in the Board of Education[2] and accordingly the part of the judgments relating to Science and Art schools and classes lost much of its significance. The delimitation of the respective spheres of elementary and secondary (and technical) education became largely a matter of administrative arrangement within one department. Moreover, as we have seen, the general plan of the higher elementary schools had already been agreed to by the Higher Grade Schools themselves in 1897 and the conference had included representatives from the Organised Science Schools. Thus the most highly organised and ambitious of the Day Science and Art Schools had already consented to a framework *broadly* within the terms of the Cockerton judgment. It was the Minute of 6th April, 1900, and the severe interpretation of that Minute which maimed the development of Day Science and Art Schools.

(2) Throughout the case the final and crucial criterion of an upper limit was age. The school boards were entitled to spend the rates upon the education of *children*. Even questions of content were subordinate to this, because if the age limit were abandoned the vital safeguard against straying far into secondary or university education had gone.

(3) The *practical* implications of the age restriction required by the judgment were most important for evening schools. It is true that the greater part of each judgment was directed to day and evening schools alike. But in actual fact the only age limit mentioned in the judgments was "somewhere between sixteen and seventeen" (Wills, J.). It is true, too, that in the course of the argument the Master of the Rolls thought this "rather high", but even if we lower it by a

---

[1] R. *v.* Cockerton, L.R., 1901, I Q.B., p. 726.
[2] Board of Education Act 1899, s. 2.

year it would still cover practically all the day pupils being educated by school boards. Moreover, as we have already seen, the upper age limit for Higher Elementary Schools had already been fixed at fifteen. This, of course, was within any legal restriction imposed by the Cockerton judgment.

(4) The restrictions mentioned on possible content of elementary education were not severe. It is true that the courts thought that school boards must not teach Hebrew and Greek; and that they might not teach the courses prescribed in the Directory, because these went to a very high level—University honours standard. It was specifically stated that some of the school board education might be technical; but, whether it was elementary or advanced, it must conform to the Whitehall Code. And whether we accept the view that it was within the Department's competence to extend the Code still further (per Wills, J., pp. 339–41) or that the Code had reached the high water mark (per Master of the Rolls, p. 729), it must be admitted that the judgments in themselves placed no serious restriction on the possibilities of technical education: Mathematics, Mechanics, Physiology, Botany, Chemistry, Physics, Agriculture, Domestic Economy, Shorthand, Horticulture, Navigation, Bookkeeping, Manual Instruction, Needlework, and Art were all included in the Code and were therefore accepted as permissible subjects for board schools to teach—so far as the Cockerton Case was concerned.

It seems a reasonable inference from the judgments that the Courts were more concerned to restrict the upward rather than the outward growth of the curriculum in the board schools: to restrain the teaching of *higher* mathematics and *advanced* chemistry rather than the addition of subjects like navigation. Indeed the technical subjects already in the Code, such as mechanics, agriculture, horticulture and navigation, were not critically mentioned throughout the case. It would be very difficult therefore to show that the Cockerton judgment in any way necessarily restricted the development of technical education in day schools.

XII

THE COCKERTON ACTS,
1901 AND 1902

*

THE Cockerton judgment convinced the government that the time was ripe for large-scale educational legislation—school board supporters indeed suggested in the Commons debates that the judgment was received by government supporters with ill-concealed joy, as a *deus ex machina* for the salvation of church schools and the destruction of school boards. But, until a great Education Bill (like that of 1902) could be passed, it was clear that temporary cover must be provided for continuing the schools and classes whose support by the rates had been declared illegal. That temporary legal authority was provided by the "Cockerton Acts": the Education Act, 1901, and the Education Act, 1901 (Renewal) Act, 1902.

The 1901 Act consisted substantially of one clause, namely:

(1) (i) Where a school board has at any time during the twelve months immediately preceding the thirty first day of July one thousand nine hundred and one maintained out of the school fund any school or class to the maintenance of which the school fund is not lawfully applicable, the council of the county or county borough within which the school or class is held, or, with the sanction of the Board of Education, any other local authority under the Technical Instruction Acts, 1889 and 1891, for the district within which the school or class is held, may empower the school board to carry on for the period of one year from that day the work of the school or class to such extent and on such terms as may be agreed on between such council or local authority and the school board, and to apply to the maintenance of the school or class such sum out of the school fund as the council or local authority may sanction.

(2) Where any expenses incurred by a school board in respect of any such school or class *before the said day* are sanctioned by the Local Government Board the legality of those expenses shall not be questioned in any court.[1]

At first reading the Act seemed to be a straight-forward solution of the difficulty. It dealt with any *previous* illegalities by providing that, so far as school boards had, before 31st July, 1901, spent rates illegally, the Local Government Board's sanction would provide complete cover. For the *following* year, all that the school board had to do was to get the permission of the rating authority—the county council or county borough council—to carry on its work as before. The original Bill was in fact put through by the Government as it stood, without accepting a single amendment; but the opposition was bitter and the debates prolonged. Analysis will reveal why this was so.

In the first place, the 1901 Cockerton Act allowed only for the continuation of schools or classes already in existence. School boards could not go on with any projected development— a serious restriction where work in evening schools, for example, was expanding rapidly.

Moreover, even within the limited field of existing classes, the county council was given power to restrict the school board's activities "to such extent and on such terms as may be agreed on". Hence, if a local authority, jealous of the competition of school board classes with its own or other technical classes, refused to "agree", under this Act it would in effect prevent the school board from holding any classes of whose legality it had any doubts.

Thirdly, the very requirement of having to go, as was said time and again, "cap in hand" to request permission to do what they had done successfully and with the open support of successive heads of the Education Department over so many years, was felt to be a poor return for the work of the school boards in the past, and indeed an unnecessary snub. Surely all that was necessary could have been achieved by a short Act, giving a general dispensation, and power to carry on as before, pending the 1902 Act?

The opponents of the 1901 Bill were on more controversial ground in contending that it was couched in unnecessarily wide terms, and that school boards need only be required to seek permission for spending school *rates*, leaving them free to use endowments as they wished. But such arguments received support from the opinion of the Law Officers (given on 24/7/01) that a school board could legally conduct science schools and science and art classes out of the

---

[1] Education Act, 1901, s. 1. (Italics mine.—E.E.)

school fund, provided that no part of the expenditure was defrayed out of the rates, or out of the government grant for elementary education, or out of any other source which would go in relief of the rates for elementary education.[1]

The government case for the Cockerton Act was first of all based on grounds of immediate necessity: partly to carry on the education of the handful of advanced students in schools of science, but mainly to deal with about 2,000 evening schools "some of which certainly will be continued, some of which certainly should be stopped, and some of which should be regulated so as to prevent them from killing existing schools which are really better than themselves."[2] Legislation was necessary because, although Technical Instruction Committees had power to carry on every subject except Latin and Greek under the Technical Instruction Act, they had not in all cases the funds, having spent both the "whiskey money" and the penny rate allocated to them. They had not the funds; but they had the legal power. The school boards had rates; but they had not power.

But the Act had a much wider significance than the mere solution of this temporary problem. It was conceived, on the one hand, as a pilot experiment, and, on the other, as establishing a principle: county and county borough councils were to be the controlling local authorities for education. Naturally the Government were attacked for introducing such major considerations on what was, after all, a side issue. They were challenged to deal with the major issue by frontal attack, which provoked a junior Member of Parliament, Mr. Winston Churchill, to retort that the Cockerton Bill was "not even a pitched battle. It was only a reconnoitring patrol sent up along the line to obtain information and cover the front of the advancing army". He suggested indeed that the information deriving from a year of operation of the Cockerton Act might either support or detract from the case for putting the county councils in control of education.[3]

This legislation was certainly neither a mere dispensing Act nor a mere experiment. Mr. Bryce described it as an attempt to snatch upon a temporary Bill "the assertion of an important and far-reaching principle. They (the government) are seeking, in fact, to effect what amounts to an educational revolution in this country and they are trying to do it by a mere side wind."[4]

The general body of Liberals in the House saw in the Bill not only a gratuitous affront to the school boards, but an attack on the educa-

[1] P.R.O. Ed. 11/2, 24/7/01.
[2] Sir John Gorst, *Parliamentary Debates*, 4th Series, xcvi, 1179.
[3] *Parliamentary Debates*, 4th Series, xcvii, 1394-5.
[4] *Parliamentary Debates*, 4th Series, xcvi, 612.

tion of the working classes, and more especially on the popular higher grade schools. They felt, too, that much of the driving force behind the Government in this unnecessarily wide measure came from the Church and its fears for the voluntary schools.

On the other hand, the importance of the Bill and its far-reaching educational implications were emphasised by Balfour himself.[1] The bitterness of the controversy was, in his view, a *necessary* result of the clash of policy involved. The Bill was to establish firmly the principle that the proper authority for organising secondary education was the local authority; that the school boards were not to be the future authorities for secondary education; that indeed no *ad hoc* authority would be accepted by the government. In this speech the 1901 Education Act was described by Balfour as establishing the fundamental principle of the great 1902 Act for which he was himself to be responsible and as being "an authoritative declaration of the general line upon which we mean to proceed in our future Bill".

The speeches of members of the government and their main supporters gave an illuminating insight into the implications of this decisive move. The main plan so far had been for some county *ad hoc* authority for secondary education. That was the idea of the Bryce Report. But the Cockerton Case, with its spotlight on the illegal expenditure of rates, made plausible the government plan of putting the school board *pro tanto* under the ratepayers' representatives, and eventually of making these representatives (in the county council), rather than any *ad hoc* body, the authority controlling secondary education.

Government supporters were against any maintenance of the *status quo* even for the period of 1901–2. They feared the power of the teachers' unions at any *ad hoc* elections, and in the meantime they feared the possibility of school boards strengthening their hold on the educational machine.

Further, Government supporters stressed the weakness and inefficiency of rural school boards, and this was tacitly accepted even by the Opposition. Nor was there serious denial of the ambitions of the greater school boards. London had made their objectives too clear; and therefore it might not have been enough to pass a simple uncontroversial Bill whereby the Board of Education would have exercised temporary dispensing powers and allowed the school boards to carry on as before.

But in debate only Balfour showed a statesman-like grasp of the principle of marrying local educational administration to local educational finance; and it was clear already that in his eyes that principle must over-ride all others.

[1] ibid., xcvii, 1358–64.

What part did the Cockerton judgment itself play in this clash of prejudices, sentiments and opinions? On the one hand government speakers tried to limit the school boards' future activities to the greatest possible extent by stating that the judgment prohibited education by school boards beyond fifteen. This they achieved by quoting Mr. Asquith's over-cautious advice to London School Board as if it were a necessary inference from the judgment—in spite of his strenuous protestations to the contrary. On the other hand, they tried to minimise the possible harmful effects of the judgment and of the 1901 Act. This Gorst did in two ways:

(a) He showed that the actual effect of the Cockerton judgment itself on higher grade schools was negligible. (And it should be noted that in this official interpretation he was using the very low age limit of fifteen):

"As regards day schools, there is not a single day school in the country that will be shut up in consequence of this judgment. Not only will no day school be shut up, but the effect produced by the judgment, even if there were no legislation at all, on the day schools, is of a very unimportant and almost infinitesimal character. . . . The higher-grade schools will not be affected by the judgment in any way whatever, except to the extent that in a few higher-grade schools there are classes which are receiving instruction in science and art; but, so far as I have been able to ascertain, those classes are only receiving instruction in elementary science and art, which is within the day school Code of the Education Department. . . . But there are forty-eight higher-grade schools in the whole of England and Wales which have what is called a science top. There is an upper division of the school which studies science under the old Science and Art Department of the Board of Education. These schools will undoubtedly be affected by the judgment."[1] But Gorst's figures showed that, even taking these into account, the effects would be small. Throughout the whole country, as regards the instruction given, a mere handful (900–1,000) of higher grade pupils would be affected. There were also some 4,000 pupils, in the ordinary elementary schools, who might be affected if one took the judgment as prohibiting school board education of any kind above fifteen. Thus, on Gorst's statement and figures, the effect of the Cockerton judgment on the day schools of England, and on the higher grade schools in particular, and even applying a very wide interpretation to that judgment, was negligible.

(b) But, in the second place, Gorst had to admit the vast numbers in the evening schools who would be affected by the judgment. There were on the rolls of these schools some 228,000 pupils above

[1] *Parliamentary Debates*, 4th Series, xcvi 1170–1.

the age of fifteen, about half of whom were in London alone. Clearly the scope of this work was beyond dispute and Gorst attacked it on two grounds—that it was poor in quality as shown by the poor attendance and trivial work, and that it was "the very worst case of overlapping in the whole of our educational system. The Education Department and the school boards for years have been in active competition with the Science and Art Department and Technical Instruction Committees, and it is only quite recently that this ruinous system of competition has been properly discouraged by the Board of Education."[1]

This is a most remarkable argument. Gorst showed that the number of pupils illegally educated in the case of day schools throughout the country was negligible. But it was vast in the case of the evening schools. Substantially, that is, the Cockerton judgment affected only evening schools. But it is clear that neither the Department nor the school boards had ever doubted the legality of the evening school work after 1890. In the Department's view the Education Code (1890) Act, 1890, had, among other things, been designed to sanction higher education in evening schools. It had been assumed to be effective in doing so. If it did not the fault was that of either the Education Department or Parliament. It is true that it might be said that some of the better evening students were working for science and art grants and that so far the London School Board were to blame; but the very evening school regulations and the attitude of the Department and of its inspectors appeared to be that of approval. And to see that grants were given only to the right students was clearly a matter for co-ordination of the work of the two departments concerned, as Gorst's own statement implies. Hence the government case against the school board evening schools on the grounds of illegality was a thin one. In so far as there was illegality the major fault was that of the two departments.

But Gorst implicitly confronted the school boards with a monstrous dilemma. If the schools were poor, they were providing an inferior article: "cheap, shoddy, education". If they were good, there would be "serious overlap" with the schools of the technical instruction committees. But one may reply to Gorst's argument with a more valid dilemma: if there was such inefficiency why was government grant being paid for it? If there was overlap as a result of school boards being over vigorous, what was the Board of Eduaction, which now controlled both types of grant, doing about it?[2]

---

[1] loc. cit., 1177.

[2] As early as 1890 Hart Dyke, the Vice-President, spoke of his planning to issue a regulation to prevent the overlapping of the functions of the Education Department and Science and Art Department. *Parliamentary Debates*, 3rd Series, cccxlv, 1135.

Since 1897–8, the year to whose accounts the Cockerton Case related, the Board of Education had come into existence, charged with the superintendence of matters relating to education in England and Wales. Accordingly, for the future, the prevention of overlapping in the evening school sphere was largely a matter of co-ordinating the two branches of his own department.

In 1901 emergency measures were certainly essential to cope with the education of adults. But these could have been provided for by legislation giving temporary dispensing power to the Board of Education (see p. 179, *infra*). It could then have been frankly acknowledged that overlapping had been merely the inevitable result of the lopsided nature of the finance administered by the two departments. And thereafter evening school administration could have been replanned more dispassionately. Instead, discussion of the best kind of arrangements for evening (as, indeed, for higher day) school education was, both in Parliament and within the Board, confused by the Government's determination to blame the school boards and thereby nullify the possibility of any form of *ad hoc* authority being retained. And, unfortunately, use of the Cockerton Case as a legal bugaboo in pursuit of this objective prevented adequate consideration of the educational implications of proposed changes.

It seems clear from the debates that the government had no case against the school boards in general on the grounds of illegal higher grade school work. Indeed, Sir William Hart Dyke himself, a former Vice-President, was quoted as having said, only a few weeks before, "He felt like the villain of the piece, for he had visited in an official position Sheffield, Birmingham, and other large towns to perform the pleasing duty of distributing prizes and certificates at those law-breaking institutions; had taken a leading part in their criminality and encouraged their career by commending their curricula in all respects and urging them to increase their efforts. . . ."[1]

It is, therefore, very difficult to find, even in the government speeches any rational ground for the restrictive, almost punitive, attitude towards the school boards which lay behind the plan of the 1901 Act, apart from the avowed policy of Balfour of seizing the opportunity of the Cockerton Case to stake the claim of the county council as the local authority for secondary education. Clearly, to establish that principle was *the* major function of the 1901 Act.

The Opposition statement of the legal implications of the Cockerton judgment came from Asquith. He emphatically denied that the judgments laid down fifteen years as the upper age-limit of elementary education, and suggested that it should be left to the Board of

---

[1] *Parliamentary Debates*, 4th Series xcvi, 1191.

Education to determine, in the light of the judgments, both the scope of elementary education and its upper age limit.[1]

Most of the Opposition, however, saw that the legal problem was merely a convenient pretext; for had not the Duke of Devonshire himself said "*Aided by the Cockerton judgment*, we shall this year have made it perfectly clear that the school boards are in future to be limited to duties connected with elementary education"?[2] But somehow Opposition speakers did not realise, or did not want to realise, that the Cockerton judgment itself scarcely touched the higher grade schools. The danger to the higher grade schools made good political propaganda; and the government attack on school boards must have appeared to many to be political suicide. The Opposition's general attitude to the government proposal to subordinate the school boards to the county councils may be summed up in the words of Bryce: "I must say that the appeal provided in this Bill from the school boards (to the county councils) appears to me to be an appeal from comparative knowledge to comparative ignorance, and from comparative zeal to comparative indifference. I absolutely deny that the Report of the Secondary Education Commission (of which he had been chairman) is in favour of this Bill. . . . The gist of this Bill is that we are to subject the school board in a borough to the borough council in that borough. We are to subject a body elected for educational purposes to a body which is not elected for those purposes, which has no educational knowledge or experience except that which has been given it in regard to technical instruction."[3]

The second Cockerton Act[4] continued the conduct of these schools and classes under authorisation of the county and county borough councils during session 1902-3, and its provisions were used to authorise the continuance of pupil teacher centres by school boards after it had been declared (in 1902) that it was not within the power of school boards to establish centres for the instruction of pupil teachers.[5]

The abolition of the school boards was effected by the 1902 Act and that statute, whatever its defects, created an educational system which worked and which effectively established municipal secondary schools. Considerations of space prevent more than a brief mention of that great measure, but we may notice that throughout the parliamentary debates the significance of the Cockerton judgments was put very differently by the two sides. Government sup-

---

[1] *Parliamentary Debates*, 4th Series, xcvii, 1376.
[2] Quoted by Macnamara. *Parliamentary Debates*, 4th Series xcvi, 1185. (Italics mine.—E.E.)
[3] ibid., 1220-1.
[4] Education Act, 1901 (Renewal) Act, 1902.
[5] Dyer and others *v*. The School Board for London (1902, 2 Ch. 768).

porters suggested that the case had rendered the school board system unworkable, that it had left the school boards with restricted powers and a somewhat uninteresting residue of primary education. The opposition pointed to the political bias behind the government's educational policy in the post-Cockerton changes, to the unnecessarily severe restrictions, and to the good work done by school boards, and suggested that, if the school boards must go, authorities for secondary education should be created on the lines suggested by the Bryce Commission.

Probably the government's most cogent arguments were, *firstly*, that the Act was to create in each district a single, paramount authority, and, *secondly*, that educational responsibility must be married to financial responsibility. The most powerful Parliamentary advocate of the one-authority principle was Balfour. "I do not believe", he argued, "that any secondary authority can carry out the work with the fullest advantage unless it has not only under its control or supervision secondary education . . . but also absolute control of the whole apparatus by which the children of the country are to be rendered fit to receive the full advantages of what we are spending on secondary schools. Apart from that, the money spent on the secondary schools is money thrown into the sea."[1] But having thus used the one authority principle to destroy school boards Balfour found it possible immediately afterwards to discard it and accept "Part III authorities" for elementary education only. The Opposition made merry at this change of front; but it had no such disastrous repercussion as a similar move with the 1896 Bill. Indeed one can scarcely read the 1902 debates without wondering at the weakness of the case put up for the school boards. Clearly the Cockerton Act of 1901 had done its work in establishing in advance the principle of the 1902 Act.

[1] *Parliamentary Debates*, 4th Series, cviii 1163–4, 2/6/02.

XIII

HIGHER DAY SCHOOLS

(Second Phase)

*

T<small>HE</small> Higher Elementary Schools Minute, of 6th April, 1900, as interpreted by the Board of Education, seriously disappointed school boards and the objections raised almost immediately called for major policy decisions. Thus Cardiff School Board wrote protesting about the possible effect of the minute on their own higher grade school. It would, they argued, not only restrict entrance to pupils coming from public elementary schools, but, a much more serious matter, its provision that attendances should not be recognised for pupils over fifteen would be fatal to the School of Science within their higher grade school. Cardiff had powerful arguments against a strict application of the Minute:—

(1) Their higher grade school was established in 1885 at the express recommendation of a circular of the Education Department.[1]

(2) Laboratories and other buildings were erected in 1892 at a cost of £11,000; and further expenditure was at that moment being incurred under the instructions of the Science and Art Department.

(3) The school filled a real need in Cardiff, catering mainly for the ordinary elementary children of the town. Some of its pupils obtained entrance to the Universities; it supplied practically all the pupil teachers; and its pupils were in constant demand for offices and as engineers and fitters.[2]

Against this memorial the Board of Education had to place a letter from the head of the local Intermediate School (J. J. Findlay,

[1] Circular No. 213, 10/8/82.
[2] P.R.O., Ed. 16/393, 30/4/00.

later Professor of Education at Manchester University), approving of the Minute and attacking the "present anomalous Higher-Grade-Organised-Science-Matriculation Schools".

What were the Board of Education to do? The Whitehall Branch proposed to reply to Cardiff School Board saying that the grants to the School of Science would be continued. The Minute need not affect the school unless Cardiff applied for its recognition as a Higher Elementary School. That is, Whitehall envisaged the continuance of Schools of Science on the previous footing; assuming that the Minute would be used to convert higher grade schools which had not schools of science (e.g. in the London area) into the new "higher elementary schools".[1]

Gorst, however, disliked this. It would leave the higher grade school in Cardiff in direct competition with the local intermediate school. He aimed at "co-ordination" as the very heart of the policy. Accordingly South Kensington was brought into the discussion. The South Kensington policy, which was adopted, started from the fundamental principle that a school board should not have the right to give an education leading up to University entrance. From this were derived the working principles which would form the basis of a reply:—

(1) No rate-aided school or school which received a government grant for elementary education should remain as a School of Science earning grants from the "Non-Elementary Branch" of the Board (i.e. from South Kensington itself).

(2) If higher elementary education was required by a locality the school must work under the Minute.

(3) Since voluntary schools were not maintained out of the rates it would not be easy to say that they could not *legally* run a School of Science alongside an elementary school receiving elementary grant. But such voluntary schools of science could be brought into line simply by refusing recognition unless they came under the Clause VII (Secondary Education) Authority.

Hence Cardiff were informed that although Schools of Science were not directly affected by the Minute they could be converted into higher elementary schools "to the maintenance of which the School Fund may in the opinion of the Board of Education be legitimately applied." Moreover, the higher elementary grants would not be paid to Standards V to VII pupils but only to specially well qualified pupils.

Thus the threat of illegality was to be used to squeeze school board

[1] ibid., 8/5/00. The Whitehall Branch appears to have been imperfectly informed about the understanding with the Treasury.

"science schools" within the strait-waistcoat of the higher elementary schools minute.

Side by side with this plan of truncating the organised science schools, the Board of Education continued the policy, which it had initiated in 1899 immediately the Cockerton Case came to its notice, of applying pressure, wherever an opportunity occurred, to make school boards come under the secondary authority for their *quasi*-secondary work. Now it is true that Clause VII (of the Science and Art Directory) explicitly stated that school boards which were already managers of schools receiving Science and Art grants were to retain the right of establishing additional schools where necessary. But this was not allowed to stand in the way of the new policy. Thus at Tottenham the Education Department had, before June 1899, approved plans and agreed to a loan for a new school which was to include a School of Science. But when the school board made application to South Kensington for recognition of a School of Science, the Middlesex Technical Education Committee were consulted as to the necessity of the school; the school board were questioned as to the use of the rates; and at the end of October 1899 they were told that the school could only be recognised if the school board applied under Clause VII of the Directory: that is, the organised science school was in effect to be brought under Middlesex Technical Education Board.[1] And a similar policy was applied elsewhere.

Meanwhile, the nature of the higher elementary schools which the Board of Education *would* recognise had been clarified.[2] The schools were to be complete in themselves and not in connection with any existing public elementary school. They would be expected to carry most of their pupils throughout the four year course. And they would be permitted to charge a substantial fee.

How, then, was the new policy applied to the London area? As a result of the school board's deliberate policy, there were only four Science Schools in London; so that the question of recognition of the non-scientific Higher Grade Schools under the new Minute assumed exceptional importance. A deputation from London School Board waited on the Education Department and suggested that there should be more elasticity as to age than was shown in the Minute; for the restriction of the grant to pupils under fifteen would seriously limit the education of pupil teachers; most of whom came from elementary schools. Again, they urged that the headmaster of a higher elementary school might also be head of the lower school attached to it. The Secretary told the deputation that he was inclined to agree with these proposals, and that doubtless experience

---

[1] M.E. Middlesex S. Major File, Part 2, 16/6/99–21/12/99.
[2] P.R.O., Ed. 16/129, 9/7/00.

would lead to a modification of the Minute. Gorst, however, thought otherwise and in a characteristically emphatic passage wrote in May, 1900, to the President: "It would be a fatal weakness to begin our attempt to organise these schools, by promising any concessions to a body like the London School Board which is avowedly trying to get the Secondary Education of London into its hands. Here you see the urgent necessity for a Secondary Education Authority for London."[1]

That same month London School Board, little knowing how their request for a liberal interpretation of the Minute had fared backstage, applied for recognition *en bloc* of 79 Higher Grade Departments as Higher Elementary Schools under the Minute. Faced with a decision on this scale the President asked how these higher grade schools or departments had in fact developed in London. The answer came from the Whitehall Branch in the form of a memorandum from the Secretary which first of all specified the four London higher grade schools which were Schools of Science and then outlined the history of the remainder:

The extent of our official knowledge of the 79 higher grade departments which the London School Board now ask to have recognised as Higher Elementary Schools, is as follows:—

They are known to us as schools where special attention is paid to the instruction of children in the higher standards, that is to say, the Fifth, Sixth and Seventh standards. Some schools were set apart with our expressed approval for this purpose in 1887: and in 1890 we approved a list of 46 schools which the Board submitted to us as "schools at which the Board propose that special attention shall be given to the teaching of the higher standards, and to which they propose that children in neighbouring schools of the Board, within a radius of half a mile of such selected school, should be admitted on the application of their parents, and be charged no higher fee than would be charged in the school from which they have been transferred."

This list of 46 schools has now grown to 79, and we have from time to time been informed by the Board of the names of the schools added to the list.

This is all that we can be said both to know officially and to have officially approved. But it appears that of late years considerable extensions have been made to the curriculum of instruction. The schools were, up till about the year 1894, known as Higher Standard Schools, but gradually since that day the term Higher Grade School has been substituted. The word, however, is merely

[1] P.R.O., Ed. 14/102, 14/5/00.

a name, and carries with it no official connotation. In 1899 Mr. Helps, H.M. Inspector for Chelsea, made a report upon the five Higher Grade Schools in Chelsea. From this report it was evident that the schools gave instruction beyond the limits of the Code, as, for instance, in preparing scholars for examinations of the Science and Art Department. Mr. Helps made certain suggestions for improving the whole curriculum of these schools. Mr. Helps' suggestions were sent by the Education Department to the London School Board who regarded them as valuable, and asked that a Conference might be arranged between the London Inspectors and the School Board, with a view to considering this subject generally through London. This letter of the London School Board so apparently suggested the existence in these Higher Grade Schools, of instruction other than that permitted by the Code, that I directed (in December 1899) that inquiries should be made of the Board upon this point. These inquiries have been continued up to the present time, but have not been concluded. The time-tables, for instance, have been sent for, and reveal the existence of classes termed Ex-VII a, b and c. Our last letter on the subject was dated 12th May 1900, and asked the Board certain questions as to classes called intermediate and commercial.

To sum up:— All that we have officially approved at present, is a system of schools for the instruction of Standards V to VII, but we have strong grounds for thinking that these limits are in fact exceeded by the Board, and we are now making inquiry upon the subject.[1]

This Kekewich memorandum is of importance as an authoritative defence of Whitehall's policy with regard to the London Schools. But it implies a more complete degree of official ignorance and detachment than the facts warranted. After the 1891 discussions,[2] the Education Department could not avoid knowing that ex-VIIth Standard work was being attempted in London; and one can scarcely see how they could avoid accepting some responsibility, since Education Department grant was being paid to schools in which some teachers were engaged in teaching both Standard and ex-Standard pupils.[3] Further, Kekewich's suggestion that London School Board's reactions to the Helps memorandum first put Whitehall in possession of the facts would be more convincing if the time-table of events were not known:—

[1] loc. cit., 19/6/00.
[2] *Supra* pp. 46–7.
[3] It must, of course, be remembered that Kekewich's arguments before the Bryce Commission suggested a transparent device whereby pupils could remain "in the standards" almost indefinitely (cf. *supra* p. 42.)

30/1/99 Helps' Memorandum to Education Department.

24/3/99 London School Board letter welcoming memorandum and suggesting conference.

26/4/99 Cockerton audit proceedings commenced.

29/4/99 Conference between officials of Education Department and London School Board on Helps' memorandum.

9/9/99 London School Board approved scheme for curriculum of Higher Grade Schools drawn up as a result of the conference.

8/12/99 Education Department letter to Local Government Board, written on Gorst's instructions, stressed importance of Cockerton Case and asked for Local Government support of auditor.

11/12/99 Whitehall directive pointed to dangers of conferences with London School Board and directed detailed consideration of their scheme for higher work.

6/4/00 Higher Elementary Schools Minute.

19/6/00 Kekewich memorandum.

It is impossible to resist the conclusions that the Education Department were well aware of the general lines of development of the London higher schools and that the Kekewich memorandum was merely a further step in the policy of disengaging the Education Department from London School Board plans, a policy which commenced in December, 1899. Gorst was certainly not impressed by the memorandum, and his control over policy in relation to higher elementary schools stiffened.

Meanwhile, London School Board continued to press for recognition as Higher Elementary Schools of "43 schools for boys and girls in 79 departments". They urged that the numbers were not excessive—43 schools for a population of $4\frac{1}{2}$ millions (1 per 100,000); that they were prepared to give reasons for any particular school; and that they could prove that pupils would stay throughout a course. But their most forceful argument was based on educational and historical considerations peculiar to London.[1]

Further, London School Board showed that they had had reason to believe that their policy was approved by the Board of Education. Thus it was true that the Science and Art Inspector of Chelsea had suggested a School of Science for that area; but the Education Department's Inspector strongly recommended that such a school should have a literary or commercial side. This, too, had been generally agreed upon at the 1899 conference, and the London School Board's subsequent modification of their timetables had been in

[1] cf. Chap. IV, *supra*.

accordance with the policy recommended by the representatives of the Board of Education.

But the strongest card in the London School Board hand was the warm support of the Technical Education Board of London County Council. Their report (of 20/2/99) had emphasised the peculiar position of London, where commercial education was of paramount importance, and had proposed that there should be organised in connection with the primary schools Higher Grade or Higher Primary Schools which should give a more specialised training to those boys who intended to enter business at about the age of fourteen. They were to have hand-writing and précis writing, French, shorthand, typewriting and the elements of bookkeeping- in other words, essentially the curriculum that the London School Board now proposed for their selected schools. The school board case was indeed a strong one: their scheme could claim the support of official reports, and passages in the Code; it was based directly on suggestions of H.M. Inspectors; it had been approved by a conference presided over by the permanent head of the Education Department; and it was strongly supported by the only other important body familiar with local educational needs.

Whitehall officials were in no doubt as to the importance of the decision. It was true, they said, that if this request was refused the school board could continue their Higher Grade Schools "as at present"; but, as they would get less grant, they would have to make it up out of the rates. The permanent officials, were in fact convinced that the case was made out.

Kekewich had already been compelled to agree to the principle that Higher Elementary Schools would only be recognised:—

(a) in substitution for existing schools of science; or

(b) where a new school of science would, for educational reasons, have been desirable had the Higher Elementary Schools Minute not been issued;

but he appreciated the force of the London School Board's arguments, and, fortified by the backing of his colleagues, put the case directly to the President, who, however, insisted on the matter coming to him via the Vice-President.

Gorst's mind was made up. He would not entertain the London School Board population argument, and indeed seemed to imply that there were fewer children in London schools than elsewhere willing and fit to receive Higher Elementary School instruction; he suggested the inferiority of the proposed commercial education to scientific education; and he entirely dissented from the view that a School of Science was unsuited to the higher elementary education of girls. The historical argument only reinforced his impression of the extent of the division between Whitehall and South Kensington; and he commented bitterly on the failure of the Education Department representatives at the 1897 conference to point out the illegality of the expenditure of the rates in these schools.

He put the case to Devonshire in his characteristic style. "The letter of the London School Board is a plea for the establishment of a type of school differing entirely from the type provided in the Higher Elementary School Minute.[1] Whether such schools should be established by means of government subsidies; whether they should be under the direction of the Primary or Secondary Authorities; and what conditions should be imposed upon them are matters which it would not be convenient now to discuss with the London School Board. I am not myself of the opinion which most of the officials of the Elementary Branch seem to hold that the letter does not admit of controversy and I have no doubt that if the letter had been referred to the Secondary Education Branch considerable criticism would be forthcoming." In the meantime he proposed to tell the Board that the Minute did not apply to these schools, but that their representations would be borne in mind if it were afterwards decided to establish commercial schools.[2] To this Devonshire agreed.

By a reply given shortly thereafter in the House of Commons Gorst made it clear that the higher grants under the Higher Elementary Schools Minute were to be given only to schools whose curriculum closely resembled that of an Organised Science School.

During the remaining period before the first Cockerton judgment (December, 1900) Gorst inflexibly insisted on this interpretation of the Minute, in spite of continued pressure to relax it. Opinion in Whitehall, on the other hand, continued to favour some relaxation of the severity of the policy, especially in view of further arguments from the Technical Education Board. Leading officials thought that the opinion of such a body deserved the most careful consideration and argued that recognition as Higher Elementary Schools should be given both to some of the existing Higher Grade Schools with a commercial bias and to others specially directed towards technical instruction; but in vain.

Then in November 1900 Gorst took the important step of transferring initial responsibility for dealing with applications for recognition as Higher Elementary Schools from Whitehall to the non-Elementary Branch at South Kensington; they knew, he argued, or ought to know, whether other secondary schools would suffer from

---

[1] This is not supported by the words of the Minute itself.
[2] P.R.O., Ed. 14/102, 24/7/00.

the competition by higher elementary schools in the area, and they had the staff experienced in making such enquiries.

By that date London School Board must have realised where the opposition to their plans for higher education lay; and how persistent that opposition was likely to be. Accordingly they whittled their demands for recognition down to eleven schools. These eleven London School Board cases were therefore referred separately to South Kensington, each with its separate curriculum and timetables, for a full report on their necessity, their proposed course of instruction, and generally. Moreover, in each case a South Kensington Inspector was joined to a Whitehall Inspector to report on the suitability of the school. The awkwardness of the situation created by a policy thus suddenly imposed by a political head with little prior consultation with his office was made clear by the queries of one inspector who, among other things, wanted to know if the "practical work" mentioned in the Minute was to include, in the case of boys, manual training and, in the case of the girls, cookery. The officials were completely at sea, but instructed him tartly that he was only asked to report whether the premises were in all respects suitable for a Higher Elementary School. H.M. Inspector, however, had the last word: "I will try to report accordingly; but even here there is a difficulty: for it is difficult to say if the premises are suited for practical work until it is settled what the practical work is to be. A similar though lesser difficulty arises with regard to the staff . . ."[1]

Thus, by November 1900, the Higher Elementary Schools Minute had been published, the policy firmly decided upon, the administrative arrangements made—a month before the *first* Cockerton judgment was given.

The policy was adhered to without relaxation throughout 1901; in spite of reiterated appeals from the London School Board for consideration of the need for commercial education, as shown by the overwhelming demand among parents for such subjects as shorthand; and in spite of continued support for London School Board in its higher elementary policy from the Technical Education Board. By the middle of 1902 it was apparent that the rigidity of the educational clauses for higher elementary schools was causing serious difficulty. It was reported that London School Board had seriously considered abandoning higher elementary schools altogether; and senior officials in the Board of Education feared that even schools of the science type were likely to be destroyed.[2]

The restrictions of the Minute, which had now become incorporated with the Elementary Schools Code, had, however, taken on

[1] P.R.O., Ed. 14/102, 5/11/00.
[2] P.R.O., Ed. 14/102, 25/7/02.

a new significance. It had, of course, been obvious from the outset that the change of policy in 1900 was going to make it difficult, if not impossible, to complete the education of pupil teachers in school board schools. Moreover, in 1902 it was decided in the Courts that, although a school board could perhaps give non-elementary education to pupil teachers in their own schools it could not transfer them to a pupil-teacher centre and train them there.[1] Hence the actual training of pupil teachers in centres was to be transferred to London County Council. But the regulations now required pupils to be sixteen before they could be accepted as pupil teachers. London School Board accordingly asked for permission to retain pupils at higher elementary or even higher grade schools (not recognised as higher elementary) until they reached the age of sixteen. To what extent would the Board agree to this request? The various issues involved were considered in a long minute by Morant (written in December, 1903, when he was in charge of the Board) stating the policy to be taken into account in answering London School Board.

"This will be a very important letter. There is, as you well know, a prospect of a considerable tussle between the school board policy on the one hand and the Technical Education Board on the other, as regards the development of instruction of pupil teachers in London. The school board are exceedingly anxious to retain the existing Pupil-Teachers' Centres, to turn each partial (*sic*) time Centre into a whole-time Secondary School with a half-time top, and probably to establish more of these Institutions.[2] The existing schools, as you know, though their teaching staff have very high paper qualifications in many cases, are really impregnated with the Elementary School tradition and atmosphere. They are almost entirely staffed with ex-elementary teachers. Even if we allowed them to be converted into Division B Secondary Schools, it would be a conversion in name only. I understand the Technical Education Board are very anxious to establish real Secondary Schools of a different type, and with a different atmosphere in various parts of London. I understand they feel that if we recognise all these existing school board centres as real Secondary Schools, we shall be really throwing back the development of true Secondary education in London. Of course, if there were no prospect of getting real Secondary Schools established, we could not in honesty refrain from accepting the existing Pupil Teacher Centres as Secondary Schools; but I gather that unless school board nominees are put on, and are very powerful

---

[1] Dyer and others *v.* the School Board for London. (1902, 2 Ch. 768)
[2] It will be realised that the Board could not retain the Pupil Teacher Centres for training pupil teachers. (Dyer *v.* School Board for London, *supra*.) But could they retain them as higher schools for education of pupils who would at sixteen become pupil teachers elsewhere?

upon, the new Education Committee of the London County Council in March next, there is no doubt that the London County Council *will* establish new Secondary Schools. Were this done, I fancy they will attempt to convert the existing Pupil-Teacher Centres into purely half-time places for the instruction of real half-time pupil-teachers towards the London Matriculation or London Intermediate, and not let them be used for the prospective Pupil-Teacher, i.e. as Preparatory Classes or Secondary Schools.

On the other hand, I am sure it is important that we should not, at this particular stage, seem, as a Board, to be standing in the way of the London School Board in its efforts to improve and extend, *as they put it,* the education of pupil-teachers. Hence there is some reason for making the letter somewhat evasive on the various important points . . ."[1]

We have seen how, right from the outset and for thirty years thereafter, the Education Department failed to keep track of the development of the main concept with which it was concerned—"elementary education". One of the main factors which vitiated its thought was the education of the pupil-teacher. The pupil-teacher was undoubtedly "elementary" in the social sense: he sprang from the working classes, his education was part of his contract within an elementary school, and under an elementary school board. And many Education Department officials could no more conceive of the pupil-teacher being entitled to a secondary education than some people today can think of prospective secondary modern school teachers being entitled to go first to a great public school and then to Oxford or Cambridge. Yet the instruction given to these pupil-teachers was inevitably more than elementary. Morant had no such doubts. He saw his state education in stages; and in the above letter he took a final slash at this Gordian Knot of the education of the pupil-teacher: his further education must be *really* secondary. Hybrid elementary-secondary education was apparently finished.

[1] M.E., London, S Major File, Part 4. 14/12/03.

XIV

EVENING SCHOOLS

(Second Phase)

*

In a previous chapter we saw how in the early days the evening school was a mere *pis aller* for the day school, and in fact in 1885 evening school education was all but extinct. There came a gradual upsurge of a new and vigorous type of evening education, partly technical and partly recreative; but unfortunately the statutory sanction for these developments was the highly misleading Education Code (1890) Act, 1890, whose weakness was unmasked during the Cockerton crisis. We shall now see how a Morant plan for the re-organisation of the administration of the evening schools was given effect in a Minute of 1901 which was subsidiary to the Cockerton Act of the same year; how Gorst enforced a re-organisation of the central administration of evening schools; and how the new policy worked out in the field.

It should be clear that, if the precipitating cause of the Cockerton Case was doubt as to the legality of science and art schools and classes generally, the most unassailable charge of illegality against the school boards was founded on their work with adults. And that work was predominantly, almost exclusively, in evening schools. Hence the impact of the Cockerton judgment was—political considerations apart—likely to be greater on evening schools.

London School Board was quick to realise these implications and, even before the judgment in the Court of Appeal, pointed out to the Board of Education the need for establishing the education entrusted to school boards on a firmer basis "both administratively, and, in some points, such as the education of adults in Evening Schools, legislatively".[1]

[1] P.R.O., Ed. 14/25, 1/3/01.

We have already seen that Morant had originally thought that the case should be based on the illegality of the higher grade schools; but like London School Board, he quickly saw what was the main *practical* effect of the case, immediately after the judgment of the Court of Queen's Bench (December 1900) and before the judgment in the Court of Appeal (April, 1901). In a long and penetrating memorandum he analysed the evening school situation and suggested a solution. That solution was in effect adopted, and, as the memorandum provides the key to evening school policy for the period to follow, it deserves careful study as a whole.[1]

We may consider Morant's suggestions briefly at this point. He argued that the evening schools had in fact become secondary schools in the course of the preceding decade. But by a fiction they had continued to be treated as elementary, since that pretence served to keep them within the orbit of the Education Department and of the school boards. But such a policy had already, in Morant's opinion, had disastrous results; for, on the one hand, it had kept the board evening schools subject to restrictions devised for elementary day schools, and, on the other, it had prevented county councils from properly developing evening school education. Worst of all had been the administrative confusion created, with wasteful competition locally and muddle and lack of co-ordination at the centre. Thus the regulations of the Science and Art Department, which were devised for both day and evening scholars, in fact suited neither.

After this analysis Morant proposed his own solutions, which, in effect, were as follows. Evening school education must be recognised as *sui generis*. Therefore it must be under *one* central authority. And, since evening school education was in the main secondary, he implied that responsibility should be given to the South Kensington branch. There should also be one set of evening school regulations fusing the relevant sections of the Directory and Code. The local authorities for evening education must clearly be the counties and county boroughs.

But in this memorandum—as in others—Morant showed a lively awareness of political implications. And, as a temporary compromise, he advised that school boards might be allowed to act as agents for the secondary authorities in spending elementary education rates on evening schools. This proposal had the further advantage that it was in line with the policy whereby Sir John Gorst had used a clause of the Directory to establish county councils as the potential local co-ordinating authority. The supreme merit of the scheme, in fact, was that it was a further step towards effective local co-ordination of higher education.

[1] Appendix D.

Morant's memorandum carried conviction with the political heads. It was obvious that drastic steps would have to be taken, for not only had the evening schools to be sheltered from possible consequences of the Cockerton judgment, but the Treasury were pressing for the position of the evening schools to be regularised. The Science and Art Department's long continued and extreme policy of payment by results had clearly contributed to the impasse to a greater extent than Morant's memorandum implied; and the Treasury were insistent that the practice of separate grants for separate science subjects should cease. It was proposed, therefore, that the Science and Art subjects should be grouped together as a balanced general preparation for technological training.[1]

The Evening Schools Minute of July, 1901, taken in conjunction with the Cockerton Act of 1901, was designed both to co-ordinate the administration of evening schools by school boards and county councils and to change the pattern of evening school work.

Before discussing its provisions, however, we must consider a momentous tussle between the Whitehall and South Kensington sections of the Board of Education, which reveals some of the issues involved; and to understand that struggle we may recall that although the Education Department (Whitehall) and the Science and Art Department (South Kensington) were, under the Board of Education Act, 1899, merged in the Board of Education as from 1st April, 1900, these two branches of the administration continued for some time to have very different points of view.

We have seen how Gorst in 1897 was very critical of the overlapping found in evening school work. In November, 1900, he set up a committee within the Board of Education to "report on the best method of administering the parliamentary grants to Science and Art Evening Continuation Schools so as to prevent overlapping."

The committee did not report until March, 1901, when the judgment of the Queen's Bench Division in the Cockerton Case was known. Accordingly to some members of the committee it must have seemed that, as the work of the evening schools was very largely with adults, it could no longer be considered as elementary and the committee's sole task was to see how best to transfer the administration of these classes to the Secondary Branch at South Kensington. That had been Gorst's intention; but it was not the view of the majority of the committee, who thought it their duty to consider the very basis of evening school work.

It was an important decision for Whitehall; for the evening schools had become an increasingly progressive and interesting part of their

---

[1] This was the natural corollary to the 22s. block grant in the 1900 Code which superseded grants for "additional subjects" in elementary schools.

educational system, and it is not surprising that the Evening Schools Committee failed to agree.[1] The Majority Report—that of the Whitehall officials—started with a division of the work into primary and secondary. Its test of "secondary" was based upon time, quantity and quality: the time which the students would devote to the course, and the quantity and quality of the work to be done. When time, quantity and quality were adequate the work was advanced and the evening school secondary.

The object of secondary evening schools was to master some specific subject or group of subjects with a view to preparation for some career or for some advanced examination. Secondary evening school courses should last for at least three years; and they would frequently require specialised premises and apparatus. The regulations for and inspection of such evening schools should be the responsibility of the non-Elementary Branch at South Kensington.

Evening schools of the primary type would aim simply at prolonging the education given in the primary school. They would employ teachers from the primary school and the general character of the work would be the same. The regulations for this type of evening school would continue to be issued by Whitehall as an annex to the Day School Code. The grant given would be a block grant and there would be *no limitation of subject matter* like that given in the Day School Code.

Even in evening schools of the primary type the county councils might help with the funds which they held under the Technical Instruction Act by paying peripatetic teachers to organise instruction "bearing on the occupation and industry of the scholars", and by supplying apparatus which it was too costly for managers to buy. But although county councils might help in such ways, it would be premature to hand over to them evening schools of the primary type.

The report of the Minority, consisting of officials of the South Kensington branch, agreed on the need for a division of evening school work into two branches. But it took a dreary, if historically justifiable, view of the work of the primary evening school. It must be confined to the three R's and the English subjects. "For administrative purposes no other satisfactory line can be fixed. Any school which extends that curriculum to other subjects should pass into the secondary class." The effect of these proposals would, of course, ultimately have been to transfer the administration of *all* evening schools to the Secondary Branch.

As between the two reports, it can hardly be doubted that the majority had a healthier attitude to the work of the evening schools;

[1] See evidence of Kekewich, *Bryce Report*, Vol. II, pp. 114–15.

but they failed to find any practicable distinction between primary and secondary school evening education, and they assumed that without drastic changes a *modus vivendi* for school boards running evening schools under Whitehall, and county councils running evening schools under South Kensington, could be arrived at. Clearly these officials had not grasped the administrative significance of the Cockerton case.

The heads of the office, however, supported the Majority Report, and even argued to the Vice-President that school boards must retain the right to give secondary as well as primary evening school education, for they had been given that power by the Education Code Act of 1890!

The decision was made by the political heads of the office. Gorst had been determined, as early as April, 1900, that the administration of the evening schools should be handed over entirely to South Kensington; and his intention in consulting the departmental committee had been that they should consider ways and means of doing so. He had little difficulty in persuading Devonshire that the Whitehall proposals for a duality of central administration were unworkable and that the only practicable step was to make a clean cut and transfer the whole administration of evening schools to South Kensington. In May, 1901, he succinctly stated that the real grounds for the transfer were:——

(1) That that Branch administers already the Evening Schools which work under the Directory. That these are the schools with which Evening Schools under the Code compete and overlap.

(2) That the Secondary Branch is in communication with the County Authorities to whose administration we look for an extension of the Evening Schools in rural places.

From an early date Gorst had firmly grasped the major fact that the school boards would, if the Queen's Bench judgment was confirmed, be unable to continue the instruction of pupils above sixteen. Accordingly, armed with the Morant memorandum (Appendix D), he now proposed that there should be a new Code for Evening Schools recognising then frankly as secondary; with a clause enabling the new secondary authorities to make school boards their agents for the management of the evening schools and permitting the latter, as such agents, to apply the rates to evening school work.[1] Devonshire agreed to this step as he did to all the later major moves.

---

[1] Morant's memorandum is undated. It seems likely, however, that it was written some time between 3rd March 1901, when the report of the Evening Schools Committee was received, and 15th March when Gorst first submitted his proposals to the President.

Gorst's descriptions certainly gave him a vivid picture of the development: "The judgment in Regina *v.* Cockerton", he wrote to Devonshire in May, "has now decided that all this development of Evening Continuation Schools by School Boards since 1893, under the auspices of the Education Department, has been illegal *ab initio*. . . . It was a bold invasion by the school boards, and by the Education Department, of the sphere of Secondary Education."[1]

Accordingly Gorst got to work with Abney (the head of South Kensington) and Morant and prepared a scheme and regulations. The plan followed the main lines of the Morant memorandum, provided for the eventual fusion of the evening school provisions in the Code and Directory, and handed final local responsibility for evening schools over to the county authorities. It envisaged some statutory measure to provide the necessary legal authority, and regulations to work out the details. We have already seen how the Cockerton Act of 1901, which was the first essential of this plan, was designed to establish the principle that county authorities were to be the co-ordinating authority of the future. One function of the Evening Schools Minute of 1901 was to ensure that school boards running evening schools would be forced to place themselves under these county authorities.

The Minute contained twenty-one clauses. Of these the first twenty applied to non-elementary evening schools. To run an evening school under these regulations a school board, if it was to be protected by the Cockerton Act, had therefore to come under the county authority. The celebrated twenty-first clause applied to *elementary* evening schools, i.e. to evening schools run by the school boards independently of the county authorities.

The salient features of the first twenty clauses were:—

(*a*) Evening school pupils had not to be under twelve, nor (with the exception of certain Art pupils) attending day school.

(*b*) The basic rate of grant was 2s. 6d. (or 3s.) for twenty hours instruction in specified subjects. Additional grant would be made for practical work in subjects involving exceptional expenditure.

(*c*) Students must not take more than four subjects in all and of these *not more than two could be in the scientific, manual and technical groups*. And for this transitional period the scientific subjects were those of the Directory; the manual subjects were woodwork and metal work; and the technological subjects were laundry work, domestic economy, cookery, gardening and "any other subject approved by the Board of Education as of educational value."

(*d*) The Minute also specified certain time requirements for

---

[1] M.E. Private Office Papers. May, 1901.

evening school courses, e.g. that to qualify for grant in a subject a student must have attended for at least fourteen hours.

But the most interesting regulation was Clause 21. This, which was Morant's creation, provided that *where it was desired to conduct an evening school as a public elementary school*, then: (i) the other regulations of the Minute would still apply; (ii) the school must observe all the provisions of the Elementary Education Acts; (iii) grants would not be given for pupils over fifteen at the commencement of the school year; (iv) separate accounts for each school must be kept; and (v) the school must not be in the same building as any non-elementary school without the Board of Education's sanction. (Events were to prove that this clause was as great a sham as the tulchan calf set up long ago to delude simple-minded Scottish cows into giving milk; but it was effective in creating an impression that school boards had an option of independence.)

The plan, of which this Minute formed the spearhead, was explained in a further memorandum by Morant (see App. E). The more detailed implications were soon made clear in operation.

Morant had been careful to investigate the difficulties likely to arise from the proposed regulations with local officials. Thus he obtained numerous criticisms and suggestions from Garnett, of the London Technical Education Board, who had estimated the probable financial effect of the new regulations on evening classes run by the London Polytechnics and Schools of Art.

Morant also obtained a statment of the school boards' reactions from Wyatt, Clerk to the Manchester School Board, that "Napoleon of School Board Clerks", who had done such outstanding work for evening schools in Manchester.[1] Wyatt frankly stated that the scheme would destroy the evening schools as carried on by the school boards. He saw, too, the further implications of the move:

"There is strong feeling abroad, particularly in the North of England, that the school boards are to be repressed. Bare justice is not done to the work we have done—we have never been taken into consultation *officially* as to any new arrangements.

"With the giving of paramount authority to the Technical Instruction Authorities how can it be expected that the school boards will have any spirit to undertake at a few weeks' notice, the recasting of the Evening Schools upon lines entirely different to those contained in the Acland Code and to fall in with South Kensington arrangements? For the spirit of the new Scheme is entirely different to that of the Acland Code, under which we have enjoyed freedom and encouragement. Our present system in Manchester has been

---

[1] cf.(*a*) *Report of Science and Art Department for 1890*, pp. 34–5.
(*b*) Sillitoe, *A History of the Teaching of Domestic Subjects*, Methuen, 1933, p. 59.

the work of twenty-five years association with the primary schools—controlled by the authorities at Whitehall—and no evening work under the Directory has ever possessed the vitality of the Evening Continuation Schools—particularly since the introduction of the present Code in 1893. . . ."

Wyatt had several objections to the details of regulations, but his most serious was to Article 18, which, in addition to prohibiting students from taking more than four subjects in all, prevented them from taking more than *two* subjects from the scientific, manual and technological groups. Thus a lad could not take all three of wood-work, metal work and physics; and a girl could not take cookery, domestic economy and chemistry. Hence, Wyatt pointed out, this article would very seriously affect the Manchester Evening Institutes for Women, where practically all the subjects were technological; Manchester had eight of these institutes with 1,400 students, all over sixteen, who must have a free choice of subjects or they would not attend. The subjects taught were: Cookery, Dressmaking, Laundrywork, Millinery, Needlework, Sick Nursing, Hygiene, Domestic Economy. Why then should the Minute prohibit these students from taking the subjects which they chose from this group, which were just as educational as those in any other?

It is indeed a serious reflection on all responsible for these regulations that, after such a warning, the Article objected to remained unaltered in the final regulations; and it was undoubtedly a serious blow to technical education; but it had nothing whatever to do with the Cockerton judgment: *firstly*, because it applied to the older *non-elementary* group, and as the school boards could not educate these lawfully at all under the Elementary Education Acts the curriculum was entirely a matter for the Board of Education to decide in its Minute; and, *secondly*, because, as we have already seen, the Cockerton judgment was not aimed at such curricula but at preventing the extension of "elementary" schooling upwards to near-University level. Such changes in the evening school regulations were purely a matter of policy and had nothing to do with the Cockerton judgments. (The age restriction of fifteen applied to the *elementary* pupils under Article 21.)

The draft Minute, as prepared by South Kensington and Morant, was now submitted to the Treasury. It was alleged in the supporting letter that, but for this Minute, the school boards would have been limited by the Cockerton judgment to a very narrow field of action in evening school work;[1] but the proposed regulations would enable them as agents of the county authorities to carry on any work they had previously been doing. At the same time the proposal would

[1] The age restriction alone would have ensured this.

ensure that the power of organising all higher evening work rested with the county and county borough councils. The Cockerton judgment had in fact provided a favourable opportunity for a scheme which was highly desirable on its own merits. The Board also relieved the Treasury mind on the financial side: the grant was calculated on a dual basis, and, "as the lower grant was for efficiency and the higher grant for increased efficiency, the actual cost will be somewhat less."

The new regulations were issued on 3rd July, 1901, and on 10th July there appeared in *The Times* a letter from Morant, on Gorst's behalf, some of which may be reproduced below, as a masterpiece of administrative salesmanship:

"Now that the advanced work done in so many of the evening schools has reached such large proportions, and in view also of the fact that the great majority of evening students are adults, it seems undesirable that evening schools, which are in reality, as the Royal (Bryce) Commission on Secondary Education pointed out, secondary schools, should still be compelled to preserve the style and title of elementary schools, so little suited to them, and be subject to all the limitations and restrictions consequent thereon. . . ." Then, after pointing out that the new regulations would free the evening schools which came under the county from various restrictions, and would also permit a developing, comprehensive co-ordinated system, Morant went on: "To sum up, then, you will see that since the evening schools to which you refer will not presumably be conducted as elementary schools,

(1) they will be under no limits as to the age of their scholars;
(2) they will at the same time be free to give elementary or advanced instruction according as the needs of the locality or the wants of individual students may require, and
(3) they will be free from the operation of the 17s. 6d. limit.

"It should be noted that wherever a school board conducts an evening school or class under the provisions of the Education Bill now before Parliament, i.e., after being empowered by the local authority to conduct such school or class beyond the limits of the Elementary Education Acts, the same freedom both as to organisation and age limits will apply in so far as the agreement with the local authority extends in each case.

"It was necessary to add Article 21 to the regulations in order to preserve to school boards the power of carrying on evening schools at the expense of the school fund, so far as the judgment in Reg. *v.* Cockerton allows, with the aid of grants from the Exchequer. Sir John Gorst does not anticipate that there will be many such schools

hereafter. The restrictions of Article 21 are the unavoidable outcome of the recent decision of the Courts of Law as to the limits
necessarily attaching to the functions and powers of School Boards
in this regard. . . ."

As an example of presenting a series of restrictions (necessary or
not) as if they were additional liberties this letter could hardly be
bettered. The preamble, gilded with a reference to the liberal and
popular Bryce Report, suggested that the elevation of evening schools
to secondary status was mainly giving increased freedoms. It is true
that the abolition of the 17s. 6d. limit might lead to some classes of
an approved type getting higher grants; but, as Gorst and Morant
knew, the regulations were so designed that the *total* financial outlay
on evening classes would be less, not more. The restrictions on courses
which the first twenty sections of the Minute contained were not
mentioned. Finally, even Article 21 was described as if it preserved
for the school boards all the powers which the Cockerton judgment
allowed them. To see how incorrect this is, we need only consider
the limits set by the Article to the age of pupils to attend these
independently run classes, and to the content to be taught in them:—

(1) The *age* limit of fifteen was not mentioned in the judgments.
It was a possible inference from the judgments; but not a necessary
one. It is more easily explained as an extension to the evening schools
of the administrative rule laid down by the Higher Elementary
Minute.

(2) As regards *content*, school board schools had previously enjoyed the full range of the Evening Continuation School Code. The
Cockerton judgment had decided, not that the Evening School
Code was excessively high, but that school boards must not educate
under the Directory. But school boards which decided to remain
independent of county councils for their evening school work, both
were subjected by the Minute to a severe age restriction, and had
their curricula curtailed by all the limitations of Articles 1–20.

The sting was, however, in the tail of Morant's letter. Gorst, it
implied, expected the new regulations virtually to end the school
boards' power to conduct evening schools independently even in the
severely limited form permitted by Article 21. In fact, as we shall
see later, Gorst took steps to ensure that this anticipation was realised.

A strange administrative situation ensued. Morant soon found
that it was necessary to explain to the county council officials how
their dispensing powers under the Minute would operate. By taking
advantage of the protecting authority of the county council a school
board would be eligible for grants under Articles 1–20. Moreover,
"the school board rate would be available for such school or schools

if and in so far as the Local Authority's decision so provided."[1] In other words, by coming under the cloak of a friendly county council a school board could enjoy the financial advantages of pre-Cockerton days. Only school boards which thought that their duty was to run elementary evening schools would have to work in relative poverty under Article 21; and not only so, they would simultaneously have to work under the *Elementary* Education Acts and also under all the other regulations of the Minute, which, let us recall, was planned specifically on the assumption that evening schools were *secondary*.

The lynch pin of the new order was to be the technical instruction committee of each county council. The secretaries of these bodies were all at sea with the regulations, and a meeting with Gorst and Morant took place on 19th July 1901, (a copy of Morant's letter to *The Times* was enclosed with each invitation). The more immediate doubts about the regulations were explained at the meeting, and subsequently Morant was busily occupied in suggesting to these secretaries how to get the new machinery in operation. The Minute was clearly designed to bring co-ordination among the various evening classes; but it was equally clearly not to encourage experimentation with classes of new types; and, though a regulation stated that "any other subjects approved by the Board as of education value" might be taken, adventurous proposals for classes in Cotton Spinning, Plumbing or Brickwork met with a cold reception at the hands of South Kensington, where details of the regulations were to be interpreted.

The new regulations were also explained in a circular letter from South Kensington to managers, which stated that, since the law courts had decided that the Elementary Education Acts gave no power to carry on public elementary schools, whether in the daytime or evening, except for children, the Board had issued these regulations to enable evening schools and classes to be carried on without the requirement that they be conducted as elementary schools—a somewhat odd description of a somewhat odd arrangement.[2] The circular went on to explain that most of what had previously been possible would continue to be permitted under the new regulations. The legality of these arrangements would be ensured by the Bill before Parliament (the Cockerton Act-to-be).

Arrangements made by the county councils varied. Some apparently simply gave the school boards blanket authority to carry on any school or class which they had previously maintained out of the School Fund and to which the School Fund had been held to be

[1] M.E. Private Office Papers. Letter to Lancashire C.C. 13/7/01.
[2] M.E. Board of Education. South Kensington. Circular 127, 31/7/01.

not lawfully applicable.[1] Other county councils interested themselves directly in the management of these classes. It is true that Gorst—carrying his post-Cockerton policy of a detached Board of Education to extremes—had expressed the view that the actual transfer of the evening schools was "a question for the Local Government Board auditor—not for us. All we can do is to decide whether to pay them grants."[2] But there was no such detachment in some of the suggestions sent out from South Kensington. Thus a letter to the county councils had suggested that they intimate to the Board their willingness to act as managers to the evening schools in their respective areas, and that although the extent of county council supervision would doubtless vary, "the Board of Education are of opinion that county council supervision will act beneficially upon the schools, and that the experience gained by county councils cannot fail to be of advantage in any future re-organisation of the system of national education."[3] The pressure on managers was of a kind not easy to resist: "The Board of Education do not propose to insist on the managers of existing Evening Schools coming within the County Organisation, but They direct me to point out to you that the schools can hardly fail to benefit in many ways (e.g. financial stability, opportunities of availing themselves of a wider experience, of co-ordinating their work with the higher education of the County, or of readily obtaining the services of teachers with special qualifications) by working in close connection with the county organisation.

"I am to request that the Managers will, at their earliest convenience, consider whether under the circumstances it would not be better that the evening school should be conducted in unison with the . . . Committee."[4]

Morant was in communication with many of the local authorities about the interpretation of the Minute. Through Nicholas, the Essex Secretary, who was also the honorary secretary of the Association of Directors and Organising Secretaries for Technical and Secondary Education, he was able both to learn of the difficulties in the various areas and to advise about the powers which the local authorities might exercise. Nicholas, on the other hand, could, through Morant, suggest such moves as that H.M. Inspectors should be brought in contact with county secretaries to settle all the details.[5]

These measures ensured that the transference of final responsibility was smoothly effected. But the school boards must quickly

---

[1] M.E. Private Office Papers. County Resolution, 1/8/01.
[2] M.E. Private Office Papers. Letter to Morant. 24/9/01.
[3] M.E. Private Office Papers. 20/8/01.
[4] M.E. Board of Education. South Kensington. Form 794/ES. November 1901. Private Office Papers.
[5] M.E. Private Office Papers. Letters from Nicholas, 24/7/01, 31/7/01, 9/8/01.

have realised that they were subject to new masters. Thus in Essex, which to some extent set the pattern, the letter sanctioning school board evening classes reserved powers of visitation by the Technical Instruction Committee.[1]

The methods, of course, varied from area to area; but as a rule the school boards came to heel without ado. The Technical Education Boards were placed firmly in the saddle, sometimes with strange results. Thus it was considered incumbent upon county administrators to tell school boards that, since they were no longer under the Elementary Education Acts, they could spend the secondary and technical grants on teaching Reading, Writing and Arithmetic!

Similar reasoning placed Morant in at least one awkward situation. In Halifax the evening classes for 1900–01 had been of two kinds. The Halifax Recreative Evening Classes (A) had on their registers some 700 scholars over sixteen and 1,400 under sixteen. The classes were managed by a voluntary committee. Maintenance was derived from government grant; from fees, which were returnable at the end of the session to scholars who had attended regularly; and from a grant of £300 from the borough technical instruction committee. The school board was friendly and lent the school free with heating and lighting; but paid nothing .The work done was admitted to be *"extremely elementary"*. Practically all the scholars were mill hands in their teens; but the schools kept them out of the street at night. The fee had a good influence—indeed many scholars regarded the school as a bank, for if they made 90 per cent attendances they had the fees returned in a lump sum.

The Halifax Technical School (B) was also occupied mainly with evening work; but it was a very different institution. It offered technical, scientific and commercial courses. "Practically all the students who go are people who mean to work, and all who mean to work go. There is nowhere else to go in Halifax. The school board has no evening classes except one for teachers working for the certificate examination." The maintenance of this institution was derived thus:—

	£
"Gin Money"	1,508
West Riding County Council	249
South Kensington	905
Clothworkers' Company	200
Fees	787
From 1d. rate under Technical Instruction Act	1,266
	£4,915

[1] ibid., Sept., 1901.

There can be no doubt that in theory Morant's conviction was that the second type of class (B) was the only serious one, and the only one worth encouraging. But in fact when in July it was protested that the Halifax *Recreative* Evening Classes (A) would lose £400 under the new Minute, he pointed out that for many of the subjects such as Drawing, Advanced Arithmetic and Mensuration, they would be eligible for payment at the higher rates given under the regulations of the Directory. That is, he advised these elementary classes to seek payment for some of their marginal work at the secondary rate.

Then in August the Principal of the Halifax Technical School (B) wrote saying that the technical instruction committee proposed to take over the former classes (A); but asked if the local taxation residue and the 1d. rate under the Technical Instruction Act could be applied to classes in evening schools under Regulations 1–20, and specifically mentioned that Reading, Writing and Arithmetic would be taught. Morant was careful to say that he could not interpret the legal position, but that, subject to that reservation, he considered that this money could be so applied, but instruction given in any elementary classes should be "distinctly preparatory to the higher work of the school". In other words, secondary or technical money could be applied to elementary work.[1]

The contrast is refreshing. Morant had now achieved the administrative arrangements which he had planned (admittedly for a transitional phase) and force of circumstances compelled him to stretch his concept of "secondary" to allow classes which their own secretary had described, two months before, as doing "extremely elementary" work, to get pay for some of that work at a secondary rate. And shortly afterwards he had to make a similar self-adjustment to allow a strictly secondary and technical body to pay, with secondary funds for work which, no matter how much Morant insisted that it must be "strictly preparatory" to higher work, was by tradition the only unquestionably elementary work in the whole curriculum.

But, although elasticity was inevitable in any sane administration of the regulations, the objective was to make evening school education secondary in reality as well as in name; and to encourage serious work as compared with recreation. This shows in the correspondence between Garnett and Morant during the summer of 1901 about the possible effects of the regulations, and their financial implications (i.e. *before* the Minute was issued). Morant, like Gorst, had a poor opinion of the work of the London School Board evening schools,

[1] M. E. Private Office Papers. Halifax correspondence, 15/5/01, 23/7/01, 26/7/01, 2/8/01.

few of whose students, according to Morant, ever put in as many as twelve attendances a year. Accordingly, the regulations were to some extent geared to the performance of classes such as those run by Garnett's Technical Education Board. On the one hand, Morant wanted to fix a minimum number of hours to exclude non-serious students; and, on the other, a maximum to prevent teachers inducing students to stay for a needless number of hours, in order to run up a maximum grant, and it was as a result of Garnett's advice on these points that Morant wrote to Gorst:

You remember how few are the school board students who make as much as *12 hours* attendance in a whole year.

I have had inquiries made as to the *Evening Classes subsidised by the London County Council T.E. Bd.* The following is actual *fact.*

On an average *every* student who entered as a student in an evening class in science or art made thirty attendances in the session; and this average is on figures that included those students who left the class altogether, from whatever cause, early in the session. Moreover this does not mean merely 30 *hours*. For *an* "attendance" at an Art School under the T.E.B. means 2 hours at least; and "an attendance" at a practical science class is generally the *whole evening*.

This is real serious work. Compare it with the very few per cent who do as much even as 12 *hours* in the school board Evening Schools.[1]

Measurement of hours is certainly one way of assessing the seriousness of work done. If, therefore, we examine the Minute to discover what was, for Garnett and Morant, the Time Criterion of serious work, we might conclude "Evening School work is serious if each course is at least twenty hours long, if each student has attended every course he commences for at least fourteen hours, if he takes not more than two hours in any one subject in an evening, and if his total number of hours instruction in the year does not exceed 160."[2]

We have already seen some of the restrictions on technical work in evening schools which the Minute imposed. Instructions to inspectors in the course of the next year made it clear that in addition to the technical subjects specified (Laundry work, Domestic Economy, Cookery and Gardening) other subjects might be recognised if "sufficiently educational and sufficiently simple". There were also manual subjects; and science subjects under the Directory.

---

[1] ibid., July (?), 1901.
[2] Minute of the Board of Education, 3rd July, 1901. (Cd 661) Article 19. (The figures given exclude subjects taken under the Directory.)

There was, too, a provision in the Directory for trade classes in science and art subjects to be taken under a recognised educational authority. But although there were these possibilities, the general effect of the Minute and of the instructions to inspectors was undoubtedly to restrict considerably the scope of technical education in evening classes.

From the point of view of the administration this was, however, only a pejorative way of saying that the classes were concentrating on serious educational work. The Board of Education were now accepting some responsibility for courses as a whole. Inspectors were to look at syllabuses and suggest alterations and additions; and the criterion of suitability of syllabuses or suggestions was that they should conform to the Directory or to the Evening Continuation School Code of 1900, or to the practice approved for the previous year. Thus the inspectors were used to bring about a measure of practical fusion of Directory and Code regulations; as well as other changes in policy such as discouraging free evening classes.

The Minute was indeed severely criticised; for it was seen to be a deliberate attack, of far-reaching consequence, on the work of the school boards. The detailed proposals also came under fire. The withdrawal of support for physical education classes was recognised as an inevitable part of Gorst's policy; but why were ambulance classes not supported? Why the restrictions on technological classes? Why could the rule against day scholars earning grants not be relaxed to allow the continuation of successful gardening classes in rural areas? Some of the pressure (by correspondence or through M.P.'s) succeeded—but the general policy was adhered to: thus in the case of the last suggestion, although Gorst himself thought that such a concession might be made to help rural gardening, the request was rejected because it would lead to similar demands for other subjects.

Some of this change in policy was a consequence of the vital changes in the machinery of administration. Regulations now came from South Kensington, and so did Inspectors. And we have already seen how pressure was put on county councils and managers alike to ensure the establishment of county councils as the local secondary authorities. It merely remains to note that the effectiveness of that pressure had been enhanced by a deliberate policy of stalling in the recognition of classes run by school boards on an independent basis (i.e. as elementary evening classes under Article 21 of the Minute).

A Board of Education directive had required that the following procedure should be adhered to when any evening school, which had existed in 1900–1, applied for recognition, under Article 21, for 1901–2:

(i) It was to be pointed out to the school board that by obtaining the sanction of the county council the school could be made into an Article 1–20 school (i.e. a *quasi-secondary* evening school).

(ii) If the school board refused to apply, the county council were to be asked if they would sanction the school (i.e. under Article 1–20, as *quasi-secondary*).

(iii) Only if the county council refused to sanction the school, and only if its grounds for so doing were unsatisfactory was the school to be recognised as an independent school board (Article 21, elementary) school.

The policy had been strictly followed. In the words of those responsible, "All through the early part of the Session (1901–2) it seemed desirable to do nothing which would tend to make the establishment of Article 21 schools easy."[1] By February, 1902, the recalcitrant school boards had been reduced to a total, in the whole country, of four, and, as it was late in the session and awkward questions might be asked in Parliament, recognition under Article 21 was granted to this rump. But the object had been achieved: independent school board evening schools had been abolished in the course of six months administration. And county authorities had been established as paramount in that field of educational administration where school board work had been most ambitious and advanced.

What of the main body of evening schools? And what was the estimate of the value of their achievement by those responsible for this administrative revolution? The following extracts from a memorandum, written early in 1902 by Sykes and Morant, give an evaluation of the changes in the evening school system as seen through the eyes of two of the officials who had been largely responsible.[2]

SYKES—MORANT MEMORANDUM ON THE EVENING SCHOOLS AND THE 1901 MINUTE

". . . One main object of the Minute of the 3rd July, 1901, and of the Education Act, 1901, and of the handing over to South Kensington of their administration, was that the education given in evening schools should be looked upon as coming within the sphere of secondary and technical education, which is the sphere to which it properly belongs, and as therefore not properly a a matter for the expenditure of the elementary education rates, except with the consent, pending the promised legislation, of the

---

[1] M.E. Private Office Papers. 30/10/01, 3/2/02.
[2] Sykes wrote the memorandum, adapting it from a draft memorandum previously written by Morant. (M.E. Private Office Papers.)

Local Authority in control of the funds legally available for secondary and technical education. It was further desired to develop this most important part of continuative education throughout the County areas, and to co-ordinate it, in the borough areas, with similar cognate forms of education that were being provided by the Local Authorities.

So far as the information at present available can be judged, the intentions and anticipations of the Government, as embodied in last year's Minute, have been satisfactorily fulfilled in all these respects. . . . There are now more than thirty county councils which have undertaken to be responsible for all Evening School work in their area on the lines of Clause VII of the Directory. It cannot be doubted that this County organisation will have a most favourable effect upon the development and improvement and correlation of all continuative education. Finally, as regards London and the County Boroughs where the Evening Schools have been very largely the work of the School Boards, the Board of Education are confident that, whatever may be the effect of the new Minute upon the mere numbers of enrolments of students as compared with those of last year, this will be no criterion at all of its educational effect. The object of the Minute was to put a premium upon solid continuous educational work by serious students, and a discount upon the production of large numbers of irregular attendances in an infinity of ill-assorted subjects. In a word, what the Government have in view in their re-organisation of Evening Schools is the prevention of waste and overlapping of effort and machinery, and the recognition of Quality rather than Quantity in all their educational output, and in the application of the public funds on this branch of education. . . .

It is particularly to be remembered that, as the Managers and Teachers of the Evening Schools in country districts are to a very large extent the same as the Managers and Teachers of the Elementary Day School, the County Councils are thus acquiring an invaluable experience of the educational condition of their area, and of the character of the Elementary School Managers and Teachers.

The Board of Education have now issued the main body of their Regulations for the Evening School Session 1902–3. In these Regulations they have amalgamated the Directory, so far as it related to Evening Schools and Classes, and last year's Evening School Minute. They have adopted the system of grants laid down in the Minute though of course the old high grants for Science and Art instruction remain. Many of the detailed restrictions surrounding these grants have been swept away, and the old Directory payments will henceforth be on the same simple lines as the payment for Literary or Commercial subjects under the Minute. In nearly all subjects the maximum prescribed by the Minute has been slightly—in some, considerably—increased. Various minor changes have also been made with the object of helping School Managers and of enabling the Regulations to be administered with smoothness."[1]

But, although Sykes and Morant here claimed to be mainly concerned with the quality rather than the quantity of evening school work, reports in the summer of 1902 of "an extraordinary decrease", not only of the numbers of enrolments, but of students attending with satisfactory regularity, produced considerable alarm in South Kensington. The causes of this fall were said to include *bona fide* uncertainty as to the future of these evening classes, sulkiness in school boards, and "cussedness" among managers and teachers (not unnatural in the circumstances). So disturbing were the omens, indeed, that it was found necessary to give a public reassurance in parliament that school boards would be safeguarded from any surcharges for carrying on their evening school work (under the county council) for the ensuing session.[2]

It is unfortunately impossible to determine exactly what effect the Minute had on numbers attending evening classes; for the statistics were so compiled that they could not be compared with previous years.[3] In view of the Board's extreme anxiety about the shrinkage of enrolments in 1902 it is difficult to resist the inference that there was no great desire to reveal the facts. Thus average attendances were no longer given in the statistics, but instead the numbers actually qualifying for grant. On the other hand, it must be borne in mind that changes in organisation had been so great that it would have been difficult to give strictly comparable figures.

There can, in any case, be little doubt that serious damage was done to the evening classes, in checking "technological" developments such as those at Manchester, and recreative classes such as those in London, and also in turning away those less tenacious students whose awakening interests would scarcely suffice to meet the stringent requirements of the Minute.

[1] M.E. Private Office Papers.
[2] *Parliamentary Debates.* 4th Series, cix, 693. 16/6/02.
[3] *Report of Board of Education,* 1902–3, p. 14.

XV
REVIEW AND CONCLUSIONS

*

THE fundamental problem behind this crisis is almost as old as civilisation itself: *aut rex aut lex*—whether to trust to the discretionary rule of an individual, or an individual institution (king, minister or school board), and thereby expect strength and flexibility, but risk tyranny; or to embody agreed policy and decisions in law and thereby ensure justice to all and freedom from individual caprice, but risk stagnation. In Anglo-Saxon countries, the choice has apparently long been made. The law is supreme; and, until recently, at least, few would have challenged the basic assumptions behind Dicey's Rule of Law.[1]

But the rapidity of social changes in democratic states today has seriously troubled modern writers on the philosophy of law. "The pressure of less immediate social interests . . .", wrote one, "has called continually for overhauling of legal precepts and for refitting them to unexpected situations. And this has led men to seek principles of legal development by which to escape authoritative rules, which they feared or did not know how to reject, but could no longer apply to advantage."[2]

The search for law, which would facilitate, rather than hamper, social development, which was suggested in Forster's speeches on the 1870 Bill, is, indeed, implicit in the writings of a large group of modern legal philosophers. "When human relationships are transforming daily", suggests one, "legal relationships cannot be expressed in enduring form. The constant development of unprecedented problems requires a legal statement capable of fluidity and pliancy. . . . *Much of the uncertainty of law is not an unfortunate accident:*

[1] Dicey, *Law of the Constitution*, Macmillan, 1927, *pp.* 179, *et seq.*
[2] Pound, *Introduction to the Philosophy of Law*, Yale U.P., 1921, pp. 18–19.

it is of immense social value."[1] Not many practising lawyers, however, would agree with such an advanced view; and the practical man of business craves both security and a considerable measure of certainty in the rules within which he must work. But, the teacher may well object, it is precisely the practical applications of legal and administrative rules that are so important and difficult in the sphere of education. In the last resort, school boards who knew what their administration meant were faced with the moral dilemma, not of *aut rex aut lex*, but of *aut pueri aut lex*: and their answer was in line with the principle advocated shortly after the Cockerton events by an outstanding supporter of the London County Council. "I am glad to think", he wrote, "that there are fervent educationists to whom the point of conscience comes in the reflection that, whilst the various other conscientious objectors are disputing as to *how they would like to alter the existing status quo in the schools*, there are 800,000 London children waiting to be taught."[2] Hence, clearly, since education concerns the learning and development of children in a society rapidly changing from a highly complex present to an unpredictably complex future, fixed and detailed rules are out of the question if education is to be a healthy and efficient service. It would be folly to make rigid law to govern a system subject to such rapid change. As Aristotle himself said, rules dealing with indeterminate matters must themselves be indeterminate.[3] On this view, therefore, whatever the eventual upshot, Forster was right in *principle* in leaving the scope of elementary education undefined.

One must admit the force of much of the above argument. "Elementary" education had to be left flexible; the initial error lay in leaving too indefinite the nature and extent of the controls restricting its possible expansion. The Education Department's main discretionary powers were concerned with the limits of *grants*. In theory, at least, no one held a similar discretionary power of defining the expanding limits of elementary education as far as *rate* expenditure was concerned. Indeed, even after 1901, these limits were not finally settled. School board "Elementary" education had, therefore, flexible limits, as defined by the *grant* regulations; and for *rate* expenditure relatively fixed limits, prescribed by Statute as interpreted by the auditors, and, ultimately, the courts. In practice, of course, these limits usually coincided; for the auditors accepted the grant limits as indicating the permissible rate limits. But this was not necessarily so; for the department might lay down conditions of grant which would apply to, say, *voluntary* evening schools, but

---

[1] Frank, *Law and the Modern Mind*, Stevens, 1949, pp. 6–7.
[2] Sidney Webb, *London Education*, Longmans, 1904, p. 211.
[3] Aristotle, *Nicomachean Ethics*, V.x.

this would not protect the school boards in their expenditure of the rates on *board* evening schools. The framers of the 1870 Act had not seen that the conditions of rate-aid must be flexible and indeed identical with the flexible conditions of grant if the system was to work.

It is, however, possible to accept the moral arguments behind the school board case and yet to doubt the practical wisdom of the policy pursued by London School Board. By its clever and, occasionally, doctrinaire arguments it rendered increasingly suspicious an Education Department which was very conscious of its own weaknesses. By its all-or-none methods it challenged the public and the Education Department with too radical changes in too rapid succession-abolition of fees in day schools, abolition of "elementary" restrictions in evening schools, wholehearted adoption of the Re-creative Evening School programme, swift expansion of evening schools, wholesale proposals for higher grade schools, abolition of evening school fees—all within ten years, and all backed by an assumption of universal educational power, and a readiness to challenge, if not to despise, the law. "If in any nation", suggests a by no means reactionary writer, "there is a group of men who are capable of disregarding the established law, then we can say that here there is a tyranny."[1] And, with all their good intentions and all their constructive work, it must be admitted that at times London School Board came near to satisfying this definition.

The approach of London School Board to the Education Department on matters of policy took too little account of practical limitations—including such realities as the departmental outlook. It is true that it tried practical experiments; but somehow such experiments were liable to appear to the department as carefully planned infiltration, aimed against accepted policy. Thus by its classes for ex-pupil teachers and assistant teachers it excited the fears of the Education Department lest a Day Training College should be established; by its exploration of endowments it seemed to aim at jumping a claim in technical and secondary education. Its attitude to higher grade schools was similarly independent. Other school boards, though disliking the narrowly scientific curriculum of the Science and Art Department, made a working compromise with official requirements, by creating higher grade schools and science schools and adjusting them in ways which seemed likely to meet official approval. London, since it could not obtain approval of its policy of commercial education, in effect deferred creation of higher grade schools during the earlier period; and eventually faced the Education Department with a demand for the recognition of a large

[1] Goodhart, *English Law and the Moral Law*, Stevens, 1953, p. 57.

batch of schools as "higher elementary". The wholesale nature of London's proposals was, of course, merely a symptom of the local trouble: on the one hand, London's problems were so vast as to render the Education Department almost helpless in coping with them, and, on the other, its size and importance made London School Board, officials and members alike, too sure of its strength and unprepared to smooth the way for a timid and apparently obtuse Department. The friction had a snowball effect, and the records of these later years suggest an almost complete absence of informal consultation; indeed, one is driven to the conclusion that tea drinking was unknown as an instrument of educational administration in London in the nineties.

One cannot, of course, do more than guess what would have been the result if London School Board had, from the outset, been content like other boards to follow lines apparently approved by the two departments, by gradually establishing higher grade and organised science schools and waiting for the amelioration of the crude methods and curriculum of the Science and Art Department (which came in 1894–5); but it seems reasonable to infer that such a policy would have created less violent hostility. Probably it would not have saved school boards; but it might have avoided the Cockerton débacle; and it would at worst have meant that London would have had more schools equipped to take advantage of the Higher Elementary Schools Minute.

The government departments concerned had a large measure of responsibility for the final breakdown of the system established in 1870. It is true, as the courts indicated, that the Education Department had no *legal* duty to restrain the expenditure of the rates by school boards. But, on the other hand, we must recall (i) that it had, in fact, on various occasions, assumed some measure of responsibility for control of such expenditure; (ii) that it had to assure itself of the methods in which buildings erected with public money (usually in the form of loans) were to be used; (iii) that its grant regulations gave it an effective instrument of control, but that the confused and bewildering nature of these regulations (especially after 1890) invited, if, as in the case of the Evening School regulations, they did not actually incite to, misuse of the rates; and, (iv) that the Education Department was, during the crucial years, reponsible for a marked change of policy with regard to appeals from auditors' decisions affecting school board expenditure of the rates. The effect of its interventions with the Local Government Board was to weaken the auditor's enforcement of existing law, when the need was for new or more explicit rules of law.

The need for clarification of the legal position with regard to the use of the rates had been obvious since 1888. It is true that the Cross Commission's emphasis had been on the "absolute necessity for *legislation*"; but, pending such legislation, the onus was on the Department to clarify its own regulations, or, if that was thought unnecessary, to enforce them as they stood.[1] For twelve years, however, the Department remained content with its ambiguous regulations and did nothing effective either to make them understandable or to enforce them, and only when trouble was clearly imminent did it, in 1900, evolve a minute which the school boards would have welcomed long before.

In fairness to the department, it must be reiterated that the ambiguity of the law affecting evening schools from 1890 onwards, was the result of hasty end-of-session legislation; but the department itself appeared to lose sight of the limited scope which it had intended to give to the Education Code (1890) Act, and it is not too much to say that, throughout the following decade, the evening school regulations implied and encouraged a sweeping interpretation of the law, which proved unfounded; and it was through acting on this departmental encouragement that the school boards suffered.

The whole period offers ample illustration of the unhappy results of lack of co-ordination between government departments. The uncertainty in the division of responsibility for audit appeal cases between the Education Department and the Local Government Board led to a serious weakening in the legal guidance which such cases gave to school boards. The Local Government Board were, of course, *technically* responsible; but some of the most important decisions were substantially made by the Education Department. On the other hand, the Education Department, though they were, when it seemed opportune, liable to give an emphatic opinion, regarded final decisions as a matter for the Local Government Board, and became, during the '90's, increasingly casual about precedents, and increasingly apt to base their advice on policy and the Code rather than law and the Acts. Indeed, it is not too much to say that they succeeded in exercising power without responsibility. In several cases they persuaded the Local Government Board to give audit appeal decisions favourable to school board higher education; but these remained Local Government decisions. Hence, when the Cockerton Case arrived, the Education Department were able to wash their hands in public of any responsibility for the blood of the school boards. Not that the public was entirely deceived. "The Education Department", ran one forthright press comment,[2] "has allowed the London School Board to do certain things, and then it

---

[1] The Brighton letter of 1887 was a first step towards clarification (*Supra* pp. 95–6).
[2] *Leicester Post*, 22/12/00.

appeared to some subtle casuist to get an auditor to disallow the charges complained of, and raise the whole question in a court of law. . . . The Education Department is more culpable than either the London School Board or any other authority." And likewise *The Guardian* not only inferred, with some justification, that Education Department jealousy of South Kensington had led it to play for its own hand as from 1890 onwards in the endeavour to win higher education for its own sphere of influence, but went so far as to suggest that the Education Department's own disregard of legal obligation had brought upon it the open contempt of the school boards throughout the country.[1]

The failure of the Education Department and the Science and Art Department to demarcate effectively their respective spheres was confusing in the extreme to the school boards. The overlapping was implicit from the outset, both in the roving commission assumed by the Science and Art Department and in the vague language of the Elementary Education Acts. It was accentuated by the method of payment by results. But the seriousness of the overlap only became apparent when it was clear that the original notions of the scope of "elementary education" had far underestimated the potentialities of school board pupils, and from the time of the Cross Commission the need for co-ordination was increasingly obvious.

The final responsibility for the administrative muddle in education in 1890–1900 was, of course, that of parliament itself, and, in particular, of the political heads of the Education Department; the institution of two overlapping departments, the ambiguities of the 1870 Act, the obscurity of the 1890 Code Act, and the continued failure to clear up the situation after the Cross Commission had emphasised the weaknesses—all were ultimately failures of the legislature and of successive governments. Indeed, until the coming of Gorst, political heads of the Education Department had openly and consistently encouraged the school boards in their adventures in higher education. Such restraint as had been imposed had been the work of the auditors and of the permanent officials of the Local Government Board and the Education Department, especially in the pre-1890 days.

It is manifest that most of the practical effects usually attributed to the Cockerton Case were the results of policy rather than law. As we have seen, the *major* consideration in the judgments was the importance of age; school boards' rights under the existing law were limited to the education of children. The practical implications of this part of the decision were two: (i) that since school boards must not educate adults, the higher grade schools must have a definite

[1] *The Guardian*, 27/12/00.

upper limit of age; and (ii) that, since evening school pupils were predominantly adult, either new legislation was necessary to enable school boards to conduct them, or they must be transferred to county councils (which clearly required legislative sanction). Neither course had implications necessarily adverse to educational progress. The other main finding was not that technical subjects should not be taught but that school board schools had to work under Whitehall. The damage done to educational development during and after the Cockerton crisis had, it is clear, political, rather than legal, sources. Gorst, Morant and their supporters disliked and, in some ways, feared the great school boards, and seized every opportunity to belittle their work by pointing to its more casual and recreative aspects. They had, too, a belief in disciplined, planned, traditional education; and it may be doubted if at this time either Gorst or Morant had any realisation of the possibilities, for a less exclusive secondary school population, of the technical and commercial education whose development they to some extent impaired; for it must be remembered that all the major investigations of the possibility of transfer of training had still to come.[1] But it seems clear that, in Gorst's case at least, the fundamental objectives were religious and political: to save the voluntary schools at all costs, and to subordinate the school boards to, and eventually replace them by, the county councils, which were for various reasons expected to be relatively conservative in their administration of education. There is evidence, too, of a genuine fear of and hostility towards elementary school teachers and their organisations. Thus, when the Cockerton decision was known and it was plain that some emergency measure to cope with the crisis was necessary, one suggestion was that the *Board of Education* should be given a dispensing power to enable school boards to carry on the work which the judgment had found to be illegal (and there can be no doubt that such a proposal would have gone through parliament without serious opposition). But Gorst opposed this obvious plan; for, he argued, the Board would be unable to withstand the pressure! "The power would be exercised under the influence of the School Boards and the National Union of Teachers", he wrote, in a revealing memorandum. "It would afford no practical check on the School Boards, who would at once occupy the whole field of Secondary Education in the great Towns."[2] Hence the dispensing

---

[1] Before judging Gorst and Morant too harshly on this issue, we should not overlook the fact that even in 1956 the main impact on organisation and methods in secondary and technical education of experimental findings on transfer of training still lies in the future.

[2] "Memorandum by Sir John Gorst upon various methods of dealing with the Cockerton difficulties." M.E. Private Office Papers. May (?), 1901.

power, with all its implications, was conferred on the County Councils.

Such measures were of ephemeral significance. The lasting importance of the educational upheaval of 1899–1902 lies in its revelation of the forces to be reconciled if a sound basis for educational progress is to be assured. Many of the problems of educational administration are *sui generis*, or, at least, so different from the ruck of administrative matters as to call for distinctive principles of organisation. It was no accident that the leading case on the discretionary powers of a governemnt department concerned the Board of Education;[1] for, as Forster had recognised in framing the 1870 Bill, education is by its very nature a living, almost unpredictably changing, social service, which cannot, as far as much of its business is concerned, be subjected to strict rules without risk of serious injury. On the other hand, some control must be exercised over the expenditure of public money; and everyone concerned should know both the limits of that control and the principles under which it will operate. How then can two such apparently conflicting sets of requirements be reconciled?

It may be objected that, far from being peculiar to education, such a dilemma is only one example of the general problem of legal control well known in the philosophy of law. "Over the inseverable phenomenal flux", writes one of the most penetrating modern thinkers, "we cast the meshes of our categories; it refuses to be bound by them, but we must be. For imaginary certainties are the artificial dykes which have won the realities of civilisation from the chaos of nature; or, to use another figure, they are the bootstraps by which men have pulled themselves up out of the primeval mud."[2] It is obvious that, however profound and true such a principle may be in general, there are extreme cases in which we may refuse to be bound by our legal "categories"—the good citizen would hardly allow the law of property to prevent his breaking into a house to save a child's life. But, extreme examples apart, if we test the principle of the quotation by applying it to the difficulties of school boards in, say, 1885, "inseverable phenomenal flux" would become a group of forty poor, but intelligent, Birmingham boys who had mastered the standards of the Code and were eager for further opportunities. The "meshes of our categories" would be the permissible limits of elementary education. Ought the school boards and the teachers to have awaited the decisions of parliament; or were they justified in stretching the meshes to meet the pupils' needs?

In such circumstances the lawyer would have no doubt. Whatever

---

[1] Board of Education *v.* Rice. House of Lords, 1911. A.C. 179.
[2] Dickinson, *Administrative Justice and the Supremacy of the Law*, Harvard 1927. p. 118.

the morality of the matter, the *legal* duty of the school board—like that of any good citizen—was to keep within the law; and, if the law was inadequate, to press for its amendment. Any teacher worth his salt would, with equal emphasis, answer that, in such circumstances, the needs of his pupils would come first, so far as he could contrive; and, rather than irreparably spoil their careers, he would strain the law, if necessary to breaking point (especially as, in educational matters, the law then lagged so far behind public opinion); and, if his pupils required science and art bread, he would scorn to give them elementary stones.

Such considerations explain, if they do not entirely justify, the extraordinary powers given to the administration by the Education Acts of 1902–44, which seem framed with the immediate objective of substituting administrative controls for legal rules wherever possible. Some sections of the 1944 Act, in particular, are couched in remarkably wide and general terms, giving extensive discretionary powers to local authorities in the first instance, but subjecting them to the almost absolute control of the Ministry of Education. In the "phenomenal flux" governed by these statutes, there is limited scope for legal rights in the usual sense; and parents, for example, get little more than a friendly wave of parliament's hand; it is suggested that the local authority "shall have regard to" their wishes.[1]

The Cockerton Case is sometimes cited as an alarming example of the dangers of any reference of educational questions to the courts of law. If the findings of this investigation are sound, its implications are very different. The harm done to education during these critical years was almost entirely of political not legal origin. The Cockerton Case provided a mere smokescreen. The crisis of 1899–1902 might, indeed, be used as a powerful argument for strengthening the administration by protecting it from politicians. But that would imply more definite and more detailed law rather than our present wide and sweeping provisions. A despotic politician, appointed to be Minister of Education, would find in the 1944 Act all the powers he needed to twist the whole administration, local and central, to suit his purposes.

How then is our educational system to grow healthily, if it must, on the one hand, avoid the paralysing restraints of a too rigid system of legal rules, and, on the other, beware of the ever-increasing danger of political control? There can be little doubt of the urgency of the problem. Education is today changing at least as rapidly as in the late nineteenth century; but there is one radical alteration: far from being the "horrid question" that it then was, education is fast becoming a matter of absorbing interest to politicians. And the statu-

---

[1] cf. Watt *v.* Kesteven County Council, L.R. 1955, 1 Q.B., 408.

tory instrument that they have to hand affords them ample scope—
the Minister, indeed, enjoys wide latitude and exercises the most
formidable powers. In fact, the language of one section of the Act
already referred to seems to put the Minister above the law.[1] Flexibility purchased at such a price tends to take the whole system out of
the region of law and put it under the control primarily of officials,
and, ultimately, of politicians.

Aristotle made politics the master of education. Dewey, in effect,
made education the master of politics. England, during the past
half-century, has aimed at establishing a working compromise, in
which representation of professional opinion on such bodies as the
Consultative Committee or the Advisory Council may provide an
invaluable counterpoise to political influence; but pressure of events
appears to be giving ever-increasing scope to political decisions in
such matters as school organisation and selection for secondary
education. The system is, indeed, without anyone's malice afore-
thought, becoming less a balance of law against administration and
more a balance of local politicians against central politicians. But
if there are few fields in which politicians have now such great
powers and opportunities lying to hand, there is none in which they
are likely to do more harm. Nor is there any other field in which
political slogans can so readily mask ignorance of fundamental
issues. It is, therefore, a problem of some urgency to make education
as independent of politics as considerations of public finance will
allow; for behind politicians, administrators, regulations and rules
of law are six million children whose paramount need is expert,
unbiased, liberal teaching. It was with this thought in mind that
Sidney Webb wrote, "The Lion in the Path of London education is
this peril of administrative perversion."[2] Today the Lions in the
educational path of the nation are the dangers of political intervention; and it is small comfort to know that the quieter ones are in
the provinces and those with the loudest roar in Westminster, or
that some are red and some are blue: all are liable to injure children
if they escape from their proper enclosures.

A modern writer, perturbed by the difficulty of maintaining the
rule of law in rapidly changing social conditions has well argued
that "it is a high and not a low conception of morality which recog-

[1] Education Act, 1944, s. 68: "If the Minister is satisfied . . . that any local
education authority or the managers or governors of any county or voluntary school
have acted or are proposing to act unreasonably with respect to the exercise of
any power conferred or the performance of any duty imposed by or under this Act
he may, notwithstanding any enactment rendering the exercise of the power or the
performance of the duty contingent upon the opinion of the authority or of the
managers or governors give such directions as to the exercise of the power or the
performance of the duty as appears to him to be expedient."

[2] *London Education*, Longmans 1904, p. 199.

nises that the State cannot enforce all men's duties, that its main business is to maintain liberties. . . . That the end of all State activity is the development of human personality can never be sufficiently recognised."[1] Political intervention in education reverses this order by subjecting the development of human personality to State activities and State aims. To devise a system of living and growing educational law and administration which gives adequate guarantees to legitimate state interests on the one hand, and adequate freedom to the schools on the other is a problem which has not yet been solved; but merely adding vast central powers of dealing with any doubts and removing any difficulties may prove to have been even more disastrous than the 1870 device of leaving the law vague and undefined.

[1] Lindsay, *The Modern Democratic State*, Oxford University Press, Vol. I, pp. 89 92.

APPENDIX A

First Morant Memorandum[1]

The Higher Grade Schools in England,
their origin, growth and present condition

. . . BEFORE ten years had elapsed from the passing of the Act of 1870, the School Boards of several large towns in the North of England had begun to set apart special schools in their towns, in which an education was given of a higher character than that in the ordinary elementary Schools. The Schools which were in each case thus set apart were usually those at which no half-time scholars attended:[2] this fact in itself made it possible to keep the education, therein given, at a higher level. A further "natural selection" of scholars took place, in most of these Schools, owing to the existence of a higher fee in them. This requirement of a higher fee arose admittedly from two causes:— (*a*) that this better class of education was more expensive, in consequence of the more highly skilled teachers which it required. (*b*) that this better education extended over a longer period of years than the mere exemption standards, and was only sought by the somewhat better social class of children—the more well-to-do—who could afford to postpone wage-earning, and were, *ipso facto*, in a position to afford more than the common 3d. fee; and, in the seventies, it was a cardinal principle, recognised both by School Boards and by the Education Department (as it is still to this date by the Science and Art Department) that parents should be made to pay as much as possible towards the school expenditure; so much so that the statutory limit of 9d. as a maximum fee was often evaded at least in the higher portion of these schools by an arrangement of lower fees in the lower school so as to bring the *average* fee of the school within statutory requirements.

[1] M.E. Private Office Papers. This memorandum was written in 1897 and revised in 1901. Amendments presumed to have been added in 1901 are shown in square brackets. The memorandum has been slightly abridged by omitting Morant's review of the history of the relevant regulations.

[2] Any considerable number of half-timers, by involving a repetition of the morning time-table in the afternoon, seriously cripples the work of the school and halves the possible progress of the whole-time scholars.]

At first it was generally the case that individual Schools in the different towns gradually *acquired* this higher character, rather than that they were specifically erected for this purpose. But when the question of actually building new schools to serve these deliberate objects had to be dealt with (the question necessarily arising on the sanction by the Education Department of the necessary loans) the Education Department was forced to consider its position in regard to what was undoubtedly a strong intention in *Northern* towns to regard the School Boards as the natural public authority for the provision of intermediate education out of the rates. (It must be remembered that there was as yet no Act empowering Municipalities to undertake educational provision, and that even up to the very eve of the 1889 Act, School Boards were very widely assumed to be natural purveyors for *local* educational needs, not only in the elementary, but also in higher, and specially in the technical, spheres.)

By the year 1879 there were already some five or six of the chief Northern School Boards that were applying to the Education Department for permission to establish such schools called Higher Grade Schools, notably Sheffield, Barrow, Bradford, Nottingham and Halifax.[1]

Accordingly, the Duke of Richmond, Lord George Hamilton and Sir Francis Sandford laid down the lines of the Education Department's policy in an important letter, on August 23rd 1879 to the Bradford School Board, in which was urged the desirability of grading all the Board Schools in a town, "adjusting as far as possible the quality of the education given to the fee paid (after the manner of the Charity Commissioners' policy with Endowed Schools) while at the same time, by means of exhibitions or otherwise, facilities are afforded for those who show capacity *to pass from the lower to the higher grade 'schools'*."

It is from this suggestion that the name commonly applied to these schools has arisen: a name which was obviously applicable at the time, but ceases to be so appropriate in these days of free board schools and specially when applied to some of the present-day schools which provide almost no teaching, (whether higher or lower in type), in the standards, and are rather *continuation* schools, than schools giving a higher grade of education in the standards.

It is obvious that—this suggestion that a School Board should maintain schools of various grades in the same town—contained within it very large possibilities of an extended provision of higher education by School Boards.

[1 The school at Sheffield was sanctioned as early as 1876 and is believed to have been the earliest true "Higher Grade" Central School. It was opened in 1880. The Birmingham Bridge Street School was probably the earliest school of the later and more developed type of Central School.]

In practice there have been three main limits upon this tendency:

(i) The first limit is the discretion of the Education Department in sanctioning or refusing School Board loans for building schools not required for ordinary school accommodation of Standard Scholars, (or at least not restricted to those requirements), but planned and equipped specially for the purpose of giving such higher education, with lecture rooms, laboratories, etc.

(ii) The second limit is the discretion of the Auditors in the different localities, in the matter of surcharging, or permitting, expenditure on this higher and ex-standard work, (whether the inevitable loan-interest for the buildings or in the less obvious and possibly avoidable expense of the salaries and maintenance incurred directly for the ex-standard classes), out of rates levied under the Act of 1870 which normally limited the School Board powers to providing, and maintaining, schools in which "the principal part of the education given shall be elementary."

(iii) The third limit is the discretion of the Education Department in permitting, or prohibiting, the Staff of the Elementary or Standard portion of the School (paid out of the Whitehall Grant and the Elementary Rates) to be used, in part at least, for the work of the upper portion, i.e. of the scholars who are usually in classes under the Science and Art Department, and who are in any case prohibited by section 66 of the Revised instructions from being on the register of the School as recognised by Whitehall. It may be added that the Science and Art Department now expressly forbids children who earn *South Kensington* Grants from being on the register of a Public Elementary School.

It is round these three points that the chief difficulties have arisen, and it is the complete or the modified application of them that alone curbed the upward growth of School Board work, previous to 1889. But for these obstacles it is possible that very little ground would have been left for the new authorities created in 1889, at all events in the lower stages of Technical instruction, a point which is sufficiently proved by the strong opposition of the greater School Boards to the introduction of the Technical Instruction Act, which they looked upon as handing over to *other* bodies powers which they themselves were already exercising with great energy and great success (*vide* School Board Chronicle Volume for 1889, *passim*).

When the question of meeting the expenditure to be incurred by the proposed Higher Board Schools was first raised, the Education Department expressly recognised the difficulty of using the rates for the purpose of ex-standard instruction, and suggested, in an important letter to the Nottingham School Board of September 3rd, 1880, that a School Board might appropriately "organise a class in connection with 'their Higher School which might obtain the Science Grants of the Science and Art Department'."[1]

[It is this suggestion which has not only rendered financially possible the great development of Higher Board Schools throughout England, but has also imprinted on them that strongly scientific and somewhat technical character as expressed in their curriculum, which has always differentiated them from ordinary Secondary Schools, and has given rise to the theory that their proper function has been until recently the preparations of boys mainly for handicraft occupations, and specially for subsequent higher technical instruction.]

The immediate reason for this tendency is to be found in the important steps taken by the Science and Art Department in 1872 (see Minutes attached) to encourage the later education, in a science direction, of children leaving the Public Elementary Schools. (Considerable influence must also be ascribed to the important report of the Royal Commission on Scientific Instruction.) For some years, however, the Department was disappointed of results from this move; most Schools preferred to adopt disjointed classes in individual Science subjects rather than the organised curriculum of the School of Science as put forward by the Science and Art Department, which compelled the teaching of some of the other proper branches of a "Real-Schule" curriculum. Indeed up till the year 1883 there were only two organised Science Schools in the country, neither of them connected with elementary schools, or under School Boards.

A second and even greater impetus, however, was undoubtedly given to the establishment of Schools of Science by School Boards, through the publication (in 1884) of the Report of the Royal Commission on Technical Instruction, which strongly urged the development of such Schools under the School Board system . . . and, while making no reference to the legal question of such expenditure, uttered strong praises of the action already taken on these lines by School Boards in certain towns.

Hence in 1885, we find that the Manchester School Board established an Organised Science School under the Science and Art Department in connection with each of the three Higher Grade

[1 It should be noted, however, that this Minute omitted the question of whence money could be derived for the *buildings*, while yet sanctioning the higher work which would inevitably in the long run demand special buildings if it were to be efficient. Hence the subsequent complications.]

Schools which already existed there,[1] while six more towns, Brighton, Gateshead, Halifax, Jarrow, Leeds and Sheffield followed suit the following year, showing clearly that the movement was mainly in the great industrial and manufacturing towns *of the North*. This was of course due to the fact that the technical requirements of their great industries naturally emphasised the need of some higher education *different in type from that given* (*almost universally in the seventies and early eighties*) *by the Endowed Secondary Schools:* and also to the fact that these same industrial developments had created a large class of well-to-do artisans who—

(*a*) by their daily work had learnt the value of education beyond that of an elementary School.

(*b*) by their wages were enabled to postpone the wage-earning of their children, and even to pay a 9d. fee without grumbling.

(*c*) from their own experiences looked naturally to the Board Schools to which they were accustomed, and to the School Boards in whose election they took a personal interest, for the provision of this higher education.

Moreover, in the seventies and early eighties, the Endowed Schools were still traditionally associated in the minds of everyone with a higher social class, and an emphasis was inevitably given to their differences and their refusal to cater for the new needs by the height of their fees. [Usually £10 or £6, as compared with 30s. or 20s. in Board Schools.]

It should be observed at this stage of our history that there had now grown up practically three different types of so called Higher Grade Board Schools:—

(*a*) Those which charged a higher fee than the other elementary Schools in the same town, while giving an education wholly confined to the Standards and differing very little if at all from the ordinary elementary school, their sole distinctive feature being a social selectness. Schools in this category still exist in considerable numbers, chiefly under Voluntary Management, though their creation, and even their continued existence where they exist, has been considerably affected by Mr. Acland's application of the Act of 1891. These Schools bring discredit on the term Higher Grade School, and as they play no part in the provision of higher or intermediate education by the Elementary Education Authorities, no further reference

[1] It would probably be more correct to say that it converted the ex-standard classes in those schools into Organised Science Schools with complete curriculum, whereas they had previously been odd and end disconnected classes in individual Science Subjects.]

need be made to them in this Memorandum, beyond the statement that they usually adopt the name Higher Grade in order to influence ignorant parents in their neighbourhood, and so increase the number of children in attendance, and the Grants earned. This type of School has lost considerably by the new Block Grant. But as a rule the School will be all the better for being restrained within proper limits and being forced to give a sound elementary education.

(b) Another type or category of Higher Grade Schools includes those Schools which, while taking children throughout *all* the Code Standards from the lowest (sometimes even from Infants) upwards, both raised the quality of the education given in those standards above that of the average elementary Schools in the same town (by adding Class and specific subjects throughout, and by having highly paid teachers) and also carried on that education beyond the Standards, by classes under the Science and Art Department or otherwise, usually called ex-standard classes. About one-third of the total number of Higher Grade Board Schools in existence in 1897 are of this category.[1]

(c) The third type or category is that specially exemplified by the Birmingham School Board, whose two Higher Schools (at Bridge Street and Waverley Road) have no standards below the seventh.[2] Schools of this type are essentially Central Schools, to which children are drafted (sometimes compulsorily) from all the elementary schools of the town, if they desire to carry their education beyond the sixth standard. The Central School at Hull is also of this category as it gives only Standard VI and ex-standard work: as also those at Huddersfield, Wolverhampton, Salford Central and Sheffield Central. In all of these the School gives an education only in one top standard of the Education Department Code with Whitehall Grants (sometimes Standard VII is provided as an *alternative* course to the Organised Science Course, after Standard VI) followed by a two, or a three years' course under the Science and Art Department regulations, and aided by their Grants.

It is this type of School which has caused the greatest difficulty, regarding the question of legality. Obviously a School intended to give a three years' course in ex-standard Science School work, prefaced by only one year of work in the Standards, can only by a

[1 Viz., those at Todmorden, Liverpool, London, Stockport, Finchley, Norwich, Leeds, Brighton, Tottenham and Oldham. All these have from Standards I (or II) up to Standards VI (or VII) inclusive; some even have infants. But several of these have since 1897 become Organised Science Schools.]

[2 The Higher Grade School at South Shields is also thus limited.]

considerable stretch of discretionary powers be sanctioned under an Act which limits School provision to Schools in which the principal part of the education given is "elementary". The first School of this type was opened at Bridge Street, Birmingham, and the question of legal possibility of a School Board building such a School was not raised, as Mr. Dixon generously lent a building to the School Board for the purpose at a peppercorn rent. Various other administrative difficulties necessarily arose of one kind and another (see correspondence re Bridge Street School and also re Waverley Road School, Birmingham) and certain rules were laid down by the Department, on one occasion and another, as to the limits within which the Education Department would sanction developments in this direction. But the attitude taken by the Education Department towards this particular type of advanced work by a School Board, under Lord Sandford and Mr. Cumin, in Mr. Mundella's regime, and again under Sir George Kekewich in the regime of Lord Cranbrook and Sir William Hart Dyke, sufficiently shows that the Department began to consider that the provision of Day Continuation Schools (even as distinct from an elementary school and giving an education of a considerably higher standard than that contemplated in 1870) might be considered as a proper duty of School Boards.

But it cannot be doubted that this policy of letting School Boards supply a sort of Pretence-Secondary School has headed off the natural local pressure in the big towns for the development of true Secondary Schools, and has considerably postponed the establishment of Local Authorities for Secondary Education, besides making such establishment [now] an infinitely more thorny question than it otherwise need have been.

[Signed] R. L. MORANT
Written 1897, revised 1901.

APPENDIX B

Second Morant Memorandum[1]

The proposed Minute of the Board of Education establishing Higher Elementary Schools

(*Copy sent to Mr. Balfour, 6th April, 1900*)

1. At the present time, owing to the steady upward growth of School Board activities in the larger towns, there is in practice no top limit to the kind of education given in Schools maintained by School Boards: e.g. Nottingham Higher Grade School successfully prepares its scholars for the Intermediate Examination for the London B.A.; at Leeds they pass the Matriculation Examination while at the Higher Grade School; and there are altogether some 1,200 scholars in Higher Grade Board Schools doing the most advanced Stage of "Science School" work, and obtaining grants up to £6 and £7 a head from the Science and Art Department.

2. At the same time this work is quite unsystematised. Different Boards organise their Higher work in different ways. Many of the Higher Grade Board Schools, having a "Science School" top portion, comprise in their lower portion both Infants and all the Standards of the Code from I to VII. Some include in their lower portion Standards III to VII, others IV to VI. Thus there is every variety of system, and no co-ordination of function between one School and another even in the same town.

3. The lower or "Standard" portions of these Schools have obtained large grants from the Education Department by taking an infinity of extra subjects on each of which grants could be earned. The new "Block" Grant [with a maximum of 22s. with a possible additional 7s. for Practical Work such as Manual Instruction or Cookery] given in the New Code now on the Table will cut down very seriously the possible "earnings" of these Schools. A great outcry has been raised at this "curtailment of the continued education of the industrial classes in the only Schools open to them, viz. the

---

[1] M.E. Private Office Papers. E.E.

public elementary schools." Unionist Members as much as the Opposition have pressed for some scheme which shall not wholly destroy the Higher Grade Schools.

4. It should be noted that, even under the new Code, the upper portion of these Schools (i.e. the Science School portion) will still be able to earn large grants from the Science and Art Department; and nothing is done under the Code as it now stands to limit their scope in this direction, nor to systematise their activities.

5. It is proposed by means of the new Scheme for Higher Elementary Schools to fix, and define precisely, the proper limit of the education to be permitted in Schools (or in higher Departments attached to Schools) maintained out of the Elementary Education Rates and aided from the Elementary Education Grants. To place this limit rigidly at 14 years as is done in Article 13 of the new Code, and thus cut off at a sweep all the Higher Grade top portions throughout the Country, would stop suddenly the education of some 14,000 children and cause very serious difficulties. It is therefore proposed to fix the 14 year old limit definitely for all *ordinary* elementary schools, but to allow certain schools under definite conditions and restrictions, and in places determined by the Central Authority, to carry on a certain fixed amount of higher elementary work, but always within limits and upon lines laid down by the Board of Education: allowing for these Schools, which will not be numerous, a higher rate of grant than that given to the ordinary elementary School, but lower than that given on the new "Block" System, so as to discourage a multiplicity of additional subjects, and to obtain a clear-cut curriculum on sound and restricted lines.

6. To carry out these objects, and at the same time to prevent any possible abuse of the system, or an extension of it hereafter into higher branches of education, many safeguards are necessary. These have been carefully elaborated in the proposed Minute. Alterations in this Minute in what might appear comparatively trivial points will doubtless be pressed for in the interests of "higher education". Such alterations might very easily reduce the scheme to an impossibility, financially. To take the points seriatim:—

7. The Schools must be called "Higher Elementary"; not "Higher Grade", because this term is used by an infinity of Schools up and down the Country and has no definite connotation whatever (very frequently it has merely a social signification); and "Higher Elementary" is preferable to "Higher Primary" because these Schools must, as will hereafter be shown, be a definite part of the Elementary System under the Elementary Education Acts—and the term Primary is not in use in the Acts or the Code. By calling them "Higher Elementary" they can at once, without legislation, be fitted into

the Elementary System, and also the more easily be kept within the proper limits.

8. The proposed curriculum of these Schools, and its higher and lower limits, may be more easily discussed after the proposed organisation of the Schools has been explained in detail. Admission to these Higher Elementary Schools must be rigorously restricted to children educated in public elementary schools, in order to prevent parents from a higher social class sending their children to them at the age of 12 or 13 to obtain a cheap higher education, and crowding out the others. (*Arts.* 1, 2 (*i*))

And no children should be permitted to enter or to stay in these Schools who are not sufficiently well grounded, and intellectually fitted, to profit by the instruction given; otherwise the higher grants . . . would be wasted. (*Arts.* 2 (*ii*) 3)

9. It is necessary to fix a rigid top limit to these Schools. An educational limit is exceedingly difficult to draw at all exactly. An age limit of fifteen is precise and cannot be evaded. It is the age up to which the State has already sanctioned Elementary Education Grants under the Act of 1891, so that it would be difficult now to fix the age limit lower: and it will just suffice to permit the scholars to have a sound education (somewhat higher than that possible in schools where most of the children leave at 12 or 13) in the new type of School in classes which will practically correspond to the present Standards V, VI a new VII, and a new higher VII, only with improved curricula. (*Art.* 4 (*i*))

10. In view of the Fee Grant and other considerations it is best to stop the grant definitely when the child is 15: but it would hardly be defensible to turn the child out of the School on a particular day, perhaps in the very middle of a school term: hence the child should be allowed to stay out the year (not earning a grant to the School), but *not beyond the year*. This point is important to prevent the present practice by which children stay on in a school, beyond the time during which they may earn the grants, without any top limit, thus taking up the accommodation needed for children below the age limit, and also gradually raising the level of the work done in the school. It is this practice which has steadily though almost imperceptibly brought about the present large number of higher classes in School Board Higher Grade Schools. (*Art.* 4 (*ii*))

11. As it is desired that the present "Schools of Science" under School Boards should transform themselves into "Higher Elementary Schools" under this Minute, it is necessary to assimilate the School year of the proposed Schools with that at present in force for the "Schools of Science" in order to facilitate the administrative transfer and the arrangement of grants. (*Art.* 5)

12. With a view to facilitating the transformation of the present Higher Grade Schools into the new "Higher Elementary School" form, it is requisite to arrange for a simple transference of children and recognition of existing qualifications during the first two years of the new experiment. (*Art.* 6)

13. In order to restrict the multiplication of these Schools, and to see that none are aided by the State except where they are really needed by the locality, and to arrange that *every* circumstance shall be taken into account in deciding for or against a given school being "necessary", it is important that the Central Authority should have absolute power to veto their establishment in every case. To give, in the Minute, the lines on which the Central Authority should or should not consider a school "necessary" would raise infinite debate in the House. It would seem wiser to reserve it for departmental consideration in every case (probably after careful enquiry on the spot as is done at present before recognising new Schools of Science), upon lines laid down with the Treasury, and so forth. (*Art.* 7A)

14. Similarly the recognition or non-recognition of buildings and premises should not be settled upon any hard and fast rule laid down now for all time. Circumstances must in every instance be carefully taken into account. Many a Higher Grade Voluntary School may apply to be recognised as a Higher Elementary School whose premises, though not on so large a scale as some of the School Board Higher Grade Schools, may yet be quite adequate for the curriculum and general course of work proposed to be given, in view of the circumstances of the neighbourhood. It would be well, therefore, to leave a fair discretion to the Central Authority in all these matters, at all events until further experience may enable definite rules to be formulated. At present this would not be possible. (*Art.* 7B)

15. In order to ensure that the Higher Grants to be offered to these Schools are really used for higher work, it is necessary to fix the proper proportion between teaching staff and children taught. The numbers here given are somewhat less rigorous than those in the Scotch Code, but they are practically consonant with the present practice of the better Higher Grade Schools in England, and are very considerably higher than is the rule for ordinary elementary schools. . . . (*Art.* 8)

16. The Grants have been fixed with the approval of the Treasury on such a scale as to keep the State Grants on these Schools well within the present limits, so far as can be estimated on the figures available.

The method of assessing and apportioning the Grants is the same sa that laid down in the new Code for the new Block Grant. . . . (*Art.* 10)

17. (This paragraph is now misleading. The Article it refers to is

not in the Minute.) The object of this article is to practically force or induce School Boards to give up their "Schools of Science" under the Science and Art Department; thus leaving that form of Education to its proper authorities—the Secondary Schools. Every large School Board will desire to adopt this new Scheme of Higher Elementary School Grants for some at least of its Higher Grade Schools; and in order to do this they will be required, under Article 11 of this Minute, to give up their at present too advanced work. It is believed that this price will be willingly paid by all the bigger School Boards. [There are comparatively few which have any "Advanced Stages" under the Science and Art Department.] At the same time it is probably not wise to attempt thus to *force* the School Boards by means of Articles in the Code. Opposition will be aroused by the wording of Clause 11. Whereas if this opposition be not aroused there are strong grounds for believing that all the School Boards will accept this new Scheme. This Clause 11 may be omitted with advantage. (*Art.* 11)

18. It is important to keep the accounts, and organisation and staff of these new Schools quite separate from those of the ordinary Elementary Schools, in order that the expenditure of these Higher Grants may be definitely noted and earmarked. At present some of the funds raised for ordinary elementary education and a portion of the elementary school teaching staff, are available to a considerable extent for carrying on advanced education in attached Higher Departments, and for the instruction of older and advanced scholars beyond the Standards. (*Arts.* 12, 13)

19. This provision already exists, practically, in regard to the "Science Schools": it is to prevent the duplication of State Grants for instructing the same children, and also to prevent overpressure for the children. (*Art.* 14)

20. It remains to state that, in view of the organisation herein proposed, the natural course of education for these Schools would be to give them (and restrict them to) a "4 Year Course"; and to comprise within the first two years the form of education now given in Standards V to VII in a good Higher Grade Elementary School, and in the last two years a course of education—with modifications to suit circumstances—more or less conforming to the present "Elementary Course of the Schools of Science" under the Science and Art Department. This will provide a good continuative education precisely suitable to, and assimilable by, children who have been educated wholly in the public elementary schools and will not compete in any real sense with, because differing widely both in character and in scope from, the education offered in Secondary Schools. It will, moreover, be mainly Elementary in character

(though on a somewhat higher plane than that suitable for Schools where most of the children leave at 12 years of age) and hence not unsuitable for recognition in the Code and under the Elementary Education Acts. It is important that these Schools should be definitely stamped as Elementary Schools: hence the importance of their name, and of their being included within the Code. For the same reason it is well that they should be eligible (as they are under this Minute) for the Fee Grant. This has been allowed for, by fixing the Grants in Article 10 of the Minute 10s. lower than would otherwise have been done. The age limit of 15 fits in with the plan: and it adds the final "cachet" of the *Elementary* character of the proposed Schools. It has received the approval of the Treasury and will not add to the present State expenditure on these Schools: and to refuse it would go very near to breaking the Act of 1891 which expressly gave the grant up to the age of 15.

R. L. M.

APPENDIX C

Gorst Memorandum[1]

SCHEME FOR NEW GRANTS
UNDER THE CODE
TO HIGHER ELEMENTARY SCHOOLS

(Abridged version of the Scheme submitted by Gorst
to the Treasury)

HIGHER GRADE SCHOOLS

... There are certain conditions and restrictions that must be strictly observed.... The Higher Elementary School must be definitely organised and staffed for a complete four years' course. It would correspond practically to the present Standard V and Standard VI, and the two years of the Elementary Course of the "School of Science" under the directory of the Science and Art Department. This would involve stopping the "Advanced Courses of the School of Science" in the few Board and Voluntary Schools that now carry it on. This, however, would only affect some 1,250 students out of 12,579, or one-tenth of the whole. The managers would willingly suffer this curtailment in order to obtain the advantages of the new system.

15. The whole of the work and the grant system of the "Higher Elementary School" would be laid down in the Code; the present separation of the upper portion of the work in the Directory would be done away with. Similarly the money now disbursed to the upper portion of these schools by the South Kensington Authorities would in future be transferred to the Whitehall Accounts and disbursed by the Whitehall Authorities—the "Science and Art" Sub-head in the Board of Education Estimates being diminished and the "Elementary Education" Vote increased by the amount (£53,843) in question, a considerable sum being saved in the process. ...

16. Various important requirements would be laid down in the Code to ensure the efficiency of the new type of school, to secure that

---

[1] M.E. Private Office Papers.

it be allowed to exist only where strictly needed, and to determine effectually the limits of its scope: e.g.,—

(a) The school must be recognised by the Board of Education as "necessary", i.e. actually required by the circumstances of the district. The sanctioning of new "Higher Elementary Schools" would have to be very carefully considered in every case in view of all the circumstances. Their increase will be very slow as the supply is already fairly complete, and the initial expense of buildings will always deter the localities considerably.

(b) It must from the outset have a staff qualified to teach the higher work of the third and fourth years of the course; no school would be recognised which provided for anything short of the full four years' curriculum. . . .

(c) Its work would be of a higher character, from the very commencement, than that of the ordinary elementary school which earns the new Block Grant of 22s. under the Code. Its curriculum would be laid down by the Board of Education mainly on the lines of the present "School of Science" Course in the Directory.

(d) Every child, in order to be admitted, would have to prove to the satisfaction of the Inspector of the Board of Education that he or she had reached the requisite standard of attainment to be able to profit by the school course. At first this would correspond roughly to the completion of the work of Standard IV in all subjects; but this requirement might be heightened in the future.

(e) Every child must have been attending an ordinary public elementary school for at least 12 months before seeking admission to the Higher Elementary School. This is to ensure that this form of State-aided education is secured to the class which needs it, and that the school shall not become a cheap resort for middle class children; it also tends to prevent competition between the Higher Elementary School and the Secondary School. This latter point is still further guarded against by the distinctly non-secondary character of the proposed curriculum, as also by the strict top limit of its scope.

(f) No child should be allowed to remain in the Higher Elementary School after he (or she) has completed (*bona fide*) the four years' course, and is upwards of 15 years old. (? Alternative regulation—No child over 15 may stay in the school.)

(g) The teachers must be certificated, and possess such other qualifications as may be laid down by the Board of Education in the Code as requisite in the case of Higher Elementary

Schools, and there must be a fully qualified teacher for every 40 (or less) scholars on the register.

(h) The Higher Elementary School must be quite distinct from the ordinary Elementary School; it must have a separate head master, separate staff, separate registers, separate accounts, etc. etc. During the present transition it may be held, under approval of the Board of Education, in the same buildings as an ordinary Elementary School, where circumstances require it; but the rule in the first sentence of paragraph (h) must still be rigidly adhered to.

[The memorandum concluded with proposals on the one hand for differentiating the Higher Elementary from the ordinary elementary schools, and on the other hand for ensuring that the latter were "strictly restrained to the ordinary Seventh Standard work".]

[Signed] JOHN E. GORST

2nd April, 1900

APPENDIX D

Third Morant Memorandum [1]

(written about February 1901)

EVENING SCHOOLS

I. *Historical Explanation of the Present Difficulties*

THE present difficulty in regard to Evening Schools arises out of the following circumstances.

In the seventies and eighties Evening Classes were held in a haphazard fashion here and there in Elementary Day School buildings by Teachers and Managers of the Day School, and grants were given to them by the Whitehall Department under the ordinary Elementary School Code which had a few Articles dealing specially with Evening Schools, giving grants for the same subjects and Standards as in the Day School, but recognising attendances of one hour only and with grants on the lower scale.

Often the Accounts of these Evening Schools were mixed up with the Accounts of the Day School; indeed this was quite usual, I

---

[1] M.E. Private Office Papers.

believe, until the Department required separate Accounts to be kept for the Evening School; this was not until 1894; so that Evening Schools may be said to have had no real separate existence until six years ago.

These Evening Schools or Classes, under the Code of the Education Department, received scholars of all ages between 12 and 21 but were not ambitious in their range of work. They were arranged according to the ordinary Standards of the Elementary Day School, and every scholar had to be in one of the seven Standards and to do one of the Standard Subjects, i.e. the three R's.

They very naturally, being in Elementary School buildings and being managed by Elementary School Managers, and providing in those days little beyond the three R's., were looked upon as part of the Elementary School System, and were practically Elementary Schools carried on in the evening, and for the most part for young persons over school age.

But after a time, as the effects of compulsory Day School Education spread, the scholars coming to Evening Schools wanted something more advanced in character than was provided for in the Standards of the Day School Code; and in time the Department frankly recognised this need, and began to meet it by removing in 1890 the requirement that every Evening scholar must take one of the Standard Subjects.

In 1892 the Department took the further step of issuing a separate Code specially for Evening Schools, and in the next year (1893) came the great Evening Schools development of Mr. Acland's Code, which frankly opened the Schools to all forms of Higher Education,[1] removed entirely the age limit of 21, that had hitherto existed, and initiated the term "Evening Continuation School" in imitation of the German term Fortbildungschule.

But though in all this the Evening Schools were now providing what was really Secondary Education, the Department, for reasons hereafter to be shown, deliberately kept these Schools and Classes within the Elementary System and labelled them (even to this day) as Elementary Schools. So obviously inaccurate, however, was this classification, that in order to make the Departmental fiction legally possible, they were obliged to pass an Act called the Code Act of 1890, which removed from these Evening Schools the restriction under which (as Elementary Schools) they would otherwise have lain, viz: that the principal part of the Education given in them must be Elementary.

[1] It is true that III(c) of the Code suggests that the principal part of the work will be preparatory to Higher Education; but in practice their scope has been very extended.

Thus the Evening Schools came to have a frankly Secondary character, although (by what has since turned out to be questionably wise policy) they were still by a fiction called Elementary Schools.[1] Two reasons are now alleged for the policy adopted at that time:— (a) that if the Evening Schools had not been classed as Elementary Schools it would have been difficult for the "Elementary Education Department" to give grants to them; and the Science and Art Department was not for some reason permitted to enlarge *its* scope and to give grants to them, as its sphere was supposed to be limited to Science and Art subjects; though it is not easy now to see why it was more correct to extend the purview of the Elementary Department into Secondary and Technical Education (as actually happened) than to widen the scope (into *general* subjects) of the Department *already* dealing with all the Scientific part of Higher Education, and (b) that it would otherwise have been impossible for School Boards to maintain them; and it was mainly the Urban School Boards that had brought the growing Evening Schools into existence and that were eager to develop evening work and to extend their function into Higher Education and to provide money for it out of the unlimited School Board Rate.[2] There was probably the supposed additional advantage of concealing the expenditure on this Higher Education development through its being merged in the local budget for Elementary Day Schools and so escaping notice.

Yet on now looking back it would seem that, seeing that—even as it was—an Act of Parliament was needed (Code Act, 1890) to make this policy possible, it would surely have been better policy in 1890 to have frankly recognised these Fortbildungschule[n] as a part of Higher Education and given them into the care of the then just created Technical Instruction Authorities, when they would have at once taken their true and proper place in the National Organisation of Education, and when they would also have been more adequately provided and financed in the County areas where School Boards were almost non-existent. Had this line been taken

[1] This was precisely the same policy, in another sphere, as that which permitted the Higher Day Schools to grow out of the Elementary Schools and to be organised and labelled as Elementary Schools when they should properly have been part of a Secondary School System. Possibly, at the time this policy seemed the line of least resistance and a process of natural development to which it was easy for the Department to yield. But the policy of drift thus adopted and the confusion of issues thereby initiated have in the long run been the direct cause of the Higher Grade difficulty and educational muddle in England—alone of civilised countries—as also of the Evening Schools chaos. And the thorough solution of the organisation difficulties was after all really only postponed, to be settled now by us at a later date under conditions which the delay has made much more difficult.

[2] This is again the same reason that has been adduced as justifying the recognition of the Higher Grade Day Schools; in both cases unfortunately the needs of rural areas were overlooked.

the only new requirement would have been perhaps to give the right to a further 1d. rate to those Authorities; and this would after all only have taken the place of the School Board Rate, which was unlimited, and which as a matter of fact has been largely drawn upon to finance these new higher Schools—only to be stopped in the long run, very naturally, by the decision in the Queen's Bench, as being an unjustifiable application of Funds intended for Elementary Education only.

But to return to the history—having by Departmental action established these Higher Schools, and given them large State subsidies in all subjects of general Secondary Education, and having also by Parliamentary action (Code Act, 1890) enabled them to pose as Elementary Schools, a quite unintentional result ensued— the Schools became, despite their giving non-Elementary Education, subject to the 17s. 6d. limit of grants laid upon all *Elementary* Schools by the Act of 1876, fourteen years before, when Evening Schools barely existed. The absurdity of this consists in the fact that the sum of 17s. 6d. in the Act of 1876 was fixed as being approximately half the then cost per child of an ordinary Day School Education; but the sum bore, and still bears, no sort of relation whatever to the cost of Evening Classes. It is in fact a purely accidental and (as the Office can testify) unintended circumstance that it applied at all to these grants for Higher Education. It may here be noted parenthetically that the original theory of the 17s. 6d. limit was of course the requirement of local funds to share with the Exchequer the cost of each School; but in the vast majority of cases (having been abolished for the Day Schools) it has now in the Evening School come to operate, and so to be looked upon generally, merely as a rough and ready limit to the State subsidy for Evening Education. At present the Exchequer saves by its operation from eight to ten thousand pounds per year in deductions under the limit; but it is believed that many Schools cease working in any Session when their expenditure had reached 17s. 6d.: so that that sum does not represent the whole effect of the limit.

We thus now have Evening Schools up and down the country giving general Higher Education (including Modern Languages, Political Economy, Science, Mathematics, and many branches of Technical Education), costing the Exchequer (in 1900) £199,451 per annum on some 23,539,298 attendances—the whole thing being nominally and administratively part of our Elementary Education System by a transparent fiction, maintained partly out of the School Board Rate under the Elementary Education Acts, and partly by County and Borough and Urban District Councils out of the Technical Instruction Rate and the Whisky Money.

Here too, however, there has arisen a quite unintentioned absurdity. Section 1 (1) (a) of the Technical Instruction Act, 1889, was intended to prevent the new Local Funds for Technical Education from being swallowed up in providing Elementary Education properly so called. But by the accident of its wording, taken in conjunction with the peculiar development of Evening Schools under the Code, it has in the event had the accidental and unintended result of greatly hampering the Counties in developing the much-needed Higher Education in Evening Schools (which is practically the main source of supply in rural areas under a proper system), though leaving them in a position to do certain limited portions thereof—a state of things wholly unintentioned by the Legislature in 1889.

But this is not the whole story. As long ago as 1852 the State had in another direction and through another Department initiated what soon grew to be a considerable expenditure from the Exchequer to promote Higher Education, in the particular directions of Art, Science, and Mathematics. A great development was brought about through these State Grants. These Grants have been made available to anybody who would organise higher instruction whether in Day Schools or in Evening Classes. The development has proceeded apace, and Public Bodies and Local Authorities of all kinds have taken advantage in a variety of ways of the Grants offered for the promotion of Higher Education.

But the South Kensington Department has until quite recently taken no measures to distinguish the work thus set going in Evening Classes from the wholly different type of Education provided, through these same money grants, by means of Classes in Secondary Day Schools as portions of an Organised Secondary School curriculum. Indeed it is only in the last year or two that any statistics have been kept of the Evening adult students taught in sporadic courses and classes at Mechanics' Institutes and so forth, as distinct from the wholly different type of work done by boys and girls who were being given, under these same grants, and under what was misleadingly called the same Sytsem, a good Secondary Day School Education in Grammar Schools. Even now only a rough estimate can be made of the real Evening work actually aided from the Exchequer in this way. So far as can be judged it seems to have amounted in 1900 to some £67,500 upon some 2,775,000 attendances.

Now these grants have been taken advantage of, and these Classes have been set going, impartially, both by Elementary Education Authorities (School Boards and Voluntary Managers) and by Higher Education Authorities alike. Sometimes they are kept going as an integral part of what is nominally an Elementary Evening

School under Whitehall, though all the students may be upwards of 25 years old and may be doing Spherical Trigonometry and Goethe's Faust in the original, on the same night—the funds being provided out of the Elementary Education Rate and the Elementary Education Vote, with a small sum from South Kensington.

Here again, curiously enough, we find an inintended absurdity, through the absence of system and organisation. While the Exchequer Grant (Whitehall) for the Goethe's Faust is subject to the 17s. 6d. limit, and the Local Rate (School Board) that goes to help it is *unlimited*, yet in a similar school across the street maintained by the Borough Council the Exchequer Grant (South Kensington) is *not* subject to the 17s. 6d. limit, while the Local Rate (Technical, Instruction Act) is *limited* to a penny. Moreover, the two Schools may be competing with each other, and underbidding each other, by means of the same State subsidies, one gradually killing the other in the struggle to get the pupils of the area, of whom there are probably barely enough to fill one good school—and this disastrous process is impartially *aided* by the State! !

It only remains to complete the history of this curious English haphazard unsystematic "drifting" development of the National provision for Higher popular Education by saying that, through the Cockerton Judgment and its practically certain confirmation on appeal, the greater part of the *Urban* portion of this varied Evening Education so needed for the Industrial Classes is now doomed to certain and immediate *extinction*—a large part of the Funds now being expended on it being cut off irrevocably and many of the Schools necessarily closed — unless Parliament within the next four months finds time and determination to inaugurate an organised and legal system, on a rational basis, into which the present complications can be transformed and by which they can be coordinated and properly developed. For while the schools in rural areas financed mainly by county councils may remain practically unaffected, all Evening students over 15 in what are far the most numerous Classes in our large and small towns—viz: School Board Classes—will be stopped; an outcome of Governmental *laissez faire* which would raise a popular agitation not lightly to be faced, and infinitely greater than the outcry occasioned by the few scholars affected in Higher Elementary Day Schools under the Minute of April 6th.

It would seem then that some comprehensive co-ordinating Scheme *must* be evolved, which shall meet the real difficulties, save what is really good in the present provision, prevent future recurrence of chaos, competition and overlapping, and set on a rational footing with an intelligible sound and properly limited financial basis, that absolutely essential structure of National Education which can only be provided in Evening Schools and Classes.

II. The problems to be solved and the difficulties in the way.

The first thing to do is to realise that this problem must be treated as a problem of Education by itself. Evening Schools and Classes are a form of Education *sui generis*. They cannot be handled or organised like Day Schools, each of which has its own clear-cut curriculum which every scholar in the School goes through in its entirety, giving his whole time to it, with but little option as to variety of subjects or hours or days, and in which home preparation plays a large part quite impossible to students in Evening Schools.

And the next thing is to make provision that as far as possible someone shall be responsible for seeing that each locality has an adequate supply (but not more than adequate and with no unnecessary competing elements) of Evening Education; and that both local and central funds shall be placed to the most economical and advantageous use in each case by having no competing centres, no overlapping jurisdictions, and no dual functions.

The obvious thing would seem to be to place under one single Department of the Central Authority with one single set of Regulations, *all* Evening Classes of whatever sort as being practically *the* means of Higher Education for the great mass of the people, and as having in no real sense anything to do with the problems incident to the kind of education given in Elementary Schools or in Grammar Schools.

We might start then by taking all the work that is done now under the Evening Continuation Schools Code, together with all the work done in Evening Classes under the S. & A. Directory and putting it into one Scheme of grants and regulations, to be called the REGULATIONS FOR EVENING SCHOOLS UNDER THE BOARD OF EDUCATION.

The sum spent from the Exchequer in 1900 under the Whitehall Evening Code was £199,451: the sum spent in Evening Classes under the South Kensington Directory was £67,500;[1] this gives us a total of £266,951 to deal with; a sum that was paid upon 26,314,398 attendances. We have only then to arrange a rational scheme for the economical expenditure of this sum on a proper basis of grants and attendances.

And whereas hitherto these two sets of grants have been given on wholly different and in each case hopelessly complicated systems of calculation, the new Regulations should lay down as simple a

[1] This sum is exclusive of certain grants made to Classes in "Schools of Art" which may perhaps best be left out of consideration here, the amount being inconsiderable, and difficult to disentangle from the Department's Statistics as now kept.

scale of grants as possible, calculated in such a way as to encourage nothing but solid work in the Classes, and to *discourage* odd-and-end disconnected bits of subjects, and at the same time not to exceed on the same number of attendances the total amount of £267,000 per annum already being furnished as above shown by the Exchequer. The drafting of such Regulations could of course be done without any great difficulty when once the principle is accepted.

It remains to consider the main difficulties that have to be met in the event of any such scheme being proposed.

A. *Treasury Objection.* These new Evening Schools will not be Elementary Schools, even by a fiction; hence the 17s. 6d. limit will not apply to them as it now does to the sum of £200,000 which you are including in your Budget, and the grant would thus be liable to indefinite increase.

Answer: If what is desired to be preserved in the 17s. 6d. limit is the local moiety principle, it could be provided either by requiring the new grants to be met penny for penny by local income, or else by letting the new grant be simply a proportion (in the case of each School) of the total expenditure. The latter method would leave the Exchequer much more in the dark as to its probable liabilities, and the former is obviously preferable and could easily be laid down. But it is believed that the 17s. 6d. limit is desired by the Treasury not so much nowadays in its aspect of a local moiety but as being practically a fixed limit of the call upon the Treasury. This being so, nothing is easier than to give what is wanted by fixing a rational limit to the new grant, by saying that not more than (—) attendances by any one scholar will be paid for in a given Session. This has been for years the plan applied to all the Evening Grants paid by the Treasury under the Science and Art Directory; and it would obviously meet the point. There will be no need to repeal Section 19 of the Act of 1876 (17s. 6d. limit) since the new Evening Schools will automatically pass away from under its influence, not being Elementary Schools and the Treasury will be no losers by allowing this to happen: on the contrary they will be more easily able to fix their limit from year to year.

B. *Cabinet Objections.*

(a) You will be organising State Aid to Secondary Education, whereas hitherto State Aid has only been given to Elementary Education and to Science and Art Instruction.

Answer: This is a fallacy. £199,451 a year is now being paid as we have seen to Higher Education outside Science and Art Subjects under the Acland Code. The new Scheme will merely organise this and not extend it; and it will cause the money so spent to be much more economically administered than hitherto; it involves no extension of principle but a systematising of one long since admitted.

(b) You will practically by your Scheme be undoing the *whole* effect of the Judgment, and legalising those very extensions of School Board Higher work, and those uses of local rates for Higher Education, which should properly be stopped as being more rightly the sphere of private enterprise and personal fees from students.

Answer: This raises the question as to the proper local bodies which shall be permitted to work under the new scheme, and will better be dealt with below. But it is clear that whatever limit may be desired as to subjects to be aided from the local rates can far more easily be laid down on one clear scheme such as is now proposed, than is possible in the present chaotic procedure. Moreover the principle of requiring fees for certain types of Education is already recognised in the Science and Art Directory as a condition of Grants; therefore this point also can if desired be more easily provided for under the new Scheme than at present.

C. *Political Objections.*

The new Evening Schools will not—even in respect of one portion of their work as at present—be Elementary Schools, and therefore, Schools Boards will be debarred from maintaining them; therefore you will rouse big political opposition. Moreover, in this case, where will you get your local subsidies from, to maintain them; since by your Scheme you must give up (as shown above) the School Board Rates now being spent on Evening Education—and not only that portion of the Rate given to Science and Art and Adult work and declared illegal by Cockerton, but also *all* the present School Board expenditure under the Evening Schools Code.

Answer: This is really *the* difficulty. But as a matter of fact it faces us inevitably, since the Judgment, *whatever* plan be proposed, and still more if no plan is proposed. It has now become impossible to avoid the raising and settling of this issue in Evening Schools work, just as it is being raised and settled in the sphere of the Day Secondary School also.

What then is to be done?

Solution.

The simplest thing would seem to be this. Avoid the mistake of 1893. Call things frankly by their right names. Let the Educational problem be clearly stated and frankly solved.

It is a question not of Elementary but of Higher Education, though it is true that on grounds of economy—as well as other points—the Classes will frequently be held in buildings that house an Elementary School in the day time, and that will have to be lent or rented for the purpose of Higher Education. This however is often done already.

Therefore, pending the establishment of one Local Authority for all grades of Education, and in case this should not arrive for many years, let us frankly recognise what is the case, that the new Evening Schools Scheme is the proper function of the new *Secondary* Education Authority under the Bill; but, to lessen political friction, and also to meet existing conditions, let there be the following modifications of this main principle:—

(x) In view of the great number of the Evening Classes needed in all the Districts of every Town (specially as compared with the *small* number of Secondary *Day* Schools needed in the same area), the Borough Councils should be much more frequently given financial and administrative independence for Evening School work—or at least fairly free play as Evening School *agents* for the County Authority—than would be the case in regard to Secondary *Day* School provision and maintenance.

It might indeed prove to be a convenient and by no means inadvisable concession to give to the non-County Boroughs and big Urban Districts, in allowing them under fixed conditions some powers as to Evening Classes for Higher Education which a proper co-ordination of Secondary Education would in the other hand make it most unwise to give them in regard to *Day* Secondary Schools; and

(y) In all places where the new Secondary Authority considers its own rating powers insufficient to provide adequately for Evening Schools or to make good the loss of the School Board Rates hitherto spent in the Town on Evening Classes, it might be made lawful by a Clause in the Secondary Education Bill this Session for the School Board to act as agents for the Secondary Education Authority in respect of Evening Schools, and to spend in the Towns the School Board Rates for this specific purpose.[1] They should of course be prevented from establishing or maintaining any School that would compete with Evening Schools (if any) belonging to or aided by the Secondary Authority itself; and other conditions and limitations might always be imposed upon this delegated power with the approval of the Central Authority.

It must be admitted that this Clause is not an ideal solution. One would not suggest it, if one had a *tabula rasa*. But something of this kind must be done (if School Boards continue to exist at all) *whatever Scheme of Evening Schools is now evolved*, if Evening Schools are not to

[1] The case of London may possibly have to be treated specially, as no doubt we shall be compelled to treat it for all Secondary Education purposes under the Bill when Committee stage is reached.

be practically shattered in the Towns when the Cockerton judgment is enforced. And this plan would be no worse from the "heavy rates" point of view, indeed it would surely be better, than the present plan of falsely calling advanced Evening Schools *Elementary* Education, and letting this form of Higher Education draw surreptitiously on the unlimited School Board Rate as hitherto.

And lastly this plan leaves the way open for an immediate improvement of the co-ordination of Higher Education in each town now, and for its easy completion hereafter in the event of School Boards ever becoming extinct. Moreover, this Clause will of course be unnecessary, and the new Scheme proposed will come into operation without any difficulty whatever, if after all we get *one* Local Authority for all Grades of Education in this present Session.

III. New Scheme for Evening Schools.

REGULATION FOR EVENING SCHOOLS
AND CLASSES
UNDER THE BOARD OF EDUCATION

(i) Abolish the Evening Continuation Schools Code altogether.

(ii) Abolish from the Directory all grants to Evening Classes.

(iii) Frame a new comprehensive Scheme of Regulations to comprise, without duplication, or overlapping, all the work now done under (i) and (ii), except such parts as the Chancellor of the Exchequer may desire to exclude from State Aid (e.g. Technical Instruction as now given under Article 3 of the Evening Schools Code.)

(iv) Let the grants under the new Regulations be free from the 17s. 6d. limit, but strictly limited to such a maximum per scholar, or per attendance, or per school, as may be agreed upon by the Treasury, as is now done in all South Kensington Grants.

(v) Let all Evening Classes and Evening Schools come under one Official in the Central Authority, to avoid the present inconsistencies of policy, and also—at least so far as ultimate control is concerned—under one Local Authority; but

(vi) As a temporary measure to meet political and financial emergencies in the Towns (the Rural Districts will not need this) let Borough Councils (and in certain cases School Boards) act as agents for the Secondary Education Authority in respect of Evening Schools work as distinct from Day Schools work.

(vii) Let the Regulations be so framed as to admit of all Evening Schools in one area being organised in one system, with no difficulties in the way of pooling the grants where necessary and sharing teachers and administration expenses and so forth. At present the 17s. 6d. limit and other conditions make it absolutely impossible for this most essential requirement of efficient organisation to obtain in most of our Evening School work; this is one of the greatest barriers to organisation and progress at present; the new Scheme will entirely remove the difficulty without legislation.

(viii) Let the grants be amalgamated as far as possible into one simple grant easily calculated, on some simple registration of attendances, and avoiding complexities and variations, and anything likely to encourage grant hunting or the piling up of odd subjects.

(ix) As far as possible let the grants be so regulated as to encourage (and perhaps in time to compel) every Evening Student to follow a proper course of studies, and so eliminate the educational and financial waste incident to the present complex system of variable grants on isolated subjects; and

(x) Lastly, above all, let all the Evening Schools in one Town be, under the Regulations, necessarily co-ordinated so as not to compete with one another unnecessarily, and so as to fit in with a logical system of higher education adapted for all persons sometimes fee-paying sometimes not, employed in the daytime in their own occupations of life.

APPENDIX E

Fourth Morant Memorandum [1]

THE SCHEME FOR THE NEW REGULATIONS FOR
EVENING SCHOOLS

(*Written in March or April, 1901*)

AFTER a historical introduction showing the weaknesses of a system whereby managers could conduct evening classes under one or other or both of two competing sets of regulations, Morant outlined his proposals for overcoming the Cockerton difficulties as follows:

7. The plan proposed to meet this situation, and to systematise all State-aided Public Education on a clear and rational basis, is, briefly, as follows:—

That the Board of Education should issue each year—

A. Its Code of Regulations for Public Elementary (Day) Schools, together with the regulations as to the Pupil Teachers and the Staff of these Schools and as to the Training Colleges for Teachers in these Schools.

B. Its Regulations for Secondary Schools inspected by the Board of Education. This would include all the Endowed School work now transferred to the Board of Education, all the Schools inspected under the Board of Education Act 1899, all the Schools of Science, and all the new 50s. Science Schools—*all* these being *Day* Schools, each with a clear curriculum of its own, taken by every pupil in the School, as distinguished from odd sets of Classes in individual subjects taken by individual students; and

C. Its Scheme of Regulations for Technological Classes and Continuation Schools and Classes. This would comprise the more or less specialised Classes of the Science and Art Directory held in the Evening or in the Day-time in Polytechnics and elsewhere, which are not parts of an organised Day-School Curriculum. In fact, it would include *all post-school work*, done mostly in the

----
[1] M.E. Private Office Papers.

Evenings, and tending towards specialisation in the majority of cases; while it would also allow for Classes giving continuation of elementary and general education for students employed in the day time and only able to spare the evenings for instruction. This is its differentiation from the Elementary School and the Secondary School of A. and B.

8. It has been found, however, that, owing to the need for issuing the South Kensington Directory this May, the above Scheme cannot be carried out *in its entirety* this year, as it would be impossible to recast the Directory in time for publication; and therefore the Directory will this year not be split up into the B. and C. above described, but will contain B. and part of C. A special document will thus be necessary this year, setting forth the Regulations for Evening Schools and Classes, as such, and referring where necessary to certain parts of the Directory which are still applicable to Evening Classes. Next year the Directory can be adequately recast on the lines above indicated.

9. This Scheme of Regulations for Evening Schools and Classes is intended to cover all the work hitherto done in the Evening Schools both under the Whitehall Evening Code and under the South Kensington Directory. . . .

[The Memorandum went on to point out that under the projected Education Bill of 1901 (eventually withdrawn and replaced, so far as this Scheme was concerned, by the Cockerton Bill) School Boards *would* be able to run evening classes provided that these did not compete with county council classes; and moreover that, since that Bill repealed s.1(i)a of the Technical Instruction Act, county councils would be able in future to aid *all* evening school work, even if it was elementary in scope. In other words county councils would in practice become the paramount authorities for evening schools.]

INDEX

Abney, Sir William, 159
Absenteeism, 110
Accommodation, School, 110–11
Acland, A. H. D., 103, 188
Acland Code, 160, 201, 207
Adult Education, 68–9, 121, 122, 127, 127–33, 154, 178, 204, 205
Age limits, 8, 31, 32, 42, 50–1, 132, 138, 140, 152, 158, 178–9, 192, 193, 196, 198; (day schools) 111–12, 131, 133; (evening schools) 61, 127–8, 129, 131, 132, 159, 161, 201
Aristotle, 174, 182
Arnold, Matthew, 30
Asquith, H. H. and Gorst's Education Bill (1896), 106; school board's counsel in Cockerton Case, 123, 124, 125, 127, 138; and age limit of elementary education, 140
Assisted Education Act (1891), 104
Assistant Teachers, further education of, 55; charging to the rates, 73–6; effect of London School Board policy concerning, 175
Auditors' control of elementary education, 5, 14, 16, 39–40, *65–87*, 186; beginnings, 65; auditors' duties, 65; large numbers of disallowances, 65–6; surcharges, 65–6; disallowances on ground of age of pupils, 68

Balfour, Arthur, 51, 107, 137, 140, 142
Barrow School Board, 185
Birmingham School Board, Seventh Standard School (Bridge Street), 22, 36, 37–8, 42, 185n, 189; evening school curriculum, 54; and higher education, 93; use of elementary staff in Science Schools, 97–8; Waverley Road School, 189
Black, Francis, 114–15

Block Grant, 156n, 189, 191, 194, 198
Board of Education, and prevention of overlapping, 140; and school boards, 145; and recognition of Higher Elementary Schools, 145
Board of Education Act (1899), 108, 132, 156, 212
Bradford School Board, 33–5, 185
Brighton School Board, and Higher Grade Schools, 40, 115, 188, 189n; and higher education in elementary schools, 93–4, 177; use of elementary school staff in Organised Science Schools, 97–8
Bryce Commission, 30, 40, 43, 44, 106, 108, 116, 137, 141, 147n, 157n, 162
Bryce, J., 136, 141
Buckmaster, J. C., 4
Burton Latimer, 111

Camden School of Art, 114–15, 119
Cardiff School Board, 143–4
Cardozo, B. N., 5
Charity Commissioners, 3, 185
Church Schools, 2, 11, 25–6, 134
Churchill, Winston, 136
City and Guilds of London Technical Institute, 46
Cockerton Acts, *see* Education Act (1901) and Education Act 1901 (Renewal) Act (1902)
Cockerton Case, 1, 62, 119, 120, 121, *122–33*, 138, 140, 154, 161, 162, 178, 181, 205, 208, 210, 212
Commercial Education, 49–50, 52, 62, 70, 148, 149, 150, 151, 166, 175, 179
Condorcet, Marquis de, 30
Connell, W. F., 30